W9-CRT-001

MANAGING

DIVERSITY IN

ORGANIZATIONS

MANAGING

DIVERSITY IN

ORGANIZATIONS

Robert T. Golembiewski

THE UNIVERSITY OF ALABAMA PRESS   *Tuscaloosa and London*

∞

The paper on which this book is printed meets the minimum requirements
of American National Standard for Information Science-Permanence of Paper
for Printed Library Materials, ANSI Z39.48-1984.

Library of Congress Cataloging-in-Publication Data

Golembiewski, Robert T.
        Managing diversity in organizations / Robert T. Golembiewski.
            p.   cm.
        Includes bibliographical references and index.
        ISBN 0-8173-0786-9 (alk. paper) :
            1. Minorities—Employment.   2. Multiculturalism.   3. Personnel management.   I. Title.
    HF5549.5.M5G65   1995
        658.3'041—dc20   94-36315

British Library Cataloguing-in-Publication Data available

To
Helen Golembiewski Yarmy,
1918–1993,
on her seventy-fifth birth date and
our last meeting-of-the-eyes

CONTENTS

PREFACE

Any effort to transcend the substance and banality that characterize human history must have failings, or even be variously false, but some efforts have a greater usefulness than others. That constitutes the challenge of the 1993 Coleman B. Ransone Lectures: to get a running head start toward dealing with diversity in organizations. Can the details be transcended in the real service of application as well as analysis? The readers will judge for themselves, but my hopeful answer to the question is, Yes, you bet.

In any case, the risk cannot be avoided. Paramountly, much social commentary—and perhaps especially that about diversity—has a historical perspective that runs the very short gamut from A to C. Indeed, most of the diversity-friendly literature implies contemporaneity, if it does not explicitly advertise itself as the future-only-just-beginning-to-emerge. Today's premium seems to go to a kind of free-floating novelty: hence the neglect of foundations on which we can build and hence also the myopia about developmental tendencies that could provide useful momentum and direction. This sacrifices too much, in the present view, and (sadly) most often for very little benefit.

The invitation to deliver the 1993 Ransone Lectures provided the immediate stimulus to try to do better, if with an eventful detour. Originally, I set out to do the lectures on the theme of "avoiding the hollow state," into which we seem to be ineluctably led by the curious concatenation of two forces otherwise in opposition: the bureaucracy-bashers of the past two decades or so, including virtually all recent presidential candidates; and several prominent defenders of our public agencies and personnel, most notably Goodsell (1982, 1985, 1993), Wamsley et al. (1983, 1990), and the Volcker Commission (1989). That initial effort became too ponderous for present purposes but has happily taken on a life of its own (Golembiewski, 1994).

So the invitation to do the Ransone Lectures did double duty, as it were. No sooner did the multiple inappropriatenesses for present purposes of what became

Beyond the Hollow State begin to impress me than my subconscious processes volunteered—or perhaps, surrendered to—the theme of diversity.

Motivators of Diversity as Theme: Proximate and Distal; Practical and Normative

Necessity vetted discovery in this case, and the trail of motivation is clear—in proximate and distal senses, as well as in practical and normative senses. Proximately, the *Public Administration Review* recently reprinted an early article of mine proposing a specific alternative to bureaucratic structures (Golembiewski, 1962b, 1992a), along with comments about what time had done to that argument (Golembiewski, 1992c). One commentator allowed that the piece was still surprisingly contemporary but advised the "good professor" to move on to today's real challenge—diversity in public organizations (Scott, 1992, p. 106).

This project instantly became a pressure on my consciousness for two basic reasons. Primarily, the 1962 article's attributed contemporaneity in effect implied—and correctly so—that little progress had been made toward basic managerial and structural reform in public administration. Despite the machinations of several commissions and multiple reorganizations, at all levels of government, we have retained as our basic public organization structure the very samenesses that we have had for the past century or so. Moreover, if both hollowers and hallowers of our public service have anything to say about it, we will forever retain that basic infrastructure for work.

So something had to be done, again, to reemphasize that without basic structural reform, our periodic managerial fads—sensitivity training, Management by Objectives, Total Quality Management, and so on—will be so many bells and whistles on the basic organizational machine that will keep generating much the same old effects.

Directly, also, the generous *Public Administration Review* commentator did not make the connection that seemed so apparent to me, in principle. To reframe the old doggerel: Diversity without appropriate infrastructure can have no roots; infrastructure without diversity will bear odd fruits. "Infrastructure" here applies in a managerial sense—to the ways work is organized or structured and also to the policies, procedures, and techniques underlying this basic organizing or structuring.

Two implied consequences of this emphasis on infrastructure are hugely consequential. First, practically, the wimpish historic record—and especially in the public sector—for basic managerial and structural change bodes ill for ongoing diversity initiatives, however well-intentioned and idealistic they may be. Briefly, for present purposes, the approach below will be broadly comparative, with a focus on the bureaucratic model and its many contrasts with a "flow-of-work" or "postbureaucratic" model. In sum, bureaucratic structures are far better designed to serve uniformity than diversity. The term "postbureaucratic" has been used elsewhere for other and more general purposes (e.g., Hummel, 1987, pp. 261–69), but convenience overbalances the risk of confusing usages. Here, "postbureaucratic" narrowly refers to the specific managerial infrastructure detailed in Chapters 3 through 6.

Second, normatively, the diversity <——> structure interface surfaces in another useful form the basic proposition that organization is a moral problem. The point has been generically argued early (e.g., Golembiewski, 1962b, 1965), as well as more recently (e.g., Golembiewski, 1992a, 1989a), and the topic of diversity provides another important venue for reinforcing the empirical and normative limitations of the bureaucratic model. Chapter 1 details numerous other motivators for dealing with the theme of diversity—practical, constitutional, demographic, and normative.

The surfaced urge to focus on diversity also has distal motivations. Conveniently, these pushes and pulls may be cataloged under four rubrics—personal, career, consulting, and research.

Personally, I early and often had to decide where my allegiances lay with respect to diversity, as well as to put real currency—sometimes in words but usually in money and actions—behind my values and emotional attachments. One issue concerned my name, with "Golden" being the most recommended alternative. "Your name can't help much, and it may hurt," I was advised at various points, in friendly if at times insistent ways by a college football recruiter, as well as later by a business school dean. These helpers proved correct, but I hung in there nonetheless.

Career connections with diversity abound—at times almost accidentally, at other times by conscious choice. For example, in 1960 I found myself, virtually at arrival on a new campus, appointed to a small committee that I learned several months later would review *all* judgments about *all* financial awards to *all* graduate students by *all* departments and schools of a huge university. Eventually, as I learned more about our monopolistic charge, I was astonished at my appointment and perhaps even more by the centralization of power it implied.

This accumulating knowledge had some humorous aspects. Thus it provided a credible explanation for an otherwise puzzling phenomenon: why my wife and I received in the month or so after arrival literally a hundred invitations to dinners and other social events. Our provisional explanation was that Champaign-Urbana was an incredibly welcoming and friendly place! That impression passed as knowledge grew even a little.

Growing knowledge proved eventful and, at times, even gut-wrenching. Thus diversity issues surfaced, although they did not dominate in our committee. And the common wisdom permitted some easy ways out: for example, "There is no point in giving financial support to women, except perhaps the very best qualified; they'll usually end up getting married and not completing their degree programs." I resisted this common wisdom, as well as its variants, and was in a strategic position to do so. There were costs, however. As a committee member, I also became part of a political battle involving my employing unit (a business school) and the central administration, among others. The safer road was clear enough, for those so inclined.

To make a long story very short, I opted for diversity, perhaps foolishly but zestfully. Did the associated battles have their cost to this faculty member, young but a teaching hotshot and already well-published? Academic politics were murky. But my school did not recommend me for promotion when I thought it should, and university administration resisted the temptation to intervene. Our family quickly pulled up stakes and went south in 1963 to an attractive job but also to participate in civil rights activities.

Consulting provided an insistent counterpoint to such personal and career stance-taking, especially in the late 1960s and early 1970s. Action research efforts variously dealt with diversity—in such efforts as the WAM (for *women and men*) task force, which sought an uncertain balance on suddenly shifting terrain, in surveys that highlighted conveniences for the disabled and nursery schools for harried parents/employees, as well as in such policies as flexible work hours that responded to the needs of a broad range of employees.

Early research tagged along in the service of diversity-relevant demands at various work sites. These demands could be generic, as in descriptive studies of gender and organizational covariants (e.g., Golembiewski, 1977a, 1977b). Or the research could be variously action-oriented, as in studies of the effects of designs for encouraging the expression of opinions and suggestions relevant to work (e.g., Golembiewski and Blumberg, 1967, 1968). That research also could focus on particular diversity-friendly programs, policies, or procedures (e.g., Golembiewski, Hilles, and Kagno, 1974). Then, again, relevant studies focused on inducing specific group or organization features—many today call that "empowerment"— to undertake various initiatives as well as facilitate the expression of opinional diversities up the hierarchy during turbulent times (e.g., Golembiewski and Carrigan, 1970, 1973; Golembiewski et al., 1972). In fuller expression, diversity-relevant perspectives also informed broad orientations to research and action (e.g., Golembiewski, 1979, Vol. 1).

A Capsule Introduction

These proximate and distal contributors to the motivation to focus on diversity get expression here in five emphases in separate chapters. They are:

1. By way of introductory guidance, several guiding orientations of these lectures need up-front owning.

2. Five developmental emphases in the growing attention to diversity will be distinguished.

3. Several major senses get detailed in which bureaucratic structures are diversity-unfriendly.

4. The attractions of an alternative structure for a diversity-friendly workplace receive substantial attention.

5. Selected aspects will be detailed of a diversity-friendly infrastructure to complement basic structural arrangements, with "infrastructure" referring to policies, procedures, and practices.

A sixth chapter, an in-process conclusion, provides temporary closure and also gives guidance for future diversity-friendly efforts.

In sum, Chapter 1 deals with kaleidoscopic perceptions of the "why" of diversity; Chapters 3–5 focus on various aspects of "how to" with emphasis on a congenial system of interaction and structure; and Chapter 6 provides a broad context for further progress toward managing diversity.

This Book's Place in Organizational Phases

This introduction to the ordering of chapters is usefully reinforced by a thematic summary. One convenient way to summarize organizational history differentiates three broad phases, based on the pathfinding applications by Frederick W. Taylor (e.g., 1911) and by others that became the common wisdom. These applications crested around the turn of this century (Grootings, Gustavsen, and Héthy, 1989, esp. pp. 27–29) and constitute the "meat" of this "sandwich" of phases:

Phase I: pre-Taylorian, or prebureaucratic

Phase II: Taylorian, or bureaucratic

Phase III: post-Taylorian, or postbureaucratic

In effect, this book reflects four thematic emphases. First, most of the world's organizations have moved beyond Phase I and have substantial experience with Phase II. Indeed, it has been a long time since observers began speaking of the bureaucratization of the world (e.g., Jacoby, 1973), with only minimal hyperbole.

Second, much of the world is moving beyond the conditions that provided a more reasonable fit with Phase II—large numbers of poorly educated workers with low expectations about workplace democracy, simple product lines, and assembly-line operations spewing out an unending flood of identical end items. Those days are going at an accelerating pace, if not yet gone. As Michael Hammer and James Champy (1993, p. 1) put it bluntly: "A set of principles laid down more than two centuries ago has shaped the structure, management, and performance of American businesses throughout the nineteenth and twentieth centuries. . . .

The time has come [for corporate America] to retire those principles and to adopt a new set [*or*] *go out of business*" (emphasis added).

Third, the critique of Phase II has taken many forms over the past three decades or so, with a definite crescendo in recent years. Among numerous other possibilities, Phase II is underwhelming from such diverse perspectives as not inducing appropriate participation, involvement, or industrial democracy; as an inadequate basis for, as well as a major motivation of, the strong movements toward "reinventing government" and "business reengineering"; as providing only a floor for the quality of goods or services rather than encouraging heightening expectations; and as negatively affecting the quality of working life—through low satisfaction, growing boredom, and feelings of alienation from work.

So tying diversity to the ongoing critique of Phase II is novel in one sense but only joins a large and increasingly clamorous chorus drawing attention to Phase II's limitations in numerous regards. Simply, this book proposes that a continuing commitment to Phase II will undercut real progress toward managing diversity. Phase II also undercuts progress toward many other goals.

Fourth, the Phase III variant emphasized here as better designed to meet the needs of diversity has been emphasized by many as meeting other needs or imperatives. What is novel here, if not unique, is tying diversity as directly to the Phase III variant as this analysis does. That many others see value in the same or related structural variants for other purposes is seen as broadening the support for the present approach to Phase III, or the postbureaucratic phase.

This Book's Place in Organizational Fashions

There is another useful way to place this book in the historic stream of organizational analysis. Directly, the development here of the diversity theme is definitely countercultural, and deliberately so.

To put it in the simplest terms, emerging fashions in organizational analysis urge that it become like unto atomic and astro physics (e.g., Wheatley, 1992) when its model is not the life or biological sciences (e.g., Kaufman, 1985, 1991). Some propose that such models reveal an underlying "physics envy" (Bygrave, 1989, p. 16). Whatever that case, and for good or ill, these now fashionable models for organizational analysis make a number of simplifying assumptions, among the most important of which are the following:

> The metaphors associated with a model are more the message than the model's methods, a triumph of sensibility over substance.
>
> Organizational dynamics are neither inherently more complicated nor analytically distinct from the models, which finesses the normative or value aspects of organizational dynamics.

Organizational dynamics can make the same or similar inferential leaps as the models, without having the benefits of the depth of development underlying the models, which is hopeful but improbable.

Oppositely, the diversity theme here is based substantially on a contrast of two *simple structures* rather than on the translation for organizational analysis of abstract ideas from the developmental histories of various physical or life sciences.

This comparison of simple structures is not undertaken casually and has strategic as well as practical motivation. Strategically, the question here takes this form: Should organization analysis encourage somehow leaning away from the consequences of the bureaucratic model—or somehow transcending those consequences —while also retaining that basic simple structure? The answer here is, No, and for the obvious reason.

Practically, the question here becomes, Is it productive—not to mention just— to encourage individuals to act in ways contrary to the action impulses generated by the bureaucratic model while retaining that simple structure? Again, the answer here is, No. That not only exposes individuals to mixed messages, if not double binds, but it also deprives them of powerful reinforcement of the attitudes and skills appropriate for the required new action impulses. Hence the comparative emphasis below on a second simple structure, one alternative to the bureaucratic model over a broad range of situations—the flow-of-work model or, at senior levels of organization, the divisional model.

Some Recognitions

The present manuscript was completely edited after its predecessor served as the basis for extemporaneous presentation and extensive discussion as the forty-third in the Coleman B. Ransone Lectures, at the Maxwell Air Force Air Command and Staff College, September 27–30, 1993. Special thanks go to Ann Riddle and William H. Stewart of the University of Alabama, as well as to Lieutenant Colonel Albert U. Mitchum, then Dean of Associate Programs at the Air Command and Staff College. They all went well beyond the calls of normal duty to make memorable and pleasant the stay of my wife, Peg, and me. Participants in the formal and informal discussions surrounding the lectures will see their influences at numerous points in the text below.

Thanks also go to William A. Osuna, for his talents and goodwill in doing research for a core paper underlying two chapters of these 1993 Ransone Lectures. Sandra Daniel provided the basic manuscript-preparing skills, with assists from Teresa Wood.

Robert T. Golembiewski
Athens, Georgia

MANAGING

DIVERSITY IN

ORGANIZATIONS

1 CIRCUMSCRIBING DIVERSITY:

ORIENTATIONS AT THE ORGANIZATIONAL

LEVEL OF ANALYSIS

Rather than circumscribing diversity, let alone defining it, many academic observers prefer to waffle or even to avoid the matter altogether. No doubt about it, diversity issues constitute a whole panoply of today's tar babies. Hence the academic literature is both sparse and underwhelming.

These 1993 Coleman B. Ransone Lectures do not have that option; they need to be deliberate and deliberative about their specific orientation. Here, two themes attempt to provide sufficient specificity for present purposes. Attention first turns to the several orientations of these lectures, and then discussion details the several attractions of an organizational level of analysis.

This approach clearly satisfices. Granted, specificity for *all* purposes is beyond the present scope, but that fact tethers rather than deters. Granted, also, different assumptions at other levels of analysis would lead these 1993 Ransone Lectures elsewhere, but substantial specificity about the present somewhere will have to do.

Much of this analysis applies to all organizations, everywhere. But the basic focus is on the public sector, especially at the federal level.

Some Orientations and Assumptions

Although intensive analysis might yield a larger inventory, nine features serve to orient these lectures. These orientations and assumptions set limits as well as open doors. Now, up-front and stage-center, is the best time to detail them.

1. *"Diversity" will (and should) be interpreted in very broad terms.* It should not be otherwise, here or anywhere; but it has been otherwise, in many sources. Thus, "diversity" now clearly encompasses race, if only after centuries of escalating consciousness; and some would prefer to restrict diversity to race. Recent decades also have seen advances by advocates of gender. "Cultural diversity" is perhaps less acknowledged. Conceptually, many propose that today's multiple ferments are more properly "cultural" than (for example) "racial." Practically, the relative neglect cannot last long even in the outermost redoubts. Certainly, local beachheads have

been established for diversity-as-culture—for example, not only in those U.S. cities where Spanish is an acknowledged official language, and perhaps even *the* language, but also clearly in those numerous and growing enclaves of people from Asia, Central and South America, Africa, Korea, the Middle East, and elsewhere. Given the recent trends in immigration (e.g., *Atlanta Constitution*, 1993), there will be much more of the same in our future.

"Diversity" here has a far broader sense, sometimes neglected but more often wished away. For example, despite advances such as those related to barrier-free design and the recent passage of the Americans with Disabilities Act, even less conceptual room in the term "diversity" often is accorded the differentially abled or the variously handicapped, to deliberately rely on the old word. The signs of neglect are everywhere. Thus a recent text in public personnel administration—subtitled, no less, *Current Concerns, Future Challenges*—contains *no* appropriate index entries (Ban and Riccucci, 1991).

And, of course, the media in recent months are full of stories dealing with policy and public opinion concerning differences in sexual preferences, especially in connection with homosexuals in military service. "Don't ask; don't tell; don't pursue" seem hardly the last words on that controversial subject. In municipal government, many cities—beginning with Houston and San Francisco, and most recently Atlanta—have been pressured to provide spousal benefits to same-sex partners. Many business and some public organizations have joined in such extensions of coverage. Problems have been experienced, as with deciding on who qualifies as "relevant other" and with angering stakeholders such as customers of a business. But the extensions roll on, buoyed by experiences of increased morale as well as low costs. The latter surprise and seem due to several facts: that few eligibles enroll, apparently still fearing disclosure; that tax implications of such declarations can be daunting; and that—at least for gays, and despite fears related to AIDS—health care costs "are often *less* than those of heterosexuals" (Jefferson, 1994, p. A–1).

These lectures will not join in fighting rear-guard actions. *Managing Diversity in Organizations* accepts the catalog above and also enlarges "diversity" to include age and economic condition, as well as differences in opinions and loyalties. Practical considerations in various organizations determine which aspects of diversity can be accommodated, as well as when and to what degree. But real organizational acceptance of diversity could hardly be exclusionist in principle.

Various factors—applicable laws, the needs of specific organizations because of their markets or clientele, and so on—will influence how fast and how far approaches to diversity will go in each organization. Those situational features cannot be anticipated here, let alone be settled. Indeed, only back-and-forth accommodations may ever be achieved.

Nonetheless, these 1993 Ransone Lectures should be held accountable to detailing an approach that will be diversity-friendly across a broad and growing range. For example, Avon Products, Inc., defined as "diverse enough" the inventory of persons in the following categories (Thomas, 1991, p. 129): women; minorities, including religious identifications and handicapped status; gay males; and employees over age forty. All persons in this collection, and perhaps more, were seen as having problems of "fit" at work and as requiring "flexibility in benefits programs."

2. *Diversity will pose major challenges over the coming decades.* The ante is being raised steadily—and at times even spectacularly—as to what constitutes caring and competent public service, and much of the related dynamics can be attributed to the long-blunted desire for recognition of various diversities. The old psychological rules of thumb put it this way: a satisfied need is an ineffective motivator of behavior; a frustrated need builds tensions that often require great forces to repress, which, in turn, may fitfully reveal the building tensions in surprising outbursts; and a need too long frustrated may become unsatisfiable, forever constituting grim unfinished business that defies resolution.

This metaphor about forces helps explain the whoosh of energy when once-suppressed diversities begin to find their voices. This is true of individuals such as blacks, women, "gray commandos," and so on and also seems to be true of many macro-systems such as Quebec, Ireland, the old Yugoslavia, the fragmented and fragmenting USSR, and so on through a formidable list.

Such whooshes of energy are ubiquitous nowadays, which is another way of saying that in the past we have poorly attended to giving timely voice to diversity. Matters great and small provide plentiful evidence. Thus Stanford University recently had seven graduation ceremonies—one general session and another half dozen in response to various diversities. On a broader canvas, the same picture gets painted throughout the world. There, whooshes of energy lead to claims for autonomy or sovereignty, as entities once assumed to be sufficiently homogeneous are shown to be veritable patchworks.

The associated dynamics typically are misinterpreted, as in what Harlan Cleveland calls (1993, p. 24) the "breakup of the great ice floes of the Cold War." He seeks to set this record straight (1993, p. 25, emphasis added): "What is most striking about that stunning series of events is not, after all, the cascade of conversions to democracy. It is the *outbreak of cultural diversity*, the boiling over of resentments in the name of almost forgotten or newly discovered cultural traditions."

No one knows—at least no one to whom I have access—why some ages seem integrative and others incline toward the pervasively distributive. In any case, the tenor of our times—which some see as their terror and in whose potential others make bold to rejoice—clearly implies an imperative toward less-inclusive and more-exclusive identifications. Simply put, we are today uncommonly busy making smaller entities out of once bigger ones. This situation contrasts markedly with just earlier times, which had strong integrative features, as can be seen in the early civil rights movement, in enthusiasms for "one world" or for a "melting pot," and so on.

Elementally, such experiences leave us with more familiar rationales for integration than for big-time diversity, with its associated fragmentation as well as potential for conflict; and this constitutes a critical shortfall. Adding fuel to this superheated situation, many propose that supportive responses to diversity are sanctioned by humanist or transcendental values, or are even required by them. Such a normative orientation clearly motivates our public foreign policy: for example, the Serbs, Croats, and Muslims have a right to express their preferences, to be self-determinative about in-ness and out-ness. Our generic problem is, of course, that the reach of my self-determination may involve someone else's nose.

This diversity shift implies major empirical and normative concerns, if not problems and dangers.

3. *The tension as well as promise of diversity both seem great.* Upwellings of arts, crafts, and commerce often seem associated with cultural diversity, *if* tolerance dominates. Many social and anthropological observers have come to such a conclusion, whether their focus is on sites such as ancient Baghdad or on the America of the early twentieth century (e.g., Cleveland, 1993, esp. pp. 16–30). Hence Cleveland concludes (1993, p. 26): "The idea of a multiracial, multicultural society with both a national gist and a global perspective, pioneered in fits and starts by the United States, Canada, and Brazil, may prove to be one of the great social innovations of the twentieth century."

This excerpt seems to refer to that innovativeness associated with "successful diversity"—that whoosh of positive energy as differences get released *and* are associated with sufficient acceptance or forbearance to permit constructive release. In much the same terms, many observers (e.g., Fernandez and Barr, 1993) see a secret weapon for American business in our diversity, rightly managed, while our international competitors not only started late on dealing with diversity but also suffer from diversity-unfriendly laws, employment and immigration policies, as well as cultural norms.

On the other hand, merry hell might well break loose as diversities threaten or even overwhelm. Or our future could contain a bit of both trouble and more pleasant discoveries.

Two quotations set the boundaries within which observers of the United States see the dynamics of diversity being played out in the convenient frame of a pro/con format that estimates the probability of America successfully coping with diversity.

Pro (Fernandez and Barr, 1993, p. 2, emphasis added): "Despite the problems with diversity experienced by the United States, it is uniquely positioned among the three economic powerhouses of the 1990s (the others being Japan and the emerging [European Community]) to grasp *the competitive advantage.*"

The *con* view is represented directly by Yuji Aida, professor emeritus at the University of Kyoto, who minces no words about what will happen when "U.S. minority groups espouse self-determination in some form." Professor Aida predicts that the "country may become ungovernable" when—*not if*, but when—that happens. Aida argues (quoted in Fernandez and Barr, 1993, pp. 2–3): "Within one hundred years, and probably sooner, most Americans will be people of color. For the first time [in the United States], Caucasians will be a minority. Illiteracy may become widespread. . . . Blacks and Hispanics will not be able to run a complex industrial society like the United States unless they dramatically raise their sights and standards in the next forty years."

The present point, however, is substantially more subtle than that diversity will (or won't) merely lead to us "doing things right" at historically acceptable levels of efficiency. That misses the heart of the tension, in fact. Witness the experience and expectations of the U.S. Forest Service, which has over the past decades sought to change as monolithic an organization as anyone is likely to see and one that *was* eminently successful in a limited niche—protect the forests, period (e.g., Kaufman, 1960). Massive expansions in agency image, missions, and culture are under way. The range of professions and skills has been enormously expanded; and an all-but-unanimously white and male work force is being diversified in race and gender to a degree far beyond the hopes of all but the most expansive visionaries of two or so decades ago. Two clear-eyed observers (Tipple and Wellman, 1991) describe the developmental progress quite precisely: "From Simplicity and Homogeneity to Complexity and Diversity."

The diversity-friendly Forest Service does not yet exist in all major dimensions, but two points provide useful guidance about progress so far. First, *the* objective was to make the service a more effective claimant for resources by sharply expanding its portfolio of clients and good works. Diversity followed that key decision; it definitely did not lead it.

Second, and related, the decades-long effort is *not* motivated by a need to "do things right." Indeed, the Forest Service had ranked very high on that dimension for a long time. Rather, the motivation was to "do the right things." As Greg Brown and Charles C. Harris conclude (1993, p. 85): "The combination of gender and professional diversification in the agency will create an organizational culture very different from the past and . . . these changes could dramatically impact future resource decisions." They have that *just perfect*, in the eyes of this participant in early Forest Service discussions—often shouting matches, to put it mildly—about whether it was not better to let the service die as it had been rather than to run the risks of diversifying its products, services, and personnel.

There is no dearth of raw material for diversity, that much is dead certain. Globally, Elise Boulding (1990) draws attention to "the 10,000 societies" she sees "living inside 168 nation states." The associated complexities for orderly life are patently great. And as Cleveland reminds us (1993, p. 25), those complexities are diminished not a whit by two facts: that many persons may have what amounts to multiple memberships and that many of "the 10,000 societies" in no reasonable sense fall "inside" some conventional political jurisdiction. So points of friction will not only exist within "societies" and their encompassing large political jurisdictions, but more particularly also in two loci—often between those large political jurisdictions and always within people. Few nerve endings will be left unaffected.

Other aspects of diversity add to these basic raw materials, heightening the tendency toward "several from all," or "everyone is in a minority," rather than toward the more comforting "one for all, and all for one." These "other aspects" include age, sexual preferences, race, gender, cultural heritages, and so on.

Major counterforces will inhibit the free play of these centripetal forces, it seems certain, of which only three get highlighted here. As Cleveland reminds us (1993, esp. pp. 28–29), diversity is tied closely to the ongoing central contention about whether rights are group-centered or whether they inhere inalienably in individuals. Bluntly, rights can come generically to all by birth or by membership in categoric groups.

How one stands on this issue makes for momentous differences. Group-centered rights raise many issues beyond the sensitivity threshold of "human rights," as in concerns about differentiating "authentic" from "unauthentic" group members. In San Francisco, for example, a number of fire fighters and police officers apparently claimed Latino or Indian backgrounds to improve their chances for promotion as members of protected categoric groups. Hence a candidate might claim "a small amount of Spanish blood." But this encouraged counterclaims concerning whether he was a true mestizo or only a European Castilian, with the latter status carrying no weight for promotion purposes. How this contention about rights—group-centered or individual—gets *worked on* will be consequential for diversity's balance of tension/promise. There seems no imminent likelihood that this contention will be worked out.

Moreover, again relying on Cleveland (1993, p. 29), the primal human penchant for "us" versus "them" distinctions also faces powerful resistance from modern science and technology. This dynamic duo encourage thinking of the world as a unity and acting as if it were or should be—in Cleveland's words, "as a global market for goods and services and money, as an integrated biosphere to be monitored and protected, as a global community in which nuclear war and human hunger could conceivably be outlawed."

Finally, for present purposes, exercises in diversity face the probability of backlashes—social, emotional, and economic. Thus Ann M. Morrison (1992, esp. p. 168) reports that most of the managers her team interviewed saw fear of backlash as one of the worst potential problems limiting efforts to deal with issues of gender in organizations. Similarly, Susan C. Faludi (1991) explores a conservative backlash against the feminist movement in particular, and against women in general. This list of backlashes could be extended easily and even interminably.

4. *Dealing with diversity will be unavoidable demographically.* The need to deal energetically with diversity in American organizations is not some wish of do-gooders. That need is solidly rooted in numbers. They urge the conclusion that now is not too early to start, although it could be too late.

These numbers can differ from one commentator to another, but not by much; and methodological issues counsel tethering short interpretations of data from popular sources (e.g., Hudson Institute, 1988). But impressive realities remain. From 1990 through 1992, the running average for legal immigrants increased by about 350 percent over the average for the post–World War II period (*Atlanta Constitution*, 1993). Illegal immigrants add impressively to this massive trend, but no one can be precise about how much.

Tomorrow's organizations will be demographically diverse far beyond today's standards—whether kicking or screaming, or as the result of effective planning, or somewhere in between. Why? Three bottom lines convey much about the dimensions of the demographic *tsunami*, whose precursor tides are already being felt (*Atlanta Constitution*, 1993). Around the pivotal year 2000, more or less 80 to 85 percent of the new entrants into our job markets will be women, people of color, or recent immigrants from non-European settings (e.g., Morrison and von Glinow, 1990). If this probable outcome does not get the reader's attention, a second prediction certainly should. Unless the demographers are all dead wrong, America will be older. Today, about one-quarter of us are fifty or older, but by 2000, nearly half of us will be over forty-five (Paul, 1993, p. 67). Looked at another way, the projections reflect eye-catching escalations. Nearly 29 million Americans in 1988 were sixty-four or older, or about 12 percent of the total population. By 2020, the total is predicted to grow to over 52 million, or 17 percent of the U.S. population (Brody, 1988). The numbers of those aged eighty-five or more will grow from about 2.5 million in 1980 to a startling 24 million in sixty years (Schneider, 1989).

The major consequences seem daunting, as Robert H. Elliott (1993) nicely frames the details. What's the bottom line? Primarily, as Raymond Pomerleau observes (1993, p. 2): "To a large extent, today's [and especially tomorrow's] workplace, shaped by the values, norms, and expectations of a homogeneous culture dominated by a dominant group, singularly white men of Western-European heritage, is [and will be] increasingly at odds with the values, needs, and desires of the new generation of workers."

If this overstates the case, it is probably not by much.

Moreover, because of these demographics and various policy initiatives at federal and local levels, the needs to recruit and train a more diverse public work force not only seem widespread but may well become unmanageable. Consider a

Table 1.1   Perceived Importance of Recruiting Specific
Cohorts to MPA Programs

	Percent reporting cohorts as "very important"
African Americans	71.4
Disabled	70.2
Hispanics	69.2
Women	67.3
Asian Americans	62.5
Native Americans	61.5
Other (e.g., "older workers", "gays/lesbians")	13.5

From Mohapatra, McDowell, and Choudhury (1993), p. 9.

survey of seven midwestern states—Illinois, Indiana, Iowa, Michigan, Minnesota, Ohio, and Wisconsin (Mohapatra, McDowell, and Choudhury, 1993). Public sector executives in those states were asked about the importance of recruiting specific cohorts of students into MPA programs. Table 1.1 reviews the results, with large proportions of all respondents indicating it is "very important" to recruit from a broad range of demographic cohorts. The ostensible motivation seems to be anticipation of the sharp increases in the number of employees and clients expected to come from those cohorts.

The impacts of this coming demographic diversity are already being felt, as noted, and even in those sectors where the white male dominated until recent years (e.g., Jackson and Associates, 1992). If nothing else, witness the popular media's fascination with "male paranoia." That state reflects various combinations. These include the sense of new opportunities relished by one gender which sets the fear of displacement gnawing at some/many of the once dominant, as well as the substantial guilt felt by many men that can be exacerbated by the apparently growing attacks on men by women (e.g., *Newsweek*, 1993b). Reference also the earlier comments about probable backlashes.

Note an often neglected point about occupational demographics: the coming several decades will see an unusually strong need to replace organizational elites and subelites. This effect will be especially marked where employment decades ago spurted in a short time frame and when, consequently, many people (and especially white males) of similar ages advanced into superior positions in which they stayed for long periods. Then, later, also in an equally short interval, that cohort becomes eligible for normal retirement.

Examples of this forced-draft circulation of the elite come from all sectors of human activity. In higher education, the spurt occurred between 1965 and 1975. By the year 2000, these entrants will fall largely in the age range fifty-five to sixty-five or older. Less dramatically, but to a similar effect, the post–World War II baby boomers will be phasing out of work or will be deliberately forced out by way of downsizing and early retirement to make room for those in the new demographic bubble coming of employment age in 2000 and later. Similarly, extensive turnover is expected at the topmost levels of the federal service (Desky, 1993a), and such effects are already being felt in many businesses, often stimulated by cutbacks and early retirement as well as by inexorable demographics (Littlejohn and Ezell, 1993).

5. *Dealing with diversity will not only be necessary, but it remains congruent with major aspects of our history, traditions, and institutions.* Consider a small sample of evidence supporting this vital view.

Constitutionally, basic U.S. political institutions are built on a foundation of the protection of minority rights, and diversity contributes a major defense against a coercive majority coalition. Among numerous others, James Madison emphasizes this crucial point in *Federalist 10*, as he explains how our pluralist model helps guarantee our rights via the interplay of "factions." Even our money proudly proclaims: "E pluribus unum," which translates loosely as "One formed out of many."

Practically, the "melting pot" approach to dealing with diversity has not worked in this country, or anywhere else, to the best of my knowledge (e.g., Fugita and O'Brien, 1991). At one time, this view of adaptation or assimilation constituted the official ideology, as in the curious concept of "individuals of all nations *melted* into a new race of men" (de Crèvecoeur, 1782, 1963, pp. 62–64, emphasis added). Hence the "melting pot."

If this ever were either practical or desirable, today is not the time. The "pot" promised somehow to render all distinctions into a homogeneous glob, but in practice that tended to require a repression of individual differences, values, and experiences via thoroughgoing pressures to conform to the dominant cultural prescriptions. Today's practical challenge is more to reduce the probability of ethnic imperialisms by responding meaningfully to the differences between people, as well as to the needs they can forcefully express. As R. Roosevelt Thomas, Jr., observes, representing many others, not only have the demographics changed, but so have some basic tendencies. Thomas explains (1991, p. 171): "Increasingly today, people are celebrating the things that make them different. They're more reluctant to put their differences on hold."

Politically, in a representative democracy, the magnitudes of our diversities demand attention. President Bill Clinton concurs and leaves little doubt about two basic points (as quoted in Pomerleau, 1993, p. 1): "We have become a diverse people of many colors, languages, and beliefs. Now we have the opportunity to insure that diversity is a source of great strength and pride around the world."

Normatively, many commentators make a strong case for progress toward diversity as a value or ethical imperative. Variants of the approach emphasize individual rights, equity, the "golden rule" of doing unto others as you would have them do unto you, and so on. This analysis joins that chorus. Basically, diversity deals with the issue of how we want our "organizations to look," and that implies fundamental value and normative choices. Illustratively, President Clinton promised that his administration's appointees "would look like America," that is, they would be more diverse than typical panels of appointees.

The present approach rests on four legs, as it were. First, as has been established elsewhere, the bureaucratic model poorly suits values underlying the Western tradition. These values, referred to as the Judaeo-Christian tradition elsewhere (Golembiewski, 1965, pp. 63–65; 1989a, pp. 70–74), include prescriptions that work must be psychologically acceptable, nonthreatening; work must allow people to develop their fuller faculties, especially cognitive and interpersonal ones; tasks at work must allow individuals room for self-determination; employees must be able to influence the broad environment within which they work; and the formal organization must not be the sole and final arbiter of behavior. The broad argument has a common thrust: an infrastructure of relationships, management styles, and the structures approaching these postbureaucratic values typically results in heightened satisfaction and often in increased output.

Second, the special burden of these Ransone Lectures involves demonstrating in detail that policies, procedures, and structures consistent with the bureaucratic model poorly serve the purposes of diversity. Substantial detail will undercut the limited counterargument that bureaucracies might actually be better at coping with diversity—at least at initial stages—because of coercive rule-making. The contrary argument here is that the bureaucratic model is diversity-unfriendly in essence and in numerous particulars. Comparative analysis will illustrate how an alternative infrastructure of policies, procedures, and work relationships is diversity-friendly.

Third, this detailed demonstration of diversity-unfriendliness also works the other side of the street, as it were. Among other features, Chapters 3 and 4 will establish that the bureaucratic model induces an infrastructure—of relationships, management styles, and the structuring of work—that undercuts diversity initiatives while (for example) also heightening threat at work and inhibiting personal development. Beyond that, Chapter 5 focuses on numerous policies and procedures that are diversity-friendly but are only mildly encouraged, if not actively undercut, by the bureaucratic model.

Fourth, detailed discussion of an alternative model—labeled "flow-of-work" or, more felicitously, "postbureaucratic"—serves two purposes in addition to being diversity-friendly in numerous particulars. Consistently, the alternative model and its associated infrastructure are better suited than the bureaucratic model to meeting such normative prescriptions as those detailed above. To illustrate, this alternative infrastructure allows individuals room for self-determination at work, reduces threat, allows for fuller personal development in and at work, and so on.

For other normatively relevant aspects of this analysis, see points 8 and 9 below.

6. *Failure to manage diversity will have high costs.* Everyone has favored lists of potentials put in jeopardy by playing Canute in connection with diversity, so this analysis must be very selective. It begins with a formidable catalog of competitive advantages available to business managements which deal with diversity quickly and efficiently (Cox and Blake, 1991). These proactive businesses can expect to

> Reduce the costs associated with high turnover and absenteeism, both among the new entrants who will find a more comfortable context at work as well as among more traditional employees who may otherwise feel threatened by the new diversity

> Ease the burdens of recruiting scarce labor

> Improve their position with minorities, for example, directly by greater sales to them and indirectly via a more positive image with minorities who are customers, clients, or service recipients

> Reduce intergroup conflict at work and ideally transform that energy into greater innovation and heightened performance

> Lower or eliminate barriers to communication, with probable improvements in problem-solving and almost certain reductions in wasted energy

> Increase the capacity for risk-taking as well as for confronting differences, which opens the possibility of greater flexibility and responsiveness

In addition, public sector observers can claim a fuller and even more impressive catalog. Thus diversity—properly understood as a respect for all individual differences—poses less of a conflict with traditional merit principles and perhaps promises less political contention than quotas and set-asides, on the basic presumption that cultural differences are both broader and less emotionally loaded than racial or gender differences (e.g., Klingner and Nalbandian, 1993, p. 133). Others tie greater efficiency and effectiveness to full-fledged diversity efforts, resulting from broader perspectives, greater innovation, and a deeper pool of talent (e.g., Tipple and Wellman, 1991). And Pomerleau flatly notes (1993, p. 19n): "It's commonly accepted wisdom that a heterogeneous bureaucracy better serves the public interest."

These two catalogs of potential effects can be viewed from two directions. The lists highlight the gains that can be expected from "doing diversity" energetically. Perhaps even more significant, the lists also imply the losses that can be expected from desultory attention to diversity.

The cost-benefit issue can be put in the starkest terms, as did Pomerleau (1993, p. 19n). In a public agency, one can work toward meeting client needs via a close fit to staff diversities and strive for caring and competent service to clients who have a greater sense of comfort in their relationships with care or service providers. Or? Pomerleau observes, matter-of-factly: "As a practical matter, addressing diversity internally is certainly less costly than litigation, not to speak of the cost of image devaluation for the agency."

In this view, attention to diversity is *neither* "nice" *nor* "politically correct." Rather, efforts toward effective diversity may be viewed as prudent, strategic, or even necessary. The evidence is neither all in, nor will it ever be. But the early evidence inclines to the view that virtue need not be its own reward with regard to diversity. So let us reinforce the point already made with a few selections from a growing literature about the covariants of effective diversity efforts:

> They can affect employees' perceptions of workplace justice and equity which, in turn, can increase productivity and innovation (e.g., Di Tomaso, Thompson, and Blake, 1988).

> They can facilitate "thinking like the customer or client" (e.g., Morrison, 1992, p. 18), which makes good sense in general and in a significant particular also is consistent with managerial and marketing ambitions to better understand and serve "ethnic micro-markets."

> They can stimulate creativity as individuals seek to respond constructively to multiple cultures, races, and values (Andersen, 1991).

> They should result in reduced intergroup conflict, as well as lessened discrimination, with huge savings in the costs of monitoring and enforcement.

But enough, already. Many minority peoples may regard such list-making as minimizations and trivializations of the real issues. "We seek some form of the American dream," goes one such view, "and these windbags want to argue about whether a dog is really a dog."

7. *Organizations provide both a strategic as well as a tactical turf to deal with diversity.* In summary of things to come, changes in the work force will require multiple changes in work settings—in structures, culture, policies, procedures, and so on. The succeeding chapters will provide chapter and verse.

Here, two emphases highlight how this simultaneity applies and attracts. Thus, *no* basis for diversity—gender, race, nationality, age, or whatever—is *ever* comprehensive or unqualified. At times, we can be led into a polarization that intends—sharply, completely—to distinguish some one from some other—the good from the bad, the blacks from the whites, and so on. This simplifies thought, feeling, and action, but at the expense of being false to reality.

Organizations also provide specific loci in which polarizations can be tested against specific contextual realities and can be remedied within them, as necessary. Consider this statement, "Men subjugate women." That issue in a specific organization relates to detailed history, contexts, and persons. In such grounding, it may be true that some men did subjugate (many, most, or—improbably—even all) women; but it typically will be the case that (many or most) men also were subjugated. Polarization by gender in this case would not only be false to reality, but it disregards what might otherwise come to be seen as a common and powerful cause.

Viewed from another angle, specific organizations—or substantial parts of them—may become inclined to act in diversity-friendly ways, may even need to do so, long before most organizations or governments respond to such urges. This motivation can come from compelling situational as well as technological determinants, with which one can argue only at great peril. Such organizations usefully can lead public policy, rather than lagging behind. The sense of it all encompasses numerous working laboratories in which new things can be tried and evaluated. This is no fantasy: it has happened—in fact, it represents the normal state of affairs. Thus some organizations had working parental leave policies twenty or more years before federal legislation even considered them, let alone adopted parental leave. Similarly, many organizations—Compaq Computers, Levi Strauss, Ben and Jerry's Ice Cream, and so on—have provided spousal benefits for same-sex partners. Only a few subfederal governments have done so.

This potential for organizations as leading was never trivial and seems destined to grow in significance. Consider today's emphasis on the "learning organization" (e.g., Vicere, 1990; Zilbert, 1991), which is traced to massive determinants that affect some organizations, although not yet most or all. The determinants include global competition, instant communication or the next closest condition to it, customized market niches and products, and so on. Here, broad diversities must be accommodated, even embraced; resources and opportunities must be tapped, whatever the skins or cultural experiences in which they come packaged; and so on.

The sense of the "learning organization" has two major features when it comes to diversity. First, any structure and associated policies or procedures are infused with values, and the products of continual learning are not like some Christmas decorations to be hung on a rigid structural framework. We know, not surprisingly, that organizations designed for stable-state conditions often become barriers to change that confound learning (e.g., Argyris and Schön, 1978). Hence, as Susan and Allan Mohrman observe (1993, p. 90): "Teaching an individual [for example] teamwork skills will not lead to a different way of enacting a role unless the organization collectively determines that organizational performance is achieved through teamwork and changes the design features to promote it." Indeed, the more successful that personal learning in a traditional organization, the worse it may be for learners who can be punished because their individual growth curve is ahead of an organization's norms and practices. That piece of wisdom has been around for a long time, at least since the puzzling results of early training programs (e.g., Fleishman, 1962).

Second, a robust sense of "learning organization" vitally deals with diversity conceived broadly. To be somewhat specific, at least three kinds of continuing learning are involved (Mohrman and Mohrman, 1993, pp. 92–93): the innovation of new processes, products, and systems; organizational improvement processes, or "doing things right"; and redesign of organizations and their subsystems, which typically relates to "doing the right things"—"to carry out new strategies . . . to embody new values and to significantly improve organizational processes." Distinguishable in practice, these three types of learning often occur together, and they relate to the basic warp and woof of the empirical and normative fabrics we weave as we live our organizational lives.

More narrowly, if the goal is really learning, one can do much worse than to prescribe max-mix of participants. Here, diversity provides rich data, challenges as well as tests assumptions, and otherwise serves learning, if with predictable untidiness and substantial uncertainty. Commitment to an organization's vision and mission serve to tether max-mix short of the condition where differences can create organizational palsy, if not paralysis.

Exploiting this potential of leading organizations does not imply a variant of one size fits all. That is, organizations in more placid environments might incline toward other goals and metaphors. For example, consider the "operating organization" —viewed as a machine or clock that, once designed properly, would simply continue operating. Here, uniformity and homogeneity may be more appropriate; constants might dominate; and loyalty or variously coerced obedience might suffice to keep people in line, at least for immediate practical purposes.

8. *Diversity is not an end value.* There is no easy way to say it, but diversity constitutes no ultimate in means-ends linkages. Indeed, diversity is one of those many good things of which one can make too much, and even with the noblest of intentions.

Some approximations of what this eighth guide means will have to do. Thus diversity can be seen as vital in fine-tuning an organization, but by itself it provides an incomplete basis for collaborative effort. Or diversity can be said to contribute to a paradoxical balance in all of life, but it *does not determine that balance.* We are all distinct and yet must do most of the important things in life together in various collectivities or communities. Everyone going his or her own way is not an open option, overall.

Much the same can be said of diversity's conceptual polar partner, uniformity. So let's say it, with feeling: We can easily have too much of that, too.

Unchecked demands for either diversity or uniformity imply that a system is out of balance. Failure to respond sensitively is wasteful and can be disastrous. Basically, we are all not only different in some regards but the same in others, at least sufficiently so for all practical purposes. The challenge is to build on the latter and expand commonalities, when and if we can, while we recognize and respect the differences.

No easy choices are involved, paramountly because no single balance point exists. If nothing else, all temporarily tolerable balance points will change over time.

So these 1993 Ransone Lectures urge caution about ideologues who offer only plain vanilla diversity. Diversity must be variously blended in organizational contexts with other value-loaded efforts. One rationale for such an effort inheres in the multiple definitions of diversity, which imply very different values and time lines. In sum, diversity is a protean target and usually a moving one. J. Kim (1991) distinguishes a quintet of escalating approaches to diversity, which rest on very different values:

> As "golden rule," by which individual responsibility and morality are engaged to encourage all organization members to "do unto others as you would have them do unto you."
>
> As righting the wrongs perpetrated against some minorities or their ancestors.
>
> As educating employees about the values and belief systems of those from other cultures so as to enhance more comfortable and effective interaction.
>
> As assimilation or adaptation to differences, as via a "melting pot" that is said to produce an idealized cultural homogeneity.
>
> As explicit training in a "multicultural approach," typically vetted by external facilitators, that seeks appreciation of group differences but may encourage ethnic separatisms.

Given that diversity by itself has no conceptual brakes, Pomerleau goes further. He urges (1993, pp. 4–6) a new synthesis in a "transcultural," "transmutational," "idealized pan-American prototype" workplace, building on Will Herberg (1960). This sharply contrasts with multiple but-largely-insular cultures. Basically, Pomerleau seems most concerned about what may be called cultural or ethnic imperialism, or the "cult of ethnicity." He explains (1993, pp. 16–17n):

> For all its nods toward pluralism and diversity, [I question] the assurance of broad social benefits of some multiculturalist thinking. For one thing, the mood associated with the deconstruction of the prevailing trend of thought can lead to regressive orthodoxies whereby "truth" might find itself encapsulated within narrowly conceived collective identities. Fueling the engine of societal balkanization or prompting ethnic nationalism or chauvinistic thinking, radical multiculturalists . . . presume that their ways were superior to those of [others].

These 1993 Ransone Lectures can be neither so comprehensive nor so hopeful. The present view is that a workable approach will have to provide a reasonable place for this diversity of diversities because no one can now predict where the wheel will stop, let alone prescribe where it should stop. Carlos E. Cortés provides a colorful view of the necessary in-betweenness by contrasting *unum* and *pluribus* in one of our national mottoes. *Unum* focuses on societal unity and integrity; *pluribus* refers to protections of individual rights, privileges, predispositions, and even flights of fancy. Cortés explains why neither should be *the* end value (1994, p. 7): "Zealots sometimes become extremists—in support of their own particular versions of *pluribus* and *unum*, of course. Yet both . . . must have limits. *Pluribus* extremism can result in societal disintegration, particularly in light of our growing racial, ethnic, and cultural diversity. However, *unum* extremism can lead to the societal oppression of individual rights and group options."

The following subsection will begin this task of providing context for protean diversity, and subsequent chapters will persevere in that challenge. For openers, we can do far worse than John Gardner's (1991, p. 16) précis of values for providing initial guidance to the exploration below:

> To prevent the wholeness from smothering diversity, there must be a philosophy of pluralism, an open climate for dissent, and an opportunity for subcommunities to retain their identity and share in the setting of larger group goals.

> To prevent the diversity from destroying the wholeness, there must be institutionalized arrangements for diminishing polarization, for coalition-building, dispute resolution, negotiation, and mediation.

Plain terms can suffice to profile diversity's appropriate boundedness. The character and degree of successive diversity blends will change over time, and there is no a priori definition of the always-appropriate balance. Tolerable balances will result only from continuing dialogue between the stakeholders, who will be making multiple asymptotic approximations that alone can better meet the changing expectations of all stakeholders. But no one will ever find a permanent equilibrium.

The situation is in some respects like that in the old commercial for Audi automobiles. "What do you mean—five cylinders?" asked a perplexed potential buyer. "Why have five cylinders?" The Audi engineer put it to the perplexed person directly. "Six cylinders are too many," he explained, "and four are too few."

But the situation with respect to diversity is also very different from that commercial. What is "too many," and what is "too few," will both change over time.

This broad sweep of the present definition of diversity cuts more than one way, of course. Thus practitioners and scholars alike assign different connotations and designations to diversity. Moreover, these differences inhere in different motivations. For example, some definitions are rooted in what is possible and/or necessary in specific organizations. And this will always be with us, and should be front and center in each organization's angle of attack on diversity. For example, also, other definitions seem rooted in a concern that broadening may diffuse if not defuse the still unsatisfactory attention to traditionally protected populations (e.g., Laudicina, 1993, p. 29).

While acknowledging the legitimate concerns underlying narrow concepts of diversity, this treatment consciously does not take that track, especially for a single but powerful reason. Absent broad cultural and structural change in any organization, that is, diversity initiatives usually will remain "out of the mainstream" and hence vulnerable to shifting fashions or even fads. Patently, a broad definition of diversity helps stereophonically motivate the required cultural and structural change. A narrow definition provides an excuse, even a rationale, for diversity as dealing with exceptional cases only.

9. *Acting on diversity without an early and simultaneous focus on performance will be chimerical: it probably will prove unsatisfying to all stakeholders in the long run; failure to insist on that coupling raises serious practical difficulties even in the short run; and, overall, that failure possibly could lead to disaster.* Put tersely, these lectures seek tethering between an impossibility and a probable disaster.

No one can specify the full range of value-loaded issues whose balancing will determine the state of the multiple and temporary equilibria attained by specific approaches to increasingly full diversity in organizations. They will be woven into the historic social fabric that not only will develop over time through the interaction among many stakeholders, but those equilibria also must survive the collisions between stakeholders, or even thrive on those collisions.

As a practical matter, nonetheless, "performance" will have to be encoded in all diversity programs very early—indeed, ideally, from the very start. The rationale is direct, in capsule form. As the next chapter shows, the prognosis does not appear favorable for diversity that rests on common approaches (Thomas, 1991): waiting for events to propel us; merely having larger proportions of various demographic cohorts "in the pipeline"; relying on legal mandates to coerce action by slow-moving or recalcitrant managements; or even increasing sensitivity to diversity. To illustrate the associated long-run inadequacies of such approaches, whatever their short-term attractions or even necessities:

The idea is to get ahead of historical waves, rather than to risk being engulfed by them.

The problem is far more to enact diversity at all levels and in all activities than it is to increase raw numbers because new employees may remain stuck at entrance levels, or thereabouts (e.g., Little, 1991).

Typical "diversity-valuing" efforts are targeted to individual and interpersonal levels to develop insight and a sense of appropriate skills/attitudes at micro-levels. All well and good, in its place. But the problem more essentially concerns developing organization cultures and structures responsive to diversity (e.g., Kilmann, Saxton, Serpa, and Associates, 1985).

External impetus *was* necessary, as via legislation and regulation, but the long-run issue is to depend less on probably variable support as political regimes change and to move decisively into continuous efforts to reformat organizations and their infrastructures.

What this means, for present purposes, is that performance and its measurement must be tied into basic ways of organizing that also serve diversity. As later chapters will show, bureaucratic ideals are awkward when it comes to estimating performance. Moreover, they poorly serve diversity in that they imply—indeed, require—a thoroughgoing *assimilation to conventional organizational policies and routines*. Some degree of assimilation always will be necessary, but the growing emphasis will be toward structures, policies, and routines that facilitate estimating performances while they proactively *respond to differences* as well as permit them scope.

Five elementals in a fuller rationale for diversity-cum-performance help detail this overall view. First, and simplest, only such an early melding will earn the continuing and committed support of the various elites, as well as meet practical needs. Some elites, or coalitions of them, may be tempted by immediate pressures to accord primacy to some categoric group, but this support will tend to be unstable, given relatively full and free information and communication. Presumably, however, managerial and military elites will have a long-run bias toward performance, especially if real competition intensifies and if real budget cuts continue to occur. Various cultural or intellectual elites also may be expected to reflect a similar emphasis, in general, as is illustrated by the opinion among many ethnic Jews about quotas or set-asides in admissions processes. Political elites also may often join the performance chorus, despite the continuing allure of going where the votes seem to be—which often has encouraged more movement toward protection than performance.

Over time, diversity-cum-performance in practice implies three kinds of passages. Barrier-free and informed entry into learning/training/apprentice situations will become increasingly possible; all entrants will have to gain confidence that their individuating characteristics do not of themselves pose additional obstacles; and, ideally, high minima will get set for staying within a job, occupation, profession, or organization. For example, assessment centers as a first sort concerning selection for supervisory training could be wide open to all employees who are eligible by experience, education, or even desire. But performance in the assessment center will be crucial—along with past performance—for gaining a priority slot for developmental activities. In turn, performance in these developmental activities as well as on the job will inform choices of those later selected for supervisory roles (e.g., Golembiewski and Kuhnert, 1994). Periodic evaluations within role will follow.

Second, a broad consensus about organizational fairness and equity must exist concerning managerial responses to diversity, and hence *some* value-loaded standards must be applied consistently. Tenure in job or seniority may provide useful backup standards, for they commonly are seen as carrying moral weight. But the positive case for them does not approach that associated with performance, especially in the context of dual urgencies: the heightening competitiveness of the global economy and the ubiquitous need to do more and more with less and less at the typical business or government work site.

Broadly, this consensus can only emerge out of—and will be a necessary contributor to—what is commonly referred to as an *organization culture*. Accumulating evidence and experience reinforce this proposition. Numerous and long-standing studies at lower organization levels (e.g., Perkins, Nieva, and Lawler, 1983; Evans, 1987; Lawler, 1981, 1992) support the criticality of the integration of culture and performance, and perhaps especially when peer-group evaluation dominates. Recent evidence suggests a similar interaction in the case of the cluster of the most senior officials in the Canadian government (Bourgault, Dion, and Lemay, 1993).

These shared agreements embodied in cultures not only serve as the immediate context for specific activities such as performance appraisal, but they also can provide social and behavioral shock absorbers that cushion the pervasive fragmenting tendencies in all organizations, and perhaps especially in public organizations. The challenge is ubiquitous and severe. As three Canadian observers note (Bourgault, Dion, and Lemay, 1993, p. 73):

> Public bureaucracies have a well-known tendency to act as a conglomerate of highly independent agencies. Each bureau tends to pursue its parochially defined interests, dictated largely by its position in the bureaucracy, the career goals of its members, relations with clients, short-term constraints, and so on. Incoherence in the policy agenda as well as budget [inflation] are the [prime] negative outcomes.

Third, psychologically, even the hint of selection by categoric groups rather than performance implies real difficulties. This holds not only for the offended losers but also in many or most cases for those selected for favorable treatment. "You were chosen only because you are an X," we have learned, serves nobody's long-run interests, whether the statement is true or constitutes a bald-faced lie. Even those successful in reality may feel the stigma of psychological failure, and the malcontents have a ready accusatory theme. Both factors may contribute, for example, to the anger felt by even objectively successful blacks. At best, in any case, performance appraisal is so difficult and delicate that it needs no conscious confounding.

Fourth, choices about performance often will be difficult, and at least the general interest is poorly served by that brand of diversity that merely changes the gender, color, or whatever of the new oligarchy. One Georgia county experiencing continuing fraud and malfeasance over the decades illustrates the sad genre: a decade or so ago, the hands of the malefactors were white, and today they are black. Does that qualify as the kind of progress on which we can confidently build? No essential difference exists, as far as I can see, in what the two elites produced. The mere "circulation of elites"—as Roberto Michels (1962) observed long ago—can be consequential, but not necessarily for responding effectively to the claims of multiple and increasingly insistent diversities.

Fifth, performance-estimating activities give tangible form to the specific set of values with which each organization is infused. Basically, organizations are perhaps best at mobilizing bias. So organizations have a good chance of mobilizing *some* bias and for substantial periods of time. But any mobilization of bias—usually sooner rather than later—has destructive effects when divorced from reasonable standards of performance. Further, the more thoroughgoing and ruthless (read "efficient") that mobilization of bias, the more traumatic the eventual negative outcomes. Witness the tragic failure of making dead certain—really, *dead* certain—that Soviet biologists once were committed to Lysenkoist theory and viewpoints, the only biology then acceptable to Communist Party elites (Medvedev, 1969).

Much is known about organizational values that are broadly accepted, as well as about those that have self-defeating aspects. More on both headings will be said in the following chapters. But, for now, note only the criticality of the specific value sets that link performance and diversity at work.

Again: Why the Organizational Level of Analysis?

This is a consequential issue, and some relevant aspects already have been mentioned in passing. Elementally, where we look determines what we will find, or miss. But the present choice of the organizational level analysis—especially in the federal government—has much to recommend it. Nothing fancy or subtle is intended by the term "organizational level of analysis." Readers are encouraged only to put themselves in the role of those managing an enterprise of some scale—let's say, with more than several hundred employees. All dynamics of interest will be generated in units meeting even that modest lower limit. Most of the treatment will apply directly to business, but the focus is more on government.

Two sections below illustrate the broader case for the emphasis on the organizational level—a few general features will get brief attention, and several more specific analytic advantages then will receive a bit more extended treatment.

1. *General Reasons for the Organization Perspective.* Two points suggest that an

organizational focus will provide a rich vantage point for developing the diversity theme. Much of what diversity becomes will be determined in our various organizations, both public and business. That will be where the rubber meets the road, concerning issues of both principle and practice. Some may not like it much (e.g., Scott and Hart, 1979), but we will remain ineluctably an organizational society unless we develop a new form of the Dark Ages. Hence this perspective.

Perhaps most persuasively to me, although some may object to the conclusion as conjectural, Woodrow Wilson seems to have gotten it right. He wrote, way back in 1887, that it was becoming "more difficult to run a constitution than to frame one" (quoted in Waldo, 1979, p. 9). Implementation is never everything, to be sure, but subsequent events certainly require no pullback from Wilson's position. In fact, this updated paraphrase may well be in order: it is becoming far more difficult to implement a policy than it is to formulate one.

2. *Some Specific Advantages of an Organizational Perspective.* To seek a broader sense of the usefulness of the organizational level of analysis, at the explicit risk of overkill, consider several specific competitive advantages of the point of approach to diversity, as here defined. Five will do for present purposes.

Organizations Are Where We Live

We speak much nowadays of "gaps" between races, genders, cultures, and so on. And we do so with good reason.

At the same time, almost all of us spend most of our adult lives in organizations, and we will continue to do so, for good or ill. *How* we will continue to do so remains in doubt, and arguably that is *the* issue of our days. This recommends a focus on the many gaps in all organizations, which may fundamentally affect our view of those gaps that get more attention. Harry C. Triandis (1974, pp. 207–8) illustrates the interaction in proposing that our problems are "*much more* of social class than of race" (emphasis added), and this encourages a new balance. Triandis explained:

> Only Malcolm X, toward the end of his life, reached the insight that is discussed here: that there is no such thing as a white culture versus a black culture, but an urban industrial culture versus a rural agricultural culture. The skilled worker in Western Europe, Russia, India, Japan, Australia, or the United States lives in ways which are strikingly similar to the skilled worker in Nigeria; the professionals in these countries are even more similar; those who belong to the jet set in these countries cannot be distinguished [except] by . . . their preferred language for communication within their families (at work they often use English). In short, industrial man, not white man, is a special type.

Implementation, as Augmented

An organizational perspective directs attention to implementation, and one can *almost* say that a policy does not exist until it is implemented. At the very least, policy takes on distinctive meaning only as implementation proceeds. This deliberately limits Karl Weick's (1979) focus on "continuous enactment" as the standard for reality, but only marginally. Indeed, the specific meaning of any policy is fugitive in the absence of close attention to the details of implementation (e.g., Pressman and Wildavsky, 1973).

Usefully, an organization focus also can serve both leading/lagging purposes in relation to public policy about diversity, and this has strategic as well as tactical value. Basically, public policy no doubt will be preoccupied with elaborating diversity for an extended period of time. Indeed, given a group-centered concept of rights, one can conceive of a large number of possible diversities that might press for accommodations. As one input into this ongoing and delicate process, organizations can on occasion lead public policy, as has often happened in the past in relation to diversity, among other issues. Later, when (and if) public policy developments definitively lead rather than lag, existing organizational experience can already have generated a sense of what can be done at which costs to meet the situational determinants operative in specific organizations. Both possibilities extend the usual sense of implementation as derivative only.

Implementation, as thus augmented, is bidirectional. Thus many or even most organizations may at times lag public policy: but some organizations also can serve to lead public policy, as in developing ways and means to serve diversity that are beyond both policy-makers and policy. Much of the history of Organization Development, or OD, was involved in developing just such ways and means—first relating to opinional diversity and more recently to race, gender, and diversity generally (e.g., Golembiewski, 1979, esp. Vol. 1; 1993a). It is for solid reasons, then, that the NTL Institute for Applied Behavioral Science is developing a report on the theme "forty years of attention to diversity" (Cross et al., 1994).

Many Flowers and No Doubt Some Weeds

The organizational focus also brings to bear powerful pluralist forces—in this case hundreds of thousands of loci in business and government will serve two purposes with respect to diversity. Thus, whatever else, diversity will come alive only in these multitudinous settings. Moreover, if we are skilled and fortunate, local experimentation and innovation will provide a major boost for dissemination and penetration of workable ways and means. This is useful and probably necessary for at least three reasons:

It is not obvious how to make all organizations diversity-friendly, but there almost certainly is no one best way.

All or most early diversity-friendly efforts will have to be tailored to individual sites, but perhaps we can learn more about the classes of situational determinants characterizing successful application. This could provide a foundation for a limited number of packages of diversity programs.

Multiple experiences might provide guidance about workable stages or phases of diversity-friendly developments, relying on advanced cases of development to indicate productive pathways for programs less far along.

This pluralist potential has its costs, of course. Hence the subsection's reference to both weeds and flowers. At the seed stage, it often will be hard or even impossible to tell the difference. Hence the special relevance of multiple experiences in how diversity can be coped with in specific contexts.

An Escape Valve

Relatedly, the focus on the organizational level of analysis highlights an "escape valve" for those times when public policy development is stuck or even regresses—as when backlashes develop or when sharply opposed political regimes succeed one another. In short, leading organizations can continue to separate the programmatic flowers from the weeds, possibly motivating other organizations and perhaps even public policy, whenever the political environment permits.

The point is a simple one, then. An active organizational focus can help release social pressures, which no doubt will build if political progress is stopped or unduly delayed. This buildup has unknown potential, but a scary one.

Grounded Experience with Diversity-Friendly Infrastructure

Public policy can mandate and even motivate appropriate change, but only an appropriate infrastructure in our numerous organizations will permit movement toward what may be called a "grounded experience." Such infrastructures include structures, policies, and procedures, as well as the cultures in which they are embedded. If such infrastructures are diversity-unfriendly, public policy will face serious challenges in being enacted and implemented with essential fidelity to the underlying intent, however prescient and well-crafted the policy.

Hence the strategic usefulness, even the necessity, of an organization level of analysis when it comes to diversity.

In addition, we know much—certainly not all, but clearly enough for solid progress—about which specific components of organizational infrastructure are diversity-friendly. This capability can make a real difference in easing the enactment of public policy about diversity. Hence, also, the present emphasis on the organizational level of analysis, as well as the following discussion of the available foundations for building diversity-friendly collective experiences.

Next Steps

Where, then, will these orienting assumptions about diversity at the organizational level of analysis take us? Diversity has been circumscribed, at least sufficiently for present purposes. And, now, four tasks remain. Each will be the burden of a separate chapter.

The first task involves distinguishing five approaches to dealing with diversity. They are here called "approaches" or "emphases," but they also roughly correspond to historical stages or phases that now variously overlap in specific settings.

The first four approaches play useful roles, but they are limited. Hence this roughly historic progression—from grudging attention to diversity when war or other necessity compels it; "leveling the playing field" by equal employment opportunity; "tilting the playing field" by schedules, goals, or quotas in an augmented affirmative action mode; and through building personal attitudes as well as skills that serve to value diversity.

Hence, also, the emphasis below goes to a fifth approach, which is labeled "managing diversity." It refers to diversity-friendly infrastructure—of structures, policies, procedures, cultures, and so on.

The three other main tasks of these 1993 Ransone Lectures are involved with elaborating the fifth approach to diversity. The first task involves detailing one basic reason why most organizations are diversity-unfriendly: the dominance of bureaucratic structures and ideas and their consequences in numerous aspects of collective life. The second main task illustrates an alternative organization structure which is more diversity-friendly, again relying on numerous aspects of organizational theory and practice to elaborate the point. And the third task involves detailing a range of contributors to a diversity-friendly infrastructure in organizations, covering policies and procedures as well as patterns of culture and of thought and feeling that can either anticipate basic structural change or build on it.

2 FIVE DEVELOPMENTAL EMPHASES IN DIVERSITY: THE PAST CAN BE PROLOGUE TO THE FUTURE, IF WE PAY ATTENTION

This chapter rests on a truism: if we do not understand our history, we will be doomed to doing it over and perhaps even more poorly than the first time. This is always wasteful, but today it may be tragic and perhaps even catastrophic. To put it bluntly, no one can confidently predict what will happen if we do not make constructive adaptations to the differentiating forces all around us. If nothing else, we are probably still in early stages of elaborating the inventory of those forces—race, gender, class, sexual orientation, inter alia—that will challenge getting minimal collective things done. Hence the shaky confidence about whether or not we will have a *good* opportunity to try again if we fall short of dealing well enough with this round of diversity.

To what features of our unfolding history should we direct attention when it comes to diversity? This chapter distinguishes five developmental emphases. Of course, one can take other routes to structuring our experience with diversity, and with value (e.g., Kellough, 1989a, esp. pp. 14–24). Nevertheless, the five approaches described below have major redeeming virtues for present purposes.

The five approaches serve to frame a basic challenge. If we fail to act successfully as well as energetically on the fifth developmental phase—by lack of wit or will or because of a run of ill fortune—we will be condemned to recycling back through the other four developmental emphases.

If we do not deal effectively with this basic challenge, these 1993 Ransone Lectures propose, our times will be troubled. Matters can get very much worse, in short; and they almost certainly will not get better if left alone. One can imagine an unredemptive fragmentation of our nation-state by class, color, or whatever. Our neighbor to the north illustrates how stubbornly those dynamics resist reversal, once engaged. Or far worse still, one can even contemplate two or more coalitions locked in genocidal conflict. For certain, humankind has been prone to deal with major differences by coercive polarization, motivated by a real or contrived enemy. Heaven help us.

The five developmental emphases detailed here, and especially the fifth, are critical in providing direction for moving toward really dealing with diversity. How and why, persevering readers will learn.

Stepping Tentatively Forward, Then Resolutely Back: Grudging and Temporary Acknowledgments of Diversity Under Duress

For most of American history, we have been better at attempting to finesse diversity than in dealing with it. This remains the essential point underlying the "melting pot" ideology, whether intended prescriptively or descriptively. That ideology implies that diverse elements could, and should, amalgamate or adapt. Put another way, diverse elements will and should wither and die. Both views involve deadening diversity rather than dealing with it.

During selected periods, typically under the impetus of dire necessity or clear convenience, diversity did get more attention. But that attention tended to be mixed or even hostile, was only grudgingly extended, and typically proved temporary and generated a backlash to boot.

Consider the question of people of color—particularly of African Americans— in the military. Many of us have definite ideas about our national record in this regard. For example, some know that the 1940 Selective Service Act signed by Franklin Delano Roosevelt contained a provision prohibiting racial discrimination in the armed forces. And no doubt more remember that Harry Truman signed Executive Order 9981 on July 26, 1948, which mandated gradual integration of the military while acknowledging that the 1940 act had failed in its basic purpose (Osuna, 1993).

Many people have clear ideas on this subject but usually incorrect ones. Consider this litmus test: When did the first black person graduate from one of our national military educational institutions—West Point, Annapolis, or Colorado Springs? The year was 1877; a second black graduate followed in 1887; and a third matriculated in 1889. The guesses of most people are off by sixty or more years.

Let us go back via a thumbnail history to gain some sense of how this early step toward acknowledging diversity came to happen, and then passed, and was later viciously repressed. For pass it soon did, as the answer to another key question implies: When did the fourth black graduate from one of our military academies? Answer: about fifty years after the third.

The degree of national need provides perspective on both early happenings as well as regression on the issue of color. Black troops served in George Washington's armies, as well as with Andrew Jackson at New Orleans, but our story begins with the first large-scale reliance on blacks during the years around the Civil War.

The years 1860–90 bracketed a period of dire national need, and diversity suddenly became more attractive. Early on, the Civil War exacted a heavy toll in casualties as well as in a deterioration of the national spirit. Hence, in semidesperation, northern authorities added black soldiers to the Union rolls, despite strong opposition from some quarters. About 180,000 blacks volunteered, that is, over 80 percent of all eligibles between the ages of eighteen and thirty-four, and they suffered a horrendous death rate of approximately 19 percent during the last year or so of the war (Leckie, 1967, p. 5).

After massive demobilization in a nation revulsed by the war, military needs persisted, and authorities continued to use African-Americans. Turmoil along the frontiers, from Kansas down to Texas and Mexico, impeded westward expansion and urged a strong military presence. At the peak of these winning-of-the-Wild-West activities, indeed, a full 20 percent of U.S. cavalry were black—the Ninth and Tenth of ten total regiments. The focus here is largely on the Tenth Regiment, often called the "Buffalo Soldiers."

This great leap forward was glorious while it lasted, and the record of the Buffaloes was dominated by persistence and gallantry under grim conditions (e.g., Leckie, 1967, pp. 71–72). The soldiers did well—protecting settlers, building outposts, fighting Indians, Mexicans, and assorted renegades, as well as winning an extraordinary number of Congressional Medals of Honor. Such events explain the first three black graduates of West Point, who were to provide up-from-the-ranks leadership for the Buffalo Soldiers, previously led by white officers because of official distrust of blacks.

After 1890, however, the history of gallantry was both cut off and forgotten. The western lands came under firmer control, and national politics shifted in Reform Darwinian directions, with an emphasis on national and local reform. An aversion to war and the military also grew, providing polar opposition to their glorification by the survival of the fittest Darwinianism that had dominated earlier (e.g., Goldman, 1952, esp. pp. 85–104, 234–36). The Buffalo Soldiers did fight gallantly in Cuba. But when their operations moved beyond our shores, popular uproar greeted the troops as they bivouacked in southern states. When Cuba was subdued, the Buffalo Soldiers were soon gone.

Hence the fifty-year gap between the third black graduate of our military academies in 1889 and the fourth in 1939.

How to summarize this dealing with diversity in grudging and temporary ways? Like other similar exemplars—the Japanese-American infantry and the Tuskegee pilots from World War II, the occasional reliance on women in out-of-home roles during several periods when large numbers of menfolk were away at war, and so on—the experiences of the Buffalo Soldiers may have contributed to an expanding sense of diversity in organizations and in society. Chairman of the Joint Chiefs of Staff General Colin L. Powell explained that, whatever else, having

African-Americans "in uniform [would challenge] the conscience of the nation" (*New York Times*, 1993).

The costs for the challengers were high, however, although tracking the trail of effects is difficult, and historical linkages are at times conjectural. Without doubt, this first developmental emphasis in dealing with diversity constitutes a shoddy model, and not for the first or the last time when applied to the Buffalo Soldiers.

This conclusion seems appropriate for at least six reasons. First, although perhaps attractive at onset, diversity motivated by immediate needs typically proves a bad bargain. As for the Buffalo Soldiers, William H. Leckie tells us (1967, p. 9): "Many young Negroes were eager to enlist because the army afforded an opportunity for social and economic betterment difficult to achieve in a society all but closed to them. Thirteen dollars a month was meager pay, but it was more than most could expect to earn as civilians, and when food, clothing, and shelter were added, a better life seemed assured."

The underlying motives promised little, however, in the longer run. Thus the reliance on black troops late in the Civil War, according to the eminent historian Bruce Catton (1956, p. 122), reflected no basic humanitarian impulse, but rather the self-interested "dawning realization that, since the Confederates were going to kill a great many more Union soldiers before the war was over, a good many white men would escape death if a considerable percentage of those soldiers were colored." Consistently, the concomitants of this first emphasis feature major assaults on character and person, not to mention nastinesses beyond even heroic endurance. For example, the Buffalo Soldiers built numerous forts and outposts at strategic points in the West, typically on high ground. But, the soldiers were themselves at times compelled to live in the unhealthy bogs nearby (Leckie, 1967, esp. pp. 13–14), with their good works (as it were) looking down on their uncomfortable and even deadly living conditions. Regulations also once provided that black and white soldiers could not get physically closer to one another than about fifty feet.

Second, desperation and necessity did motivate official coercion of those opposing the reliance on "nontraditional resources," but not always benign neglect nonetheless dominated in matters both great and small involving the Buffalo Soldiers. For example, army recalcitrants were officially warned that they might well get a bullet for their resistance to blacks (Williams, 1888, p. 110). Beyond that basic decision, reinforced by legislation, however, the new recruits fared poorly. As a case in point, complaints about the dire condition of their horseflesh persisted for years after start-up (Leckie, 1967, p. 15), and that sorry status was generic to the full range of support and equipment of the Buffalo Soldiers.

Third, the "diverse elements" were typically kept out of the military mainstream. The Buffalo Soldiers were segregated by color, specific loci of service, as well as numerous practices and policies. When a precious few black enlisted men received appointments to West Point for the explicit (and apparently sole) purpose of providing leadership for the Buffaloes, they got harsh treatment, both during and after their education. One man apparently was shunned for four years at the Point. Others were court-martialed after graduation (e.g., Marszalek, 1972, 1974).

Fourth, superior performance did not seem to matter much in the final analysis. When the specific need passed, so did the grudging acceptance of diversity. Leckie concludes (1967, p. viii) that the only obstacles the Buffalo Soldiers "could not overcome were those of prejudice and discrimination."

Fifth, this first approach brought a vicious backlash when the late-1800s crises abated, as they usually will. Consider the fifty years intervening between the third and fourth black graduates of West Point, as well as the tragic treatment of the "diverse" (e.g., Marszalek, 1972, 1974) and also the unconscionable lag in owning up to the wrongs (e.g., *New York Times*, 1994).

Sixth, official memory was energized eventually. Thus the Buffalo Soldiers were memorialized at Fort Leavenworth, Kansas, an outpost they founded earlier. The ceremony was July 25, 1992, presided over by General Colin L. Powell, who "set in motion the effort to recognize the black regiments" nearly a decade earlier, about a century after the fact.

Leveling the Playing Field: Legislating Equal Opportunity

Sour experiences with this first approach to diversity left many unsatisfied, and a growing body of opinion began to marshal behind several reinforcing propositions, which combine values, preferences, and statements/predictions about empirical regularities. These evolving propositions took many forms during the turbulent century rushing into the 1960s. The first approach was flatly inconsistent with widely held ethical views and our basic political philosophy. Particularly during times of great economic advance, and with promise of more to come, this normative shortfall grew increasingly unacceptable to more and more people. As a further impetus for some, the service to country in several wars by women and numerous minorities destroyed any vestige of a rationale for their exclusion from all that the American way of life had to offer. Hence some real things should and could be done about the exclusions from the better things of American life, especially for women and all minorities excluded by prejudice and discrimination. Hence, also, social as well as legal forces could and should be increasingly mobilized to include all for shares in what was available.

Such reinforcing propositions led to a second developmental phase in acknowledging diversity in organizations. To rely on metaphors, supporters focus on "leveling the playing field," "equal opportunity," or similar descriptors.

The purpose here is elemental, as other metaphors express. This leveling at entry will soon get all kinds of people "in the pipeline," goes the vernacular. Then, given time as well as appropriate selection, socialization, training, and development, a diverse work force will soon wend its way up organizational hierarchies. *Voilà!* A fair opportunity for all at entry—given various simplifying assumptions about the distribution of skills, ambitions, goodwill, and good fortune—soon will generate a representative distribution of all people throughout all systems.

Numerous examples of this bias toward leveling exist over time, beginning at least as early as Rooseveltian initiatives in 1939 and 1940, which proved more symbolic than effectual. President Truman's 1948 Executive Order 9981 with respect to racial integration in the military also fits the genre (e.g., Dalfiume, 1969; Osuna, 1993). The Equal Pay Act of 1963 applied to men and women in certain businesses. In 1965, President Lyndon Johnson signed Executive Order 11246, which assigned oversight over private sector employment discrimination—from Title VII of the 1964 Civil Rights Act—to the U.S. Civil Service Commission. These were precursors of the 1972 Equal Employment Opportunity Act, which embodied equal employment opportunity (EEO) in federal legislation and represents the high-water mark of the leveling emphasis.

The equal opportunity or leveling emphasis can be dated roughly through 1972 or so. Then, serious efforts sought to bolster the approach because of its uneven achievements, as we will see later.

How did equal opportunity fare? One can easily go bug-eyed investigating various arrays of data. Broadly, however, the representation of both females and minorities increased overall, but this growth was both limited and uneven. Thus growth was greatest for females as well as for those in lower-status jobs (e.g., Rosenbloom, 1981; Edmond, 1993). Females who were also minorities reflected a kind of double whammy—their representation showed only small increases.

Table 2.1 provides more evidence about how far the leveling approach had yet to go than on how far it had come through the early 1970s. As with most data arrays, where you sit determines what you see in the table. Clearly, whatever one's standards, females and minorities remain grossly underrepresented, especially at the senior levels. Despite signs of progress, then, Table 2.1 implies that substantial shortfalls still plagued efforts at diversity in federal employment. As one further sign, the aggregate data in Table 2.1 camouflage substantial asymmetries between the personnel performances of the several agencies of the federal government (Kellough, 1990). Diversity hardly touched some agencies.

Getting people in the pipeline, then, had clear limitations as a total strategy for diversity.

Table 2.1 Percentages of Women and Minorities among Federal Civilian
Employees at Selected Levels, 1970

	Total general schedule	GS 9–12	GS 13–15	Executive grades
Women	33.2%	15.3	4.1	1.7
Minorities[a]				
Total	14.1%	7.4	3.9	2.2
Blacks	11.1%	4.7	2.3	1.5

From Kellough (1992), p. 125.

[a]Blacks, Hispanics, Asians, and Native Americans. See also the notes to Table 2.2.

Tilting the Playing Field: Augmenting EEO via Affirmative Action

Most influential observers saw such trends as underwhelming, and public policy moved toward a search for—and often political warfare over—ways of augmenting equal opportunity. Dates are always troublesome, but the year 1978 certainly identifies a peak in the transition toward "tilting the playing field," as contrasted with "leveling" it. That year saw the passage of the Civil Service Reform Act (CSRA), which contributed to a definite tilt in at least three major ways (Kellough, 1989b, esp. pp. 314–15). First, the legislation clearly called for a representative bureaucracy —a "work force reflective of the Nation's diversity" (*U.S. Statutes at Large*, 1978, p. 1112). Second, contributions toward diversity would become a specific criterion in evaluations of satisfactory performance in all federal jobs. Third, a related shift in administrative responsibilities (Reorganization Plan No. 1 of 1978) framed the movement toward diversity through a decidedly more vigorous use of numerical goals and timetables. This was possible earlier, but the original enforcing agency provided only a gentle impetus toward goals and timetables (see also Kellough, 1992).

Conveniently, as does Norma M. Riccucci (1991, pp. 89–90), let us label as "affirmative action" this tilting of the playing field to force outcomes favoring diversity.

The phrase "affirmative action" seems to have originated in President John F. Kennedy's Executive Order 10925, which emphasized recruiting and training programs, and was executed under orders through the early 1970s. In 1971, to augment the milder reliance on "plans," goals and timetables were introduced for hiring and promotion at the federal level and soon were mandated for state and local personnel management. The protections of affirmative action also spread, quickly and broadly, and the list of protected categoric groups soon grew. As David H. Rosenbloom (1984, p. 32) explains:

> Originally, goals and timetables were to be used for minorities, which overwhelmingly meant blacks, but included Hispanics, Native Americans and

Asian-Americans as well. It quickly expanded to include women (Rosenbloom, 1977) and was more forcefully applied to Hispanics. But the major programmatic change has been the inclusion of the physically and mentally handicapped, rehabilitated offenders ("ex cons"), and veterans within the program.

Despite various threats such as the Supreme Court's decision in *City of Richmond, Va. v. J.A. Croson Company*, 109 S. Ct. 706 (1989), this augmentation of equal opportunity essentially remains, with complex interpellations. Thus aggressive uses of goals and timetables have proved judicially acceptable, as long as they "stop short of setting quotas" (*Johnson* v. *Transportation Agency* . . . [107 S. Ct. 1442 (1987)]). Similar subtleties limit state and local government reliance on aggressive programs, which must pass "strict scrutiny." Nonetheless, many "tilting" programs remain in effect (e.g., Kellough, 1991).

Tilting the playing field, in contrast to equal opportunity, can be accomplished at various stages of the employment cycle—during recruitment, early socialization, training and development, or promotion. Exemplars employed in the federal service tend to cluster at the recruitment stage (Laudicina, 1993, p. 15). In addition to conventional responses to judicial set-asides and administrative orders, this third approach to diversity can make use of such tactics, among numerous others, as partnerships with schools or colleges that have distinctive student bodies, black, Hispanic, disabled, or differentially abled (FDIC, 1992), and reliance on early retirement or separation to create an enlarged pool of openings at senior or middle levels especially in the context of strict controls on "head count." Efforts to increase targeted upward mobility also exist, for example, arrangements to encourage networking about job or promotion opportunities or mandated developmental programs.

Such details aside, goals and timetables became the primary tools of affirmative action for a definite "tilting of the playing field"; and some advocated flat-out quotas to close the representational gaps, *and fast* (e.g., Edmond, 1993). The question focused on the rate of redistribution: *equality of opportunity* could be augmented by goals and timetables, but insistence on *equality of results* via explicit quotas was clearly more ambitious.

Analytic razors often are required for the distinction-making that goes on in this critical area of public policy. At times, only the subtle can distinguish robust uses of "goals and timetables" from "quotas," despite the political comfort that the distinction provides some observers.

Even if the balance may seem in doubt at times, today's public policy basically relies on equality of opportunity, as enhanced unevenly by goals and timetables that permit greater flexibility and room for maneuvering in cases of egregious exclusionism. "Quota" has become a political boo-word, overall, and President Clinton took pains to distance himself from those who advocated quotas (Edmond,

1993, p. 3). Nor have public officials (e.g., Daley, 1984) or the general public (e.g., Gallup, 1992, esp. pp. 166–70) warmed to ambitious goals and timetables, despite reliance on them by courts in cases of employers with records of stark aversion to diversity in their employment practices. Indeed, some signs can be interpreted as a backlash against the third approach to diversity (Brice, 1994). The broadly political issues are suggested in an editorial by Joe Klein (1993, p. 29). He highlights three escalating central questions in dispute:

How does one define quality?

Does one favor equality of opportunity, of outcomes, or some subtle mix?

Does one acknowledge rights in individuals only, or do groups also have them? Or both?

Klein reflects the very real potential for social and political conflict in how such questions are worded. He concludes that the "mainstream of the civil-rights movement . . . has gone off the deep end" following great progress on desegregation —"*the* great moral cause of 20th-century America." Klein adds (1993, p. 29): "But the limits of legislative action were soon reached, and the movement lurched off-course when the focus shifted from equal rights to race-specific remedies. It has stagnated ever since, poisoned by the shakedowns and bean counting inherent in the legalistic search for 'equality of results' rooted in a strong sense of 'group rights.'"

Despite such disjoints of principle and practice, the diversity ball is clearly rolling at the federal level. Table 2.2 suggests the point, with economy, considering only federal employment at GS-13 and above. These grades encompass the most senior positions, of course.

The overall trend toward greater diversity or representativeness seems clear enough, and other sources permit important nuances beyond the scope of Table 2.2 (Lewis, 1988, p. 702). Thus the proportion of women in the most senior jobs has increased between 1970 and 1990 by almost seven times and that of blacks increased by over 200 percent.

So the augmentation of equal opportunity after the early 1970s had real effects, but that still leaves a very long way to go, which shortfalls extend from bad to worse, as it were. Thus data not in Table 2.2 establish that white non-Hispanic women show the greatest change in representation at senior levels, 1976–86, from 4.6 to 10.5 percent (Rosenbloom, 1987, p. 67). This does not suggest "substantial representation," not to mention "equal representation." Other women fare even more poorly. Specifically, white non-Hispanic women account for over 80 percent of the increase in female representation.

The case for males between 1976 and 1986 is a little more complicated, but shortfalls also dominate. Broadly, minority males show only tiny increases in representation.

Table 2.2   Some Results of Hiring Practices, 1970–1990

Total and selected grades	Women	Minorities[a]	
		Total	Blacks
1970			
Total GS	33.2	14.7	11.1
GS 9–12	15.3	7.4	4.7
GS 13–15	4.1	3.9	2.3
Executive grades	1.7	2.2	1.5
1980			
Total GS	45.3	20.8	14.5
GS 9–12	27.2	14.8	9.1
GS 13–15	8.3	8.5	4.8
Executive grades	6.2	7.0	5.0
1990			
Total GS	50.2	26.4	16.5
GS 9–12	39.0	21.3	8.4
GS 13–15	18.7	12.7	6.4
Executive grades	11.1	7.7	4.7

From Kellough (1992), p. 125; U.S. Civil Service Commission, *Study of Minority Group Employment in the Federal Government*, Nov. 30, 1970; idem, *Study of Employment of Women in the Federal Government*, Oct. 31, 1970; U.S., Office of Personnel Management, *Equal Employment Opportunity Statistics*, Nov. 30, 1980; idem, *Affirmative Action Statistics*, Sept. 30, 1990.

Note: Federal civilian employees are those in General Schedule (GS) and equivalent grades; executive grades include the Senior Executive Service and GS 16–18.

[a] Blacks, Hispanics, Asians, and Native Americans.

So Table 2.2 and other data encourage only a diluted optimism about the success of ongoing efforts to "tilt the playing field," at least at the federal level. Much the same conclusion applies to more subtle analysis, such as considering the compensation trends that are also obviously a great part of any effort at true diversity (e.g., Lewis, 1988). Updates require no fundamental change in this federal overview (e.g., Guy, 1993a).

An attractive silver lining does exist in the near future in the form of a bonanza of openings at senior federal levels if there are no major cutbacks in total management. By 1994, close observers expect an exodus of up to 40 to 50 percent of *all* current members of the Senior Executive Service (Desky, 1993a). Selected populations in business apparently will provide even greater opportunities for nontraditional employees (e.g., Littlejohn and Ezell, 1993). In both sectors, then, opportunities for upward mobility for protected populations seem imminent (e.g., Walker, 1993).

Why this mixed record for augmented affirmative action? That question cannot be satisfactorily answered here, but five major contributors to an answer seem clear enough. First, if an initiative lives by the sword of political action, it can also be diminished by the same sword, or even die by it. All the evidence is not in, but the Reagan-Bush years not only reduced the pressure on the accelerator but also on occasion stepped on the brakes. Overall, those regimes did not gut diversity efforts, but they clearly did not spur progress. As Gregory B. Lewis concludes (1988, p. 705): "Women and minorities made progress toward greater representation and more equal job rewards throughout the 1976–87 period. The pace was not rapid. It will take another 30 years *at this rate* before women and minorities fill [their proportion of] the positions at GS-13 and above, and unexplained salary differences will still remain." Others read the personnel tea leaves differently (e.g., Guy, 1993b, p. 281), but the basic conclusion still applies.

Second, the "pipeline hypothesis" even with the augmenting of equal opportunity initiatives—clearly appears simplistic, at least in retrospect. Thus simply increasing the proportions of diverse subpopulations at entry levels does not mean that, over the passage of time, similarly robust cohorts will appear throughout a system. For example, consider the attention to the "glass ceiling" said to separate, in far too many cases, women from the most senior levels of management (e.g., U.S. Department of Labor, 1991; Naff, 1992). The conclusion seems to hold not only at the federal level but also for state and local governments and in business as well (Bullard and Wright, 1993, esp. pp. 189, 199–200).

In short, "flow through the pipeline" seems to rest on a complicated calculus and certainly is not tied in any direct way to mere numerical increases at entry levels. There, forcing and coercive strategies may do tolerably well, but promotions from within constitute a less tractable challenge unless organization cultures and norms are congenial, and they typically require fundamental change.

Third, the "tilting" either went too far, or "equal outcomes" were considered bad policy by influential interests as well as by general opinion (e.g., Riccucci, 1991, pp. 90–91). For example, Supreme Court decisions seek an uncertain *media via* in this dynamic and contentious arena. As John Nalbandian concludes (1989, p. 44):

> Putting together the present configuration of the Court, its respect for precedent, and the value patterns implied in past decisions, one could hardly conclude that affirmative action is dead, as some might believe. However, the emphasis on social equity *is likely to shift somewhat in favor of a new balance*—perhaps tempered by a renewed concern for organizational efficiency—based on complementary rather than opposing expressions of social equity and individual rights.

Nalbandian adds (1989, p. 44): "Moreover, the legitimacy of affirmative action over the longer haul depends on incorporating the value of efficiency more consistently into formal channels of judicial review as well as public policy forums and organizational practices."

Major forces, then, are engaged in a reequilibration of both "leveling" and "tilting" of the organizational playing fields. The magnitudes of multiple backlashes increased, if to different degrees, as the environment changed—first, by nearly two decades of more conservative regimes at the federal level, and recently by what seems to be a swing back toward equal opportunity. Such comings and goings contribute to up and down—but hardly on and off—attention to diversity.

Two further generalizations conclude this exercise, and they continue the mode—on the one hand . . . on the other hand.

Fourth, the augmentation of equal opportunity by goals and timetables for protected groups has no-win features but was almost certainly necessary at early stages of public action. As Pomerleau concludes (1993, p. 8): "Paradoxically, while racial classifications may engender hostility, not making such classifications may generate even more hostility." Other observers similarly see a balance of effects but lean in a direction opposite to Pomerleau's. For example, Cresencio Torres and Mary Bruxelles (1992, p. 31) agree that the fourth phase opened "doors of opportunity [for] many who were previously excluded." But they emphasize the "new hurdles" created by "the unnatural focus on special target groups in organizations, the perception by white managers that standards were being lowered to accommodate minorities and women, and the perception that EEO and AA programs were artificial methods forced upon organizations [to] pay for the historical sins of U.S. society." Torres and Bruxelles see a resulting "cycle of disillusionment" created by "catch-up programs" often initiated in haste that featured hiring policies that "were designed to increase numbers, in the short term, with little concern for long-term minority support and development."

Fifth, although at early stages they are useful and even necessary for most employers, the emphases on "leveling" and "tilting" the playing field are not sufficient in themselves to assure continuous progress toward diversity. Hence the following attention to two further developmental emphases. They move beyond legislation and regulations, although they were inspired or goaded by legislatures and courts. Commonly, these last two developmental emphases envision the development of diversity-friendly contexts at work.

Moving Toward Diversity-Friendly Relationships: Valuing Differences in People and between Persons

Any dating of *the* decisive step toward fuller diversity at the federal level must be arbitrary, but 1978 constitutes a fair approximation. In what came to signal a major broadening of affirmative action, that year's Civil Service Reform Act emphasized that a truly efficient work force would reflect a "demographic heterogeneity" that represents the nation's profile of diversities. CSRA was not the first major nudge toward full diversity, but it was a prominent one. Moreover, many careful observers see the linkage in very direct terms: "Affirmative action is simply a political stage [that] America needed to transit on its way to accepting increased cultural and, therefore, workforce diversity" (Klingner and Nalbandian, 1993, p. 134).

Whatever that case, there seems little doubt that the CSRA shifted the focus toward *individual differences*, as well as away from the protection of categoric groups that had been harmed by injustice and prejudice.

In capsule terms, two "P's" are involved in this shift. *Polarization* often occurred in connection with augmented affirmative action, especially, and sometimes was deliberately engineered. Elementally, at least in the short run, progress for some could mean losses for others. Hence even once staunch allies found themselves at cross-purposes, as in the case of American Jews and various minorities, especially African-Americans, when it came to the equal outcomes associated with an augmented equal opportunity. Finally, whether polarization occurs or not, relationships between *people* are always involved for good, or ill, or any point in between.

The recognition of the second "P"—of the need for diversity-friendly relationships between *people*—got reinforced by the common desire to avoid the first "P." The result was a fourth developmental emphasis—the "valuing of differences." At times, recognition came easily, but most often learning was delayed (e.g., Rosenbloom, 1981).

In organizations, attempts to encourage the "valuing of differences" are generally associated with "diversity training." Diversity training rests on substantial as well as growing agreements, at both system and individual levels. Thus most organizations —especially those of any size—have come to a major conclusion, if grudgingly in cases. As one federal employee observes (Jiang, 1993, p. 8): "The expectation that a workplace be homogeneous is obsolete. Save for a few holdouts, public and private corporations are now attempting to embrace the diversity which is now their employee pool and workforce. A workshop or class on diversity has become a standard for professional conferences and supervisory and managerial training."

For individuals, moreover, significant rites of passage are often involved. Laws, court decisions, and organization policies can point the way, giving marching orders to the recalcitrant and even sending warnings to them. Perhaps even more important, such formalities give heart to those basically predisposed toward diversity-friendly relationships. But affirming diversity in a big way requires supportive attitudes and often new skills. Individual reevaluation and change often are required to move beyond any but grudging and grinding recognition of differences.

Such increasingly consensual understandings imply a real role for diversity training. As Elaine Lowry (1993, p. 8) explains: "In diversity training, participants become more aware of themselves. If we are not aware of our own feelings and prejudices and stereotypes, we will never be able to open up enough to look at someone's else's differences positively." How does diversity training move toward such objectives? Thomas (1991, p. 25) provides useful overview. Such training fosters awareness and acceptance of individual differences, targets greater understanding of the nature and dynamics of individual differences, helps participants understand their own feelings and attitudes about people who are "different," explores how differences might be tapped as assets in the workplace, and enhances work relations between people who are "different."

No doubt, then, "diversity training" encompasses a huge territory and very diverse terrain. For example, the label has been applied to this range of activities, not to mention many variants in between. One example is diversity workshops, typically one to three hours in length, which seek to sensitize participants to diversity issues either by leader-led confrontations or more likely (and more gently) by lectures and role-plays. Another is the Defense Employment Opportunity Management Institute's (DEOMI) three-month program for "stranger" military personnel who will serve in equal opportunity advisor positions. The program features approximately two hundred hours spent in small, unstructured groups of mixed composition, with a facilitator, whose task involves exploring members' stereotypes, attitudes, and skills related to diversity—initially with respect to race and now also in connection with gender.

The numbers of people exposed to such variants are sometimes known precisely, but, mostly, only informed guesses are possible. The DEOMI program at a 1991 reckoning had over eleven thousand graduates from all U.S. military services. At the other pole, short workshops have been ubiquitous, with probably conservative estimates ranging upward of several millions of U.S. participants from government and business.

The content of this continuum of designs varies across many dimensions. Exhibit 2.1 illustrates four and distinguishes for each dimension several modes in which those dimensions are explored. Typically, the modes for each dimension are arrayed in ascending order of their challenges for training, as well as of their progressive ambitions for the effects of training.

A few details help elaborate the usefulness of Exhibit 2.1. At one pole, diversity training can have an intellectual bias, as in lectures about diversity issues. Most diversity training fits this profile. At the other pole, the activities have a close similarity to T-Groups or to sensitivity training. Such variants emphasize here-and-now events among group members who were strangers, to encourage the disclosure and sharing of feelings in an environment of intendedly high trust (e.g., Golembiewski and Blumberg, 1970, 1973, 1977). The DEOMI design fits this profile. The DEOMI small groups seem to differ from sensitivity training only in their focus on diversity. The ways in which that focus evolves will be idiosyncratic to specific DEOMI groups.

Exhibit 2.1   Three Dimensions of Diversity Training

Focus	Depth of attention	Locus of training
Facts and stereotypes about diverse subpopulations or individuals	Cognitive	An audience
Exploring personal attitudes and values related to diversity issues	Consciousness raising	Interacting individuals, as in role-plays
Venting and extensive dealing with personal feelings	Catharsis and personal growth	Long-term learning groups
Exploring deep-seated personal predispositions, e.g., about "racism," and working toward change	Experiential and skill- : based	Learning and counseling about "deep changes," even therapy

Although the debate about diversity training goes on—largely pro (e.g., Lowry, 1993) but also con (e.g., Jiang, 1993; Egan, 1993)—five shortfalls of its typical expressions at the workplace seem beyond dispute. First, the target usually overwhelms both the time and techniques devoted to the training activities. Valuing differences touches central life processes—in Stephen P. Jiang's terms (1993, p. 8), the target is a "personal process which requires open-mindedness and unprejudiced acceptance of people as individuals." This encompasses a broad terrain as well as digs deep. As Jiang observes: "Diversity is rooted in the definition of an individual's personality, and characteristics of an individual's personality are affected by culture (including subcultures), gender, sexual preference, religious affiliation, current and former socioeconomic status, physical appearance (including any disabilities), intelligence, immigration or native-born residency (and if an immigrant, at what age), and the list goes on and on."

These are no easy targets for brief classes or workshops. Nor is the target approached by categoric discussions resting on generalized definitions and assumptions. Neither "black" nor "white," for example, is a homogeneous category, although much diversity training fixates on them as if they were.

Exhibit 2.2   **Programmatic Elements in "Valuing Differences" at Digital**

Workshops related to multiculturalism: what can be expected, group norms concerning what is acceptable/unacceptable, skills building

A "Celebrating Differences" calendar of cultural and educational activities

Cross-cultural or intercultural workshops to learn the norms and practices of different countries or geographic regions

Team building and values clarification to work on "local" differences

Personal development concerning differences between self and others, typically via dialogue in small groups

From Walker and Hanson (1992).

Some organizations have done far better than average, fortunately. The Valuing Differences program at Digital Equipment Corporation, for example, is unusually comprehensive (Walker and Hanson, 1992). See Exhibit 2.2 for an overview of its major features.

Second, variants of "diversity training" have diverse goals and formats. Among other variants, these training goals or formats encompass

Basically cognitive efforts, as in reviews of demographic trends.

A kind of shock therapy, sometimes for blacks and minorities but usually for whites and males, which implies the message: "However things used to be, this is the way they are going to be. Get ready. It will be rough."

More or less subtle invitations to assimilate to the dominant culture, as in the implicit message: "We are really well-intentioned, and our diversity system works. We know you may be uncomfortable for a while, but we will be patient. Try it, you'll like it."

Experiential sessions, in which personal confrontations are allowed or encouraged, consistent with such rationales: "We all have stereotypes, but some we're not aware of, and others we hide. Here, you can test all kinds, while you also can deal with the stereotypes others have about you, or about the categoric groups you may be seen as representing."

Third, consequently, uniform effects could hardly be expected, and even gross extremes might occur. Hence no one can answer definitively whether—as an explicit opener—typical diversity training does significantly more good than harm. Indeed, the question is far too unspecific. Consciousness may be raised even by blunderbuss efforts; much early opinion was accepting of, if not always enamored with, "shock" approaches (e.g., Church and Carnes, 1972); and "no pain, no gain" not only has a long tradition in personal learning, but many still emphasize that prescription's efficacy and necessity (e.g., Lowry, 1993). The sparse available evidence, however, reinforces common sense: the issue seems to relate to the degree of the "pain" or discrepancy. Too little may fail to motivate learning or change, and too much may inhibit them (e.g., Golembiewski, 1990, esp. pp. 61–86). This does not leave everything for the imagination: we have useful benchmarks as to what constitutes "too little" or "too much." Nonetheless, skilled choice-making is always useful and sometimes is essential.

The evaluative literature on diversity training is very thin. Hence the anecdotal dominates (e.g., Egan, 1993).

Fourth, programs of valuing diversity may be useful and even necessary, but even the best among them do not appear sufficient in large systems. Thomas (1991, pp. 25, 26) provides useful point/counterpoint here. He begins with the point: "Companies where the quality of relationships among diverse employees is less than desired often find valuing differences [programs are] attractive [because they] can be very effective in enhancing relationships and minimizing blatant 'isms'." Thomas then adds a telling counterpoint: "But acceptance, tolerance, and understanding of diversity are not by themselves enough to create an empowered work force. To empower a diverse group of employees to reach their full potential, managing diversity is needed. . . . That means *changing the system and modifying the core culture.*"

Put in other terms, the valuing of differences targets interpersonal and small group learning and often does so in off-site settings that leave concerns about their later transfer to, and staying power in, the organizational hurly-burly (Egan, 1993). Hence the concerns about the impact of an off-site experience by an African-American woman, an account executive in a consumer products firm (Williams, 1992, p. D20): "It's all this touchy-feely stuff—'I'll respect you, if you respect me.' [However, once] you leave the [training] room, it's back to business as usual. Nobody wants to hear about your day-care problems or your sick parent." Such out-of-work activities clearly have their place; but emphasis on them also has substantial limits in large organizations, as the early experience with Organization Development clearly demonstrates (e.g., Golembiewski, 1979, Vol. 2). Intact work teams increasingly will have to be the loci for "valuing differences" which, in effect, moves such learning into the fifth phase—what is here called managing diversity.

The history of the Buffalo Soldiers also clearly implies the crucial shortfalls of even sincere efforts to value diversity, absent great complementary attention to contextual changes in structures, policies, procedures, and cultures. Thus, back then, a few white officers in the field either were predisposed philosophically to good relationships with black soldiers, or came to develop them because of African-American successes and gallantries in action (e.g., Leckie, 1967, pp. 41–44). But these relationships typically wilted in the face of army policies, procedures, and practices. Witness the inhumane treatment of Buffalo Soldier candidates at West Point and their marked tendency to run afoul of courts-martial and other aspects of the formal military infrastructure, especially after the need for their services abated.

That such backlashes occurred in the context of the overall success of the Buffalo Soldiers implies much about three major points. Thus the early official and coercive support for African-American enlistments—in the extreme case, a bullet for each resistor—did not over several decades induce the required changes in infrastructure. Moreover, one can safely speculate about the monumental grimness of the backlash had failure dominated the record of African-American service. In addition, "natural" building of effective interpersonal and intergroup relationships will neither suffice nor persist, absent great good luck. "Natural" improvements can occur but typically are too little and too late.

Fifth, only a few efforts at valuing diversity have developed beyond the limits common to the genre, especially in government. As one exception, DEOMI seeks to provide assistance for commanders in all military services (U.S. Department of Defense, 1993), with a focus on "readiness"—that is, on maximizing the capacity of service units to respond to their missions, both combat and supporting. In addition to off-site training, consequently, DEOMI also provides a mobile training team for dispatch to field locations to deal with diversity issues. More broadly, moving into the managing of diversity, DEOMI also can conduct Military Equal Employment Opportunity Surveys to assess specific cultures in the field as a prelude to identifying and diagnosing possible targets for action planning (Laudicina, 1993, pp. 18–19).

Moving toward Diversity-Friendly Systems: Managing Diversity in Organizations

Even if some or even many individuals develop diversity-friendly relationships in a large system, it is not at all clear that systemic behaviors and attitudes will change sufficiently to make the difference. Cultures and routines can blunt such 1:1 transformations, inhibiting their diffusion, stunting their early growth, or even swamping great progress as conditions change and priorities shift, *which always happens.*

Common sense and much historical evidence support the basic point of the need for intentionally systemic change as a valuable—indeed, probably necessary—complement to all other approaches to moving toward diversity-friendly systems. Let us put the point in another way. We have examples of diversity-friendly organizations—the Metropolitan Atlanta Rapid Transit Authority in the public sector (e.g., Golembiewski and Kiepper, 1988) and Avon Products, Inc., in business (Thomas, 1991). But we have *no* evidence of such approaches working in the absence of close attention to systemic policies, procedures, and practices.

Following Thomas (1991) and others, let us, for want of a better label, call this fifth emphasis "managing diversity." The direct point? Effective approaches to diversity have to be deeply rooted in the complex infrastructures of organizations. Hence the powerful prescription of Ord Elliott and Donald D. Penner (1974, p. 285), writing about one aspect of diversity:

> The American manager cannot wait sixty generations for the physical assimilation of the races. . . .
>
> Organizations are in a position to affect the social structure by redefining the structures of their own organizations to include structural assimilation of blacks without modifying their unique identity. This is quite simply a prescription for recognizing and practicing equity.

It will take the remainder of these 1993 Ransone Lectures to sketch what managing diversity can encompass. Certainly, there will be no single model (e.g., Thomas, 1990, pp. 111, 113, 115), but some generic principles seem to apply to diversity-friendly approaches.

Managing diversity can be reflected in many ways, but one element is all but universal in organizations self-consciously adopting the fifth approach to diversity —a mission statement, typically originating at (or at least vetted by) senior levels and bought into at all levels. Illustrations include Fannie Mae's "Corporate Philosophy on Diversity," with a code of conduct to which employees must assent by personal signatures (Laudicina, 1993, p. 25). Numerous "cultural statements" also exist.

In broader summary, organizations oriented toward managing diversity also reflect some programmatic commonalities. Eleanor V. Laudicina (1992, 1993) identifies nine features, among the most prominent of which are

> A strong and continuing support from top leadership, especially because major cultural changes are required for coming to view "diversity" broadly as related to race and gender, but also to personal features and background, cultural heritages, age and life conditions as well as work experiences and opinions
>
> A concern for the fit of the existing culture or subcultures with diversity goals and approaches

A conviction that managing diversity is related to bottom-line performance or even organizational survival, as contrasted with moral or legal motivators

Progressive integration with managerial performance/reward systems, which puts organization muscle behind diversity and, in effect, affirms that managing diversity is necessary and not merely nice

Searching for career pathways for upward mobility, often idiosyncratic to specific organizations, to serve the purposes of diversity at all levels

What is the incidence of such developmental profiles associated with managing diversity? No unqualified estimates tell us about the penetration into U.S. organizations, but three working conclusions seem safe enough. First, only a minority of businesses seem to have definitely moved in this direction. One study of 121 firms reveals that a mere 15 percent even had written policies for managing diversity that went beyond stages 2–4 identified above (Matthes, 1991), let alone fielded robust stage 5 efforts. Second, the federal government seems to lag behind in this regard. Laudicina (1993, pp. 13–21) implies that only one of twelve federal departments can be considered as having entered the fifth phase distinguished here, and she also notes that only four of the numerous federal agencies have active and well-known programs of managing diversity—Fannie Mae, Environmental Protection Agency, NASA, and Forest Service. Third, active innovation seems somewhat greater in government at state and local levels.

Preliminary to providing details in Chapters 4 and 5 about the building of such diversity-friendliness, consider how the lesson of the primacy of managing diversity has been unevenly learned and poorly applied. For example, the best among the few learning resources targeted to managing diversity typically do not pay much attention to basic structural features (e.g., Gardenswartz and Rowe, 1993). Moreover, otherwise comprehensive efforts (e.g., Jackson and Associates, 1992) fail consistently and insistently to penetrate beyond run-of-the-mill views of equal employment, affirmative action, and valuing differences.

These limitations will not wash (Ritter, 1978), as useful as each emphasis was and remains. Two mini-cases serve to make the basic point in different ways. The first neglects the systemic context of dealing with diversity; and the other attempts in various ways to build around a sensitivity to the associated realities.

1. *The U.S. Navy and the Z-Model.* Admiral Elmo Zumwalt tried to jump-start the navy's attention to diversity via the Human Goals Program, or HGP, which sensitized personnel to differences between people, especially concerning race. HGP essentially bypassed the command structure (e.g., Golembiewski, 1993a, esp. pp. 268–71, 288–92). Consider only two design details. Thus major reliance was placed on ad hoc learning collectivities to raise the basic issues of discrimination, dislike, and distance between whites and blacks. Sensitivity training–like sessions, often presided over by a facilitator, became the prime vehicle for raising conscious-

ness about racism in short-term sessions involving naval personnel at mostly low hierarchical levels. The program was steered from the top, and "Z-grams" cascaded from on high, telling one and all about the ways the newly raised consciousness about racism would be responded to in programmatic ways. Z-grams typically solicited the upward flow of communications directly from all sailors.

No comprehensive provisions for including the large and crucial "middle" were made, however. Indeed, those in middle management often were seen as a major part of the problem and as resisting Zumwaltian initiatives. Some middle managers did participate in the consciousness-raising sessions; and all personnel at this level were expected to be loyal links in the chain of command. Beyond those features, however, those in the "middle" were more acted upon than explicit sharers in the design of the new "color-blind" navy.

The experience seems to have been very uneven. The "sensitivity sessions" usually were active and at times had positive impacts on participants. But transferring such insight into action came hard, in general. Thus, among all the U.S. armed forces, the navy was perhaps the least culturally prepared to deal with racism (e.g., Polmar and Allen, 1982, esp. pp. 47–51, 189–94). Typically, management issues were related to various aspects of racism, but the focus was on the latter rather than the former. Moreover, few Naval Academy attendees were black; few officers were minorities; and the few blacks and other minorities often were assigned to unattractive if not servile billets, as in Filipino "mess boys." In addition, evidence exists that the navy's "middle" managers could be troublesome passive-aggressives. Close observers often heard the taunt: "So Admiral Z wants to run the navy. Well, let him try!" Although cause and effect cannot be established, and should not be assumed casually, some middle managers seem to have "let him" try to do precisely that, with the result that some important things fell between the cracks. At a minimum, accidents and sabotage seem to have peaked during the relevant interval (U.S. Congress, House Committee on Armed Services, 1974).

2. *The U.S. Army and the OE Model.* The army version—or OE, for Organization Effectiveness—differed from the navy's in vital regards. Here, the focus was determinedly managerial, although the "presenting symptoms" often included many relevant to diversity—race, life-styles, gender, differences of opinion, and so on. Moreover, the ties to the management structure were ubiquitous. The army ran a large school for OE facilitators, for which competition was strong and successful candidates had to present substantial line experience as well as midlevel officer's ranks; OEers were assigned directly to specific major line commands; and an OE assignment was seen as a very valuable addition to one's career profile. In short, line officials not only were involved in the OE program; OE was also built around the line, as well as subtly into the line.

Perhaps most important, the army had been more culturally prepared for its early dealings with diversity than was the navy. The unsatisfactory experience with the brainwashing of the Korean era, and especially the profound malaise associated with Vietnam greviously challenged the army, and low enlistment and especially reenlistment rates reinforced the conclusion that serious managerial changes were in order. "Panic" is no doubt a bit strong for describing the then prevailing emotional tone among military officials, but the concern was deep and general that the United States might get involved in a war and not enough folks would agree to go.

Generally, OE operated to increase the tolerance for diversity, broadly defined, and ideally to capture the synergy associated with it. Typically, the major contending forces involved were the "old army" versus the "new army," with OE serving to help target shifting balance points, as well as to provide skills to facilitate movement toward those new points.

3. *A Takeoff Point.* The Z-Model quickly came and went; OE thrived for decades as a major command and still survives within several of the component armies after some major wing-clipping (e.g., Deaner, 1991). To some degree, OEers shot themselves in the foot by too prominently parading their own version of diversity, as in an oft-noted "beads and sandals" approach to military life. In larger part, OE also grew too powerful for the tastes of many and perhaps even succeeded too much. Specifically, enlistment and reenlistment rates attained robust levels. No one would allow those effects to be orphans, and many made strong claims that they were the parents. OE lost in those scuffles, generally.

More broadly, the two mini-cases provide the point of departure for the following three chapters. These three chapters elaborate a basic point of view by providing various details about how diversity can be managed—beginning with a consideration of two basic organization structures and concluding with a review of various diversity-friendly policies and procedures.

Just a few words about what motivates this detailed development of the management of diversity before we embark on it. The relevant evidence is not all in, of course, but we have solid reasons to expect good things from the effective management of diversity. At various points, later analysis will emphasize the supporting rationale, which reflects empirical evidence as well as reasonable summaries based on experience.

For now, consider only one component of this supporting rationale. Exhibit 2.3 summarizes eleven common perspectives on managing diversity. Some are advantages of doing it well, others identify disadvantages of doing diversity poorly or sadly neglecting it. The list is tailored to the public sector and is inspired by a list of arguments for diversity in business (Cox and Blake, 1991, esp. p. 47). Subsequent discussion will explain and elaborate these major sources of advantage/disadvantages inherent in how we deal with diversity.

The point behind Exhibit 2.3 is not that managing diversity—the fifth emphasis distinguished here—constitutes some be-all and end-all. This text does not deal

Exhibit 2.3 Major Sources of Advantage/Disadvantage in Managing Diversity in the Public Sector

1. Legal: failure to manage diversity will result in high costs of litigation as well as of adverse judgments by the courts
2. Costs: the costs of doing business will be higher with failure to manage diversity—communication will be more difficult, employee involvement will be reduced, relationships will be strained if not adversarial, and so on, as organizations become more diverse
3. Intergroup Conflict: a special case of costs, with broad implications for the quality of working life, labor-management relationships, the quality of unionization—conflict will be greater where managing diversity is less successful
4. Attractiveness to Potential and Actual Employees: failure in managing diversity will be a major disincentive for existing as well as potential employees, which is of special significance in the public sector which has well-known disadvantages in recruitment and retention. This attractiveness holds not only for minorities, who will form larger portions of the pool of employees, but also for others interested in a public work force that "looks like America" (e.g., Schmidt, 1988)
5. Attractiveness to Budgeting Authorities: government agencies derive their life's blood from complex executive-legislative views of requests for appropriations, and poor performance in managing diversity may well become a growing factor in adverse reviews
6. Attractiveness to Clientele or Customer: unsuccessful diversity efforts may well have direct implications for how an agency serves its clients or customers. The latter will become increasingly diverse over time, their needs presumably will be more accessible to diverse work forces and managements, and the comfort level for both service provider and client/customer should increase (esp. Thomas, 1990, 1991)
7. Attractiveness to Managers and Executives: more managements are not only tasking subordinates with diversity goals, but performance on those goals is taken into increasing account re promotions and salary judgments (e.g., Brown and Harris, 1993)
8. Creativity and Problem-Solving: many observers argue that organizations successful in managing diversity will bring broader perspectives, different experiences, and lessened attachment to past norms and practices, all of which can be expected to have a positive effect on creativity and problem-solving
9. System Flexibility: agencies with successful diversity efforts will be more accustomed to dealing comprehensively with a changing environment, and hence more fluid and perhaps less standardized, as well as arguably more efficient and effective in responding to environmental turbulence
10. System Legitimacy: success in managing diversity is associated with core values in our political and social philosophy, and hence that success also should have regime-enhancing tendencies
11. System Image: successfully managing diversity provides another opportunity for government to exercise leadership as model employer

Exhibit 2.4 Six Questions about Five Approaches to Diversity

	Diversity under duress	Equal opportunity
How driven?	Situationally, by a pressing problem	Legally, resting on widely shared sense of discrimination too long ignored or tolerated
Posture re differences?	Minimal tolerance and time-bounded only	Focuses on basic equality in one particular and hence does not emphasize range of personal differences
Dominant metaphor?	Diversity as temporary deviation	"Open doors to all"
Basic orientation?	Ad hoc, with minimal or no intent to maintain	Remedy past wrongs by broad proclamation applicable to all new job entrants
Underlying model of integration (or lack thereof)?	Rigidly enforced parallelism or separatism of new entrants	Assimilation over time to existing norms and practices by new entrants—an organizational "melting pot" or successful adaptation by individuals to existing structure, policies, and culture
Basic limitations?	Intended return to status quo ante, with a probable backlash	Assumes that "equal opportunity" over time will result in equitable allocations to all ranks

Augmented affirmative action	Valuing differences	Managing diversity
Legally and politically, reinforced by special extensions beyond equal opportunity—in legislation, the courts, and political mandates in contention	Interpersonally, by emphasizing greater inclusion for all and, hence, higher comfort levels	Strategically, by tying progress on diversity to organization goals, cultures, structures, policies, and reward systems
Focuses on preferential treatment for specific interests or protected groups	Acknowledges differences, and seeks to reduce potential for conflict between them	Builds cultures, norms, structures, and skills so that all employees can fully develop their differences, personal as well as social-cultural
Encouraging, or forcing, preferential allocations by schedules, timetables or quotas	Raising consciousness about differences and their significance	Reinventing or reengineering work to accommodate diversities
Remedy past wrongs with great urgency and targeting	Enhance appreciation of differences and, ideally, acceptance of them	Build infrastructure, culture, and skills that maximize learning for individuals and organizations
A congeries of protected interests as contesting with, if not dominating over, the traditional concept of a loyal and efficient work force	Diverse entrants retain own features, at least for an extended period, but with lessened abrasion for all and with the possibility of some emergent common ground	Organization policies, structures, and cultures will induce systems appropriate for specific collections of employees, different work histories, and developmental stages
Violates sense of equity of meritocrats; may risk lower competence and performance; and raises probability of a backlash	Generically, may reduce creative tension, lower frequency of useful confrontations, and diminish sense of urgency about moving toward common goals. Specifically, focuses on personal rather than organizational performance	Requires long-term, intensive effort; traditional prescriptions for management infrastructure are not helpful models

with specific guides to implementation, for example, even as it dwells on structure and infrastructure. Useful catalogs of such specific guides for implementation appear in other places (e.g., Cox, 1993, esp. pp. 207–22; Morrison, 1992, esp. pp. 77–265; Thomas, 1990, 1991; Gardenswartz and Rowe, 1993). Nor will this fifth approach necessarily overcome an unfavorable environment, even if the internal or managerial challenges get dealt with successfully.

Nonetheless, the management of diversity is both significant as well as neglected; and at least for the foreseeable future, the definite balance of environmental forces demands a persisting focus on diversity. Hence the following chapters emphasize the leverage for advantage sketched in Exhibit 2.3.

An Overview: Six Questions about the Five Approaches

As a useful preliminary to this descriptive and analytic detail, Exhibit 2.4 asks six key questions about the five approaches to diversity and also provides capsule answers. The exhibit does a bit of switch-hitting, as it were. The provisional answers summarize the earlier discussion and also provide a convenient way to frame and motivate the chapters that follow.

But Exhibit 2.4 can overwhelm with complexity what is a simple progression. Directly, diversity under duress has occurred several times in our history and typically ended with a backlash like that mounted against the Buffalo Soldier. The accumulation of steps forward <——> backward eventually led to equal opportunity, whose limits encouraged affirmative action as augmented. Some backlash has occurred, but at this time is overbalanced by efforts to provide a more broadly acceptable context for diversity efforts. The general progression of developments has been from augmented affirmative action to valuing differences and then to managing diversity.

Valuing differences and especially managing diversity seek two objectives. Thus they attempt to build on as well as beyond augmented affirmative action and equal opportunity. Moreover, valuing differences and especially managing diversity seek to avoid backlashes and also to avoid a return to the base strategy of diversity under duress.

3 A, MAYBE *THE*, REASON WHY MOST SYSTEMS ARE DIVERSITY-UNFRIENDLY: BUREAUCRATIC STRUCTURES AS BARRIERS

This chapter rests on the basic assumption that among the most important things about virtually any arena are how it is organized and managed. As Jay R. Galbraith and Edward E. Lawler put the point, unequivocally (1993, p. 3): "Ultimately, there may be no long-term sustainable advantage except the ability to organize and manage." It could hardly be different for diversity.

This chapter also rests on a caveat concerning what is *not* the present purpose. The bashing of bureaucracy has become something of a national pastime and has unfairly been extended in our political life to savaging Bonnie and Bill Bureaucrat, especially in the public sector but not exclusively so. Hence the need for a sharp distinction. The critical focus here is on a body of thought <———> practice which spread almost everywhere, mercurially. The diffusion occurred especially in the last century or so (e.g., Golembiewski, 1985, esp. pp. 148–70) but with clear precursors that go back to Moses and Jethro in the biblical times chronicled in the Book of Exodus. Without hyperbole, observers have long since spoken of the globalization of bureaucracy (Jacoby, 1973).

This analysis does not intend to bash bureaucrats, despite its critical stance about bureaucratic ideas. Public *and* business bureaucrats cannot be chided because they do what they are paid for or because they respect the mandates of common structures, policies, and procedures. Otherwise, they might get into more trouble than anyone needs, with "whistle-blowers" or ethical resisters being the most extreme case in point (e.g., Glazer and Glazer, 1989). Moreover, criticism of bureaucrats also should be restrained because the balance of evidence indicates they often do not like the very behaviors and attitudes their role prescribes (e.g., Rainey, 1991, esp. pp. 32–36).

As much as Charles Goodsell (1985) is to be admired for his defense of public managers, then, he got it only half-right. He titled his book *The Case for Bureaucracy*, which is much different than a defense of *bureaucrats*. The latter are people, typically doing their best within a system that often has awkward effects. Those people deserve support, in the present view, while the system within which they operate is fair game for criticism.

So what of the present approach? This analysis raises serious questions about bureaucracy, as a preliminary to prescribing in the next two chapters what better can come the way of our public and business bureaucrats. Specifically, this chapter shows how bureaucratic structures are diversity-unfriendly, with special emphasis on seven managerial features.

By way of introduction, three points heighten the motivation for this analysis— or better said, this sketch of an analysis—of a very basic way in which to develop a managerial approach to dealing with diversity. Thus if this approach is at all apt, the ubiquity of the bureaucratic model—even though times are a-changin' a bit— helps explain why diversity is such an issue in almost all organizations, far above and beyond the challenges of dealing with diversity itself. As the chapter heading proposes, bureaucratic structures constitute barriers to diversity.

In an elemental sense, then, this chapter stands in solidarity with much work that rejects the basically exclusionist character of the bureaucratic model (e.g., Calás and Smircich, 1992). At the same time, it rushes to note that not only women, or blacks, get excluded. The bureaucratic structure is an affirmative action excluder, as it were. Its ideation rests firmly on homogeneity and seeks to build to- ward it.

Perhaps the most vivid and substantially intact remaining reflection of this deep- seated yearning for ascriptive and behavioral uniformity in bureaucracies involves dress codes (e.g., Bowman and Hooper, 1991), particularly restrictions related to reli- giously distinctive dress or appearance at work (e.g., Schachter, 1993). This has be- come a last or next-to-last refuge for the robust animus against diversity. As was the historic case with other diversities—especially race and gender—generic claims still surface in court to uphold organizational limitations on religiously based garb or ap- pearance. That is, prohibitions typically have been upheld by the courts on indirect grounds—that distinctiveness might detract from performance, as by the potential to induce conflict with co-workers. Or agencies could propose that the distinc- tiveness draws attention away from work toward the difference in question by im- plying a special status for the distinction that runs counter to the neutrality-centered arguments commonly used to support bureaucracies.

Revealingly, organizations seldom try to legitimate such restrictions on the basis of their negative impact on performance. This was true, for example, of the recent nondecision about homosexuals in the military—don't ask, don't tell, don't pur- sue. Here major negative effects on morale were forecast, but little clear evidence of adverse effects on work was presented. The counterargument to racial and gender diversity had, and still retains, such a character. One of the apparently few excep- tions to the generalization involves the proscription of turbans in a work force that uses helmets as part of their normal work (*Sherwood* v. *Brown*, 1980).

One by one, the courts or policy-makers have removed various differentia from organizational control—gender, age and so on—but the animus against religiously distinctive dress or appearance substantially remains. As Hindy L. Schachter concludes (1993, p. 39): "The courts allow agencies to limit employee action stemming from religious convictions in ways that they would never tolerate in matters relating to race or gender."

Compounding the first motivator of this analysis, few observers have drawn attention to the connections between structure and diversity, let alone to highlighting the basic need for structural change as a prerequisite for successfully managing diversity. On occasion, some analysts knock on this particular door (e.g., Thomas, 1991, esp. pp. 12–26; Cox, 1993), but they are hurried census-takers, as it were. Overwhelmingly, even those few analysts generally fail to wait long enough to learn who is at home, let alone to provide detailed characteristics of those living in the organizational house that would manage diversity. Specifically, Taylor Cox, Jr. (1993, pp. 212–14), devotes less than 0.7 of 1 percent of the total pages in a recent volume on diversity to "the bureaucratic model."

In sum, the critiques of bureaucracy have long been with us, antedating even Herbert Simon's demolition of the "proverbs of administration" (1957, pp. 20–44). Nonetheless, the model has proved resilient. Hence this reemphasis on the limitations of the bureaucratic model, this time with respect to diversity.

This second point is common, if curious, because even the most caustic critics of the bureaucratic model may have provided useful perspectives on why the model presents problems, but they typically leave that basic structure in place. Thus Simon (e.g., 1957, esp. pp. 20–44) logically devastates the "proverbs of administration," but then not only leaves them essentially in place during his career to this point but also devotes great energy and talent to reinforcing that place in the several editions of his landmark *Administrative Behavior* (e.g., Simon, 1947, 1957, 1976).

Similarly, Thomas J. Peters and Robert H. Waterman, Jr., advise that organizations be "culture-driven" (1982), but they give only modest attention to the bureaucratic features that usually provide that drive, and they offer little advice about practical culture-building beyond warning that some "tight cultures" can be a very bad bargain (1982, esp. pp. 77–81).

Finally, on this short list of three factors motivating this analysis of bureaucratic structure and diversity, even otherwise prescient students seem inclined to deny or neglect the structural aspects of presenting symptoms or problems. For example, Gareth Morgan (1993) basically advises us to "imaginize" our way out of managerial problems, even when—as is often the case—they have roots in bureaucratic notions. And Weick (1979) in effect tells us not to worry. We "enact" the bureaucratic model and, one supposes, we need only to enact its replacement. Weick, however, does not dwell on the structural details for this crucial act of will. Still other observers encourage us to "vision" our way toward a better organizational tomorrow, with scant attention to two stark pieces of data: visions are often seen as a way of breaking barriers that bureaucracy has inspired; and bureaucratic structures can powerfully impact the implementation of even superior visioning processes.

The organization researchers who do not fall into this neoclassical trap are few (e.g., Mintzberg, 1979) but, to be fair, some rationale does support their self-limiting circularity. For example, complex details of environment, history, technology, coalitions, and so on often influence specific structural choices, and these cannot be taken into easy and general account.

Such fastidiousness does have its attractions, but a kind of first cut preoccupies this analysis. In sum, logically analyze, enact, imaginize, or culturize, as you will; but if bureaucratic ideation remains, serious shortfalls can be anticipated. The present purpose is to emphasize that shortfalls will characterize managing diversity, to the degree that bureaucratic notions persist in specific action settings. Directly, I imagine that what follows meets at least a 75 percent rule of reliability and validity.[1]

Diversity and Bureaucratic Structure

Although neglected, the diversity <——> structure interface qualifies as critical. No one can easily explain the neglect, but the criticality seems patent. Directly, if this argument is substantially correct, efforts to value or manage diversity can anticipate serious structurally associated impediments in most organizations. Why? Most organizations, and especially public ones, feature bureaucratic variants; and the general argument here proposes that the bureaucratic approach provides an awkward foundation for responding to diversity—not only in the seven particular features emphasized here but also in many others.

The special burden here involves reinforcing in detail the ways in which bureaucratic structures poorly serve diversity. Seven selected managerial features illustrate the multiple consequences—positive and negative—inherent in structure-specific approaches to diversity. The emphases will be on the character of interaction; job rotation; job enrichment; performance appraisal; the basic issue of whether a structure builds around heterogeneity or homogeneity; wrongdoing and whistle-blowing; and leadership.

The evidence seems convincing, overall, that these seven managerial features can be diversity-serving. Consider the following skeletal rationales:

> The quality of interaction constitutes the spirit that activates structure and policy. Interaction that is "regenerative"—high openness, owning, and trust, with low risk—is at once organizational glue and grease, as it were. Regenerative interaction helps bond those many forces tending toward fragmentation in organizations; and it eases the interaction that gets the work done,

helps identify and meet diverse needs, and permits the time to pass in need-serving ways.

Job rotation facilitates the cross-training so useful in today's "lean and mean" organizations; and it also permits some variety at work, as well as reduces tedium, thereby responding to deep human needs to express a fuller sense of self at work.

Job enrichment simplifies the oversight of work, enlarges discretion, and permits self-responsibility and self-discipline at work, all of which are increasingly needed in today's organizations and will be significant in managing diversity under tomorrow's conditions, when many nontraditional employees will enter the work force and spritely decisions about career paths will be required.

Performance appraisal is critical in recognizing and rewarding what needs doing, and it also contributes to the sense of equity at the heart of organizations as a moral endeavor to which people can safely and enthusiastically commit themselves.

Ideally, a diversity-friendly structure should build around, as well as accommodate to, heterogeneity across a broad range of human qualities. Absent such a feature, even sincere attempts to "value differences" are likely to encounter serious cross-pressures, even if they have staunch and persisting executive support. And "managing diversity" will tend to give way to variously slick offers to conform or to subtle coercion to adapt to an organization at serious costs to one's distinguishing features.

Effective managerial structures will accommodate both a concern about wrongdoing as well as a reasonable tolerance of whistle-blowing, better identified as ethical resistance. Indeed, ideally, ethical resisters can help identify as well as curb wrongdoing in organizations; and even sincere commitment to diversity probably will be dulled in its absence.

Leadership is a quintessential activity. Strong support exists in the literature for supportive and transformational forms, along with serious attention to the limits of autocratic and transactional leadership. The latter are not likely to support the valuing of diversity or its management.

Two important questions—perhaps even *the* crucial questions—preoccupy this chapter, as well as the next. Do bureaucratic structures enhance these seven managerial features? And if they do not, can alternative structures lay a greater claim to being diversity-friendly?

For those interested in the bottom line, the two working answers are no and yes, respectively.

Case for Bureaucracy as Diversity-Unfriendly

Although others may see the matter differently, this observer has no doubt about the first question. The subhead says it all.

How is the present case made, if admittedly in a suggestive way? The following discussion sketches the bureaucratic structure and then illustrates how it is diversity-unfriendly in terms of each of the seven attractive conditions identified above. Although not comprehensively, this section builds on one generalization and toward a second: most organizations, and especially those in the public sector, are structured in a bureaucratic mode, and bureaucratic approaches and structures inhibit or confound movement toward diversity in organizations.

In the absence of basic structural reform, then, the success of diversity efforts will be problematic. At best, the cost-benefit ratio will be unattractive.

Skeletal Bureaucratic Structure

Exhibit 3.1 presents a familiar if simplified bureaucratic structure and also sketches the properties underlying it. It deals with the flow-of-work A+B+C, which activities can be considered either functions or processes—at high or low levels of organization, respectively—as the reader pleases. The integration of A, B, and C yields some product, service, discrete sub-assembly, or major step in processing.

This approach represents regression in the service of analysis. Thus Exhibit 3.1 does not detail all aspects of real work sites. For example, it does not explicitly provide for the line-staff relationships that often are so big a part of bureaucratic dynamics. But Exhibit 3.1 is consistent with the traditional line-staff model (e.g., Golembiewski, 1967). In the particular of line-staff relations as well as in other convenient omissions, Exhibit 3.1 avoids some complications but can be extended to encompass them.[2]

Not all organizations are bureaucratic, of course, so my argument is limited to those which are. Not to worry, though, that this limits our analysis to an exotic species. Many organizations respect the basic bureaucratic principles in high degrees; and close analogues abound in business and especially in government. Moreover, the treatment here will not be exhaustive, but the selectivity will do no disservice to organizational realities. Other sources broaden and deepen the following discussion (e.g., Golembiewski, 1983, 1987, 1994).

Degenerative Interaction

Perhaps basically, the bureaucratic structure implies a degenerative system of interaction, with the serious consequences that Exhibit 3.2 samples. In degenerative interaction, people often fail to bring to the surface authentic ideas, feelings, and

Exhibit 3.1 Traditional Bureaucratic Model

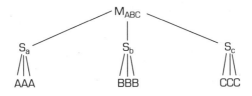

Properties

Basic departmentation puts *the same or similar* activities together—functions at highest levels, processes at middle levels, and micro-motions or "therbligs" at lowest levels.

Specialization by simplification dominates, which eases training at many levels and seeks to control errors of commission by precluding a single individual or unit from handling a complete transaction.

Authority and responsibility are basically *vertical*, following the chain of command, and each member reports to a single superior.

The span of control is narrow: each hierarchical superior monitors a small number of subordinates, given the need to oversee individual performance closely and to integrate the several particularistic components of the workflow A+B+C.

The primacy is on particularistic role and jurisdictional issues to avoid overlap while covering all contingencies.

Key: M=manager, S=supervisor, A, B, C=performers of specific contributors to a full flow of work.

issues, and they also avoid personal responsibility even when being open about specific ideas, feelings, and issues. Witness the phantom Valentine from "guess who?," for example, or the common organization charge that some "they" are out to get "me" or "us." Both of these features are reinforced and exacerbated by perceived riskiness, as well as by maudlin trust that things will work out tolerably. High trust provides a useful hedge against risky conditions.

Chapter 4 will provide the case for regenerative interaction, which contrasts sharply with the degenerative mode. So the discussion here and there will attempt to compartmentalize attention to each of the two modes, conveniently, even though one cannot really understand the one without also grasping the other.

Exhibit 3.2   Degenerative Interaction and Some Major Consequences

Degenerative Interaction

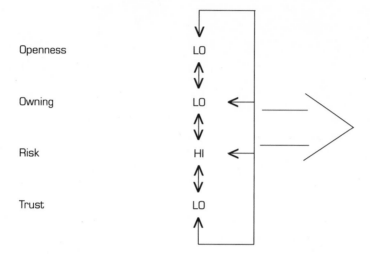

Openness	LO
Owning	LO
Risk	HI
Trust	LO

Some Consequences of Degenerative Interaction

Spurious or even false issues, ideas, and feelings tend to be raised.

Even when valid issues are raised, people will avoid ownership, as by identifying "them" as the source.

Decision making will either be short-lived, or it "solves" some apparent problems only in costly ways by avoiding real problems or by creating new and more serious ones.

Psychological success will tend to be low.

When energy levels are high, degenerative systems will tend to induce and sustain high degrees of conflict.

Over time, however, energy levels will tend to fall: consequently, the conflict potential will be reduced, but at the expense of diminished problem-solving energies and of reduced personal involvement as well as commitment.

Much of the world features degenerative interaction and, once enmeshed in it, people find it hard to escape because (for one thing) the four variables are interactive and self-heightening, as Exhibit 3.2 suggests. Bluntly, one cannot win for losing in degenerative interaction. Even well-intentioned initiatives often will be blunted, if not turned into their opposites. Consider only the relevant other returning from a long trip with a bouquet who inspires the degenerative query: What have you been doing now? More broadly, high risk and low trust complicate if they do not preclude being open and owning about ideas, feelings, and issues. In turn, this limits the capabilities of raising and solving real problems that stay solved without creating other and perhaps less tractable problems.

Exhibit 3.2 provides a substantial list of the other awkward consequences often associated with degenerative interaction.

Moreover, finessing degenerative interaction will not do, for two basic reasons. Directly, bureaucratic structures dominate in both business and government. In powerful addition, associating bureaucratic structures with degenerative interaction rests on substantial research (e.g., Zand, 1972; Golembiewski and McConkie, 1975; Boss, 1978), and informed extensions from that research also support the basic association and a formidable catalog of adverse consequences. Abundant details are available elsewhere (e.g., Golembiewski, 1979, Vol. 1; 1983; 1994). In sum, the bureaucratic structure reinforces with powerful social and psychological identifications the basic functional departmentation in the bureaucratic model which focuses on the parts of work. Hence the recent premium placed on integrating what the bureaucratic model and degenerative interaction tend to set in opposition in both government (e.g., Barzelay, 1992) as well as in business (e.g., Galbraith, Lawler, and Associates, 1993).

This fateful organizing bias of the bureaucratic model at once puts the premium on integrating the parts while raising the probabilities of interests in opposition. Why? A complete answer cannot be given here, but it has two essential aspects—between S-units and within them. The between-units case is easier to illustrate and to understand. Directly, the bureaucratic structure generates ubiquitous fragmenting forces that complicate the smooth flow of work, deriving from such persistent sources as win-lose budget decisions and cost-accounting allocations that often set unit S_A against S_B or S_C; concerns about salary increases, promotions, and career progression which reinforce vertical ties; individuating socialization and work experiences in the several S-units; and so on. The degenerative potential here also should be obvious, with (for example) depressing effects on trust and openness between S-units. Such effects have a historic prominence in the literatures of both government and business (e.g., Dalton, 1959; Golembiewski, 1962a).

The case for degenerative interaction within an S-unit is both more problematic and complicated. Thus, M_{ABC} often will lack information about S-unit performance, as later discussion will emphasize. Hence the temptation to use "staff" officials to induce upward communication and/or to employ various bypasses (including informants in an S-unit) for the purpose of catching someone doing something wrong. Such features are common and can constipate interaction within S-units and reduce trust between them and M_{ABC}, as by encouraging bypasses between operators and the M_{ABC} level. Here, risk levels will be high, and this encourages conditions favorable to degenerative interaction.

Moreover, these overall fragmenting tendencies worsen as any bureaucratic subunit develops robust features—a "strong culture," if you will. This constitutes a bad combination. Generally, for example, S-units will feature degenerative interaction as well as low cohesiveness, defined as the resultant of forces keeping an individual in a group, as discounted by those encouraging departure. As cohesiveness grows, so also does a group's control over members' behavior via conformity or consensus (e.g., Golembiewski, 1962c).

These typical conditions impoverish group and individual experiences but, paradoxically, dangers inhere in trying to improve these conditions in bureaucratic systems. Why? Consider that, in a minority of cases, regenerative interaction *may exist within any S-unit*, as may a high level of cohesiveness. To the degrees that both exist, however, this heightens the disjoint between subunits. Since degenerative interaction will tend to exist *between the S-units* in a bureaucratic structure, high cohesiveness within any S-unit will tend to heighten the defensive forces that can be mobilized to protect members from other S-units as well as from management (e.g., Golembiewski, 1962c, esp. pp. 149–70). These differentiating dynamics are critical because, for example, only *all* of the S-units working together harmoniously can create a win-win work environment or can raise productivity and improve quality, *in a bureaucratic structure*. Details are provided later.

This basic disjoint is beyond any serious debate. Witness the incredible energies directed at seeking to build normative or cultural overlays to bridge the vertical fragmentation between S-units induced by the base bureaucratic model (e.g., Golembiewski, 1993a). These overlays include the self-forcing, self-enforcing model at NASA (Sayles and Chandler, 1971, 1992); energetic efforts virtually everywhere with "team-building" to overcome degenerative interaction at executive and supervisory levels (e.g., Dyer, 1987; Golembiewski and Kiepper, 1988); Total Quality Management (TQM) programs (e.g., Deming, 1982); various Management by Objectives (MBO) efforts (e.g., McConkie, 1979); and so on. Witness, also, the greater difficulty of energizing such efforts in ongoing versus start-up settings (e.g., Golembiewski and Kiepper, 1988), as well as the need for periodic reinforcement in bureaucratic systems of even very successful programs of normative relearning or cultural change targeted to reduce degenerative interaction. Cases in point exist, both early (e.g., Golembiewski and Blumberg, 1967) and recently (e.g., Lawler, 1992). See in particular the all-but-universal prescription for basic changes in bureaucratic structures to reinforce integrative reeducation (e.g., Perkins, Nieva, and Lawler, 1983).

In conclusion, the association of the bureaucratic model and degenerative interaction may not be invariant, but it nonetheless appears to be close to that status. Much is known about why and how degenerative interaction is likely to manifest itself, and the linkages to the bureaucratic model are stout although not invariable. Moreover, we have a good sense of the basic types of relationships within as well as between S-units and also of their high incidence in organizations (e.g., Chapple and Sayles, 1961, esp. pp. 88–96).

So marked is this basic—even prototypical—association that standard designs reliably prescribe how and why to remedy degenerative effects under various conditions (e.g., Dyer, 1987). Such designs have high success rates (e.g., Golembiewski and Sun, 1993; Nicholas, 1982), and this suggests that available theory and experience qualify as serviceable if still imperfect guides. Moreover, in the absence of structural change, periodic booster shots of appropriate interventions seem necessary to inhibit the fade-out of regenerative relationships (e.g., Golembiewski and Kiepper, 1988). Again, this marked tendency implies the potency of the basic association of bureaucratic model and degenerative interaction.

So much the worse, then, for the dominant tendency to neglect the structural piece, as in the several encouragements to "reinvent government" (e.g., Osborne and Gaebler, 1992). Thus public managers are encouraged to be "entrepreneurs" while the bureaucratic tethers remain stout and tight, and this may only inspire foolhardiness within the unforgiving bureaucratic contexts that still dominate in business and especially in government. So this analysis joins the reinventors in their critique of the consequences of the bureaucratic model but also encourages looking for specific replacements of that model in structures, policies, and procedures. That concern with replacements, in any case, characterizes these Ransone Lectures, with one exemplar of the postbureaucratic structure later preoccupying Chapter 4, and policies/procedures getting substantial attention in Chapters 5 and 6.

Two high-frequency modes in degenerative interaction
The two most probable modes in which degenerative interaction works itself out not only seem clear enough, but neither is particularly helpful in efforts to value or manage diversity in bureaucracies or anywhere else. Individuals or groups within an S-unit most often generate degenerative features and, in self-heightening ways, can reinforce that outcome in one or both of two modes:

1. Withdrawal and a low energy level: here the sense of it features individuals walking in an area with many buried land mines—carefully, with trepidation, and with the pervasive sense that the greatest safety is in remaining where you are and presenting a low profile.

2. Defensiveness with a variable energy level: here the aversive stimuli are competition, different ideas or opinions, uncertainties or imponderables, and so on, with the protection taking the form of "groupthink" (e.g., Janis, 1972, 1982), which emphasizes an unquestioned belief in an S-unit's purposes and inherent morality; stereotyped views of other S-units as (e.g.) weak, dull, evil, or at least different and dangerous; and safeguards against adverse information that might lead to questions about stereotypes of others.

The energy level in the second case often heightens when the core beliefs are under attack or can be made to appear so. Dynamically, as has long been known (e.g., Festinger, Riecken, and Schachter, 1956), energies may be mobilized to urge conformity or to enforce rejection, both with great force. Typically, indeed, true believers at first direct at violators a barrage of reminders about their transgressions and later forcefully reject those who fail to respond penitently (e.g., Taras, 1991). Hence the criticality in these settings of such beliefs: "This is war, and those not with us are our enemies," to paraphrase the Nixonian variety of this genre (Raven, 1974).

Degenerative mode as a poor context for diversity
Neither of these two common variants seems of much use in efforts either to value or to manage diversity, which are the fourth and fifth approaches distinguished in Chapter 2. Indeed, in their basic and shared atavism they engage processes—isolation, fear, conformity, and so on—that seek to negate diversity, if they cannot transform it to a benign uniformity.

Consequences for diversity worsen the more one looks. Quickly, for example, the low-energy condition has limited applicability to expansions of diversity. Typically, these expansions require great energies and are impeded only by the perceived riskiness of any movement or change. This first condition helps little in dealing with diversity.

The same bottom line applies to the second mode of response to degenerative interaction, on a bit more thought and reference to experience. Although some managements may be tempted to mobilize group forces to coerce diversity, this is oxymoronic in both practice and principle. In sum, inducing conformity—as contrasted with supporting a consensus arrived at in a participative spirit—fits neither the spirit nor the profile of successful diversity-oriented systems (e.g., Jackson and Associates, 1992, esp. pp. 320–38). This fact has not precluded such attempts, but it usually dooms them.

Consider only two ways in which the second high-frequency mode of reaction to degenerative systems—an aggressive groupthink—implies potential dangers. This is patently the case when the reaction is overtly antidiversity, *as is the usual case* (e.g., Festinger, Riecken, and Schachter, 1956). It is also possible that the core

Table 3.1   Most/Least Significant Managerial
Competencies in Culturally Diverse Work Forces

	Percent reporting competency as "very important"
Interpersonal communication	89.4
Problem-solving and decision-making	85.6
Motivating employees	84.6
Building teamwork in the work group	78.8
Managing conflict in the work group	75.0
Knowledge of managerial ethics	74.0
Evaluating employee productivity	68.3
. . .	
Commitment to democratic values	46.2
Developing monetary budgets	46.2
Influencing superiors or peers	36.5
Mentoring employees in career development	35.6
Knowledge of legal processes	30.8
Using computer packages	29.8
Designing research studies or program evaluations	10.6

From Mohapatra, McDowell, and Choudhury (1993), p. 11.

beliefs might only appear to be diversity-friendly—as in the double-edged authoritarianism reflected in the dictum, "We'll do anything to help you—even if it requires hurting you" (Church and Carnes, 1972). The prognosis in this latter case does not appear positive for diversity, reasonably defined, at least over the long run.

Critical competencies for diversity stifled
by degenerative interaction
In whichever high-frequency mode, moreover, the tendencies above seem poorly adapted to the competencies that will be useful in diversity-friendly organizations. Numerous ways of supporting this point exist, and Table 3.1 takes a convenient approach. Public sector executives in seven midwestern states were asked to rank the significance of competencies in promoting culturally diverse work forces. Table 3.1 presents fourteen competencies and roughly distinguishes two clusters of them based on the highest and lowest proportions of respondents who saw them as "very important." Seven rated competencies falling in the mid-range are eliminated, and that collection of competencies is indicated by . . . in Table 3.1.

The competencies most frequently rated as "very important" have, on balance, unmistakable associations with an organization's style of interaction. In quite direct ways, degenerative interaction poorly serves these highest-rated competencies. This generalization can be seriously questioned only for one item—knowledge of managerial ethics—which may be interpreted narrowly as cognitive knowledge only. Any operational knowledge of managerial ethics, as reasonably concerned, will be diluted in multiple ways by degenerative interaction (e.g., Golembiewski, 1993a, esp. pp. 78–87).

In contrast, the competencies rated less frequently as "very important" are—as a cluster—only associated at a distance with the character and quality of interaction in an organization. Even there—as in mentoring employees or in developing monetary budgets—associations with interaction appear relatively close to the surface.

Bureaucratic structure, degenerative interaction, and gender

That bureaucratic structures and the degenerative interaction associated with them are diversity-unfriendly should already be tolerably clear, but a few words on gender should help specifically frame future elaborations of the general point. Both the bureaucratic structure and degenerative interaction literally ooze conventional "masculinity," and early observers such as Douglas McGregor (1967, p. 23) got the message, clearly and directly. No doubt about it, to him the "model of the successful manager in our culture" is definitely "masculine." McGregor adds: "The good manager is aggressive, competitive, firm, just. He is not feminine, he is not soft or yielding or dependent or intuitive in the womanly sense. The very expression of emotion is widely viewed as a feminine weakness that would interfere with effective [managerial] processes."

Broad social conditioning can reinforce this gender stereotyping relevant to organizations and their management. Thus men often are portrayed as more competent and task-oriented, while women tend to be seen as warmer and more expressive (e.g., Bem, 1974; Cahoon and Rowney, 1993, pp. 341–43). And observed behavior shows a definite tendency for both genders to play these roles—not uniformly, but substantially more rather than less (e.g., Lockheed and Hall, 1976). This closes a diversity-unfriendly loop, as it were, even as clear-eyed observers like McGregor recognize the essentially superficial character of the role-plays. He observes (1967, p. 23): "All these [alleged differences] are part of the human nature of men and women alike. Cultural forces have shaped not their existence *but their acceptability*" (emphasis added).

Job Rotation

This simple managerial technique has been a tonic at many levels of organization[3]— for production workers, air traffic controllers, nurses in pediatric oncology, even baseball umpires—and job rotation could clearly serve the purposes of diversity programs in the critical particular of heightening individual mastery at work. Needless to emphasize, the lack of mastery in numerous guises underlies the concerns of many who evaluate and experience diversity programs (e.g., Riccucci,

1991, pp. 89–97). Hence, also, the typical emphasis on the need for empowerment in connection with diversity efforts. In its baldest form, the concern is that members of minorities will be restricted to the lowest-status and even menial jobs. Job rotation fundamentally challenges that possibility, which will be heightened by acting consistently with bureaucratic ideation.

Here, consider only a few of the senses in which job rotation can contribute to mastery. In addition to providing valuable respite from boredom or stressful aspects of some tasks as well as in making the employee more valuable, job rotation—plus the cross-training it implies—can increase one's network of contacts and heighten one's sense of broader aspects of an enterprise. These common consequences are valuable in and of themselves but never more so than in organizations seeking to assess performance as a prelude to making credible promotions and career-enhancing reassignments.

Such features imply the growing usefulness of job rotation as a flood of nontraditional employees will come to challenge even well-intentioned managements. Based on past history (e.g., Jackson and Associates, 1992, pp. xvi–xvii), the temptation may be to put these new recruits in routinized jobs and to keep them there. Historical evidence from all epochs demonstrates that this temptation has proved difficult to avoid. Patently, this dour track record poorly serves the goal of valuing diversity; and it may build a legacy of mistrust and frustration.

Moreover, in addition to the obvious association with the new crowds on the "in" lanes to the new work force, job rotation and cross-training also attract in a second major sense. Specifically, the demographics imply that the "out" lanes will be unusually full in the next decade or so (Towers Perrin & Hudson Institute, 1990, esp. pp. 76–85)—that is, not only from normal retirements, but perhaps especially from cutbacks and early retirement, although the highest stages of the latter flood may have passed. Even given major economic troubles, this out-migration implies an often unrecognized need for great upward mobility, and in double-time (e.g., Littlejohn and Ezell, 1993).

Job rotation has both real requirements as well as potential costs, especially in bureaucratic organizations. Consider only the following illustrative list with details of how job rotation applications can be problematic and even troublesome in traditional structures.

Signing up Hosts. For job rotation to get started, let alone to have broad impact in any bureaucratic structure, all (or most) of the S-units must participate. This derives from the basic departmentation around the same or similar particularistic activities and hence reflects an objective dilemma rather than some personal shortcomings of people in bureaucratic structures. Directly, no single S-unit has sufficient scope for job rotation. This is obviously the case in Exhibit 3.1, and nature provides a horde of similar cases, especially at low but also at middle levels of organization.

Even at this elemental stage, then, bureaucratic structures facilitate neither job rotation nor cross-training. The barriers to start-up inherent in bureaucratic structures include multiple points of possible resistance, which encourage the manipulation or coercion from above that typically sets the teeth of all Ss on edge. Indeed, even a single S-unit with veto power—typically, a unit at the end of a long line of serially dependent units—may prevent a job rotation program, or seriously limit it, in bureaucratic systems. Perhaps more commonly, job rotation efforts can wilt from lack of attention by even less powerful S-units and their supervisors.

Such capabilities have an ironic character: management choosing bureaucratic structures often cannot win for losing. These structures often encourage job rotation, if only as a palliative to boredom; but such structures complicate if not doom what is needed. Typically, as observers have long known (e.g., Chapple and Sayles, 1961, esp. pp. 92–93), managements have been aware of the power of well-situated S-units to generate resistance to overhead direction and hence have been consciously or intuitively responsive to their needs and even whims. For example, wildcat strikes or other work stoppages occur with greatest frequency in S-units toward or at the end of long lines of sequential specialties in common flows of work, and hence employees there often receive higher wages or other benefits for not doing what bureaucratic structures permit or even encourage.

Anticipating Rewards/Punishments. Given the high probability that all Ss will urge that they already have enough to do, a major part of the difficulty in sign-up for job rotation relates to an unattractive asymmetry caused by the bureaucratic structure. Ss will pay most of the costs, whether job rotation succeeds or fails. But it seems probable that, if it succeeds, payoffs will go to either M_{ABC} or to the rotatees.

This often seems an unattractive bargain to Ss. Not only does it discourage signing on as a host, but it also diminishes the motivation to hang in there as the program unfolds and all-but-inevitable problems in implementation develop. Incentives are not everything in life, but managements are poorly advised to institutionalize basic disincentives.

The point is *not* that job rotation is always doomed to failure in bureaucratic structures. Rather, success will require that Ss transcend their immediate interests, and betting on that is a good way to go broke. Some organizations try to supply such an immediate self-interest, as by specifying in MBO agreements that an S commit to providing X employees considered promotable over some time interval. Even here, the issue remains the priorities assigned to job rotation by each S and M_{ABC}, which will tend to differ because of where they sit.

Selecting Candidates for Rotation. One cost is easy for Ss to anticipate. Ideally, rotatees should come from their best or better performers; but the practical temptation is to unload one's walking wounded. Losses to each S are possible, whatever eventuates. Thus idealistic Ss will not only be urged to sacrifice temporarily their best or better people to rotation stints, but there is no guarantee that valued resources will return. Incautious Ss may end up with rotatees who are someone else's problem.

The objective dilemma can constitute a major barrier to smoothly run job rotation efforts. Even guarantees about returning all rotatees to home bases will not resolve the issue. The reasons will become clear in the next two subsections, especially the second one.

Socializing Rotatees. As plenty of evidence indicates, and has for a long time (e.g., Blake, Mouton, Barnes, and Greiner, 1964), learning has start-up costs associated in substantial part with "comfortable uncertainty"—finding a place for oneself, being accepted, and so on, in the new learning context. Many employees will reject the risk, and particularly when they come from an attractive or powerful S-unit as well as when degenerative interaction exists in other units.

Here, traditional structures also can be troublesome. Elementally, the several S-units often will be standoffish, if not in actual conflict about budgets, in contests over the relative worth of their narrow contributions, and so on. Hence S-unit defenses often will be up, on many occasions so much so that reasonable candidates for rotation will view their "opportunity" cautiously, if not negatively. The hosts of candidates also may be cautious, in direct proportion to how many "dead cats" have been thrown into the backyards of hosts by the home S-units of specific rotatees; the number and importance of proprietary secrets that a potential host unit may be profiting from at the expense of other S-units; and so on.

Fundamentally, perhaps, S-units in traditional structures are often locked into divisive games about relative contributions to performance. Staff units may be assigned to policing such judgments, which produce and enforce wage-and-salary schedules or time standards; or the results of scuffling may appear in negotiating looser budgets or in higher success rates in gaining promotions. In any case, bureaucratic structures encourage Ss to look out primarily for self and their own, rather than for the integrative flow of work. In contrast, rotation programs require attention to the needs of other Ss, to temporary rotatees and employees, as well as to systemic needs. These two pathways of concern may not meet and, in the usual case, will not track one another for very long if they do.

This common fundamental can encourage a trying time for rotatees. Indeed, in extreme cases of the fragmenting political games that bureaucratic structures encourage, rotatee failure will be interpreted by the self-serving as validating the self-proclaimed high status of the host S-unit, as well as justifying the lower status attributed by the host to the home S-unit. In sum, rotatees can become pawns in power games.

Catching people doing something wrong is a game that has real downside potential for all parties. Such fragmenting conditions, in virtually all cases, are poorly matched to the valuing of diversity, and even less so to its successful management.

Managing Successful Rotatees. This point often gets neglected, but the plain fact is that traditional structures provide no convenient place for successful rotatees to go. Again, this is a direct structural consequence rather than an idiosyncratic perversity.

All too often, the paradoxical result of successful rotation is to heighten the competition for S positions. This, of course, brings us back to the first point above. Or successful rotatees can return to their original unit, which, unfortunately, provides no easy way to use their new skills. Worse still, this return to the status quo ante in effect constitutes a regression in terms of Herzbergian motivators (Herzberg, Snyderman, and Mausner, 1959) or of Argyrian dimensions for self-actualization (Argyris, 1957). Dynamically, this has self-defeating features. The more a job rotation program succeeds in creating new skills and greater mastery, given placement difficulties, the more will such programs fail in the more important senses of promoting human growth and empowerment.

This dreary catalog could be extended and expanded, but the bottom line should be clear. Generic features associated with bureaucratic approaches can complicate—if not always pollute—specific initiatives such as job rotation and cross-training that otherwise have diversity-friendly potential. Diversity initiatives will powerfully escalate these generic tendencies toward organizational mischief. Particular problems might be anticipated in selection, socialization, and rating of rotatees' performance. Such anticipated difficulties might well encourage S-unit heads into trying to raise their drawbridges when it comes to job rotation or cross-training.

These probabilities suggest real lost opportunities, or at least great costs. Let us consider a positive (if brief) case for how a well-done rotation effort, with associated cross-training, can be responsive to all major stakeholders interested in diversity-friendly work—employees as well as management. Temporary overloads or absenteeism at A or B or C can be responded to easily, even spontaneously, often because the situation demands it rather than because of supervisory order. This reduces the reliance on command ——> obey linkages, and this will support maturing diversity. In contrast, overloads or absenteeism in any S-unit in a bureaucratic structure can sharply limit output, and this often encourages efforts to overstaff as a supervisory defense against eventualities or probabilities. The powerful S-unit typically does best in such anticipatory hoarding of resources, which adds immediate self-interest to the list of fragmenting tendencies in bureaucratic structures. Clear winners do not seem likely, however, because other S-units will be similarly tempted.

These bureaucratic inflexibilities imply serious problems. Note the little-remarked fact that at least one-half of all mothers in the work force have children under age 1, and about two-thirds have children under age 7. The numbers encourage incredulity but come from a distinguished student of management (Ginzberg, 1992, p. xvii).

Even when a second parent is present in the family, this situation implies serious cross-pressures for the mother, who will most often—if present tendencies continue —be the primary emergency caregiver whenever problems occur with children, as they often do.

The implied attractions of job rotation and cross-training should be obvious in the case of working mothers as well as more generally. Cross-training will reduce the work-site effects of any required absences for child rearing or other reasons. Cross-training also makes it simpler to use such features as flexible work hours, whose basic motivation also derives in large part from the special needs of nontraditional work forces (e.g., Golembiewski, Hilles, and Kagno, 1974). Chapter 5 adds detail about this significant point, as well as others.

Job Enrichment

Much the same case applies to job enrichment, which has a holistic view of work and aggregates activities into jobs that increase workers' control over a set of related activities. In the present case, several enlarged jobs are possible: A+B, B+C, A+C, and, penultimately, A+B+C. The positive case is straightforward: individual needs often will be served by the expanding knowledge, skills, and orientations associated with job enrichment; and most organizations, goaded by our ongoing revolution in electronic data storage and processing as well as by the need for lean work forces, frequently give clearer-eyed recognition to job enrichment and cross-training as practical necessities. Earlier rationales for job enrichment emphasized value and humanistic issues (e.g., Argyris, 1957), and practical considerations increasingly give such ideals solid reinforcement (e.g., Lawler, 1992, esp. pp. 80–88). In their most elaborated form, these practical urgencies call for "learning organizations" in our managerial future (e.g., Garvin, 1993).

In sum, then, the sub-sections below emphasize two themes. Job enrichment variously serves diversity. However, the bureaucratic structure poorly suits job enrichment.

Diversity

Until recently, job enrichment has been avoided by believers in the traditional structure, poorly serving diversity in the process. Thus job enrichment requires trained and motivated employees, acting so as to satisfy the "higher-order needs" identified by Chris Argyris (1957) and others. Oppositely, nontraditional employees in past times often were sloughed-off into the narrow jobs prescribed by the bureaucratic model.

Nowadays, this cavalier approach has sharply-increasing costs. Consider only four senses in which this stark statement applies. First, job enrichment applications have substantial success rates in today's organizations (e.g., Alber, 1978; Lawler, 1992, esp. pp. 80–88). Hence the design will be in the inventory of many employing firms and agencies for a simple reason: it "works."

Second, to elaborate on how it "works," job enrichment has been used to induce a range of effects attractive to both employees and employing organizations. To sample only, this management strategy has attractive consequences for both individuals and work design:

- The attractions for individuals include greater autonomy and control at work, which are central in many theories concerning healthy adjustments to work (e.g., Katzell, 1994, pp. 22–25); high satisfaction and involvement; lower absenteeism and turnover (Mobley, 1982); and greater senses of involvement in work and ownership of its products (Perkins, Nieva, and Lawler, 1983; Lawler, 1993).
- The attractions for the design of work and its consequences include greater flexibility in mobilizing human resources and equipment (Lawler, 1992, pp. 87–88); higher quality, often "dramatically" (Lawler, 1992, p. 82), because of greater responsibility of specific employees for a "total job" and their consequent identification with work; higher productivity often results but, on specific tasks, modest decreases may occur as narrow specialization decreases (Prokesh, 1991); and sharp reductions often occur in "overhead"—in supervision, middle management, and staff services (Lawler, 1992, p. 82).

Hence growing numbers of employees will be exposed to job enrichment and often will find it attractive.

Third, the years beyond 2000 will see a growing crunch to replace aging supervision and management. Job enrichment will provide useful developmental experiences that inform selection processes and at multiple levels. Job enrichment can provide early tests for work force entrants as they progress through the ranks, which alone will give fuller meaning to managing diversity.

Fourth, the case for job enrichment as diversity-friendly as well as managerially useful can be boldly made in the context of the aging of our work force that is in our immediate future because of lengthening lives and the all-but-inevitable increases in the age of mandatory retirement, among many other reasons that include the sharp decline in physically exhausting work as well as the labor shortages in some job categories anticipated in the next decades (e.g., Towers Perrin & Hudson Institute, 1990). In the federal service, aging will be especially pronounced. Indeed, the projections of *Civil Service 2000* are startling (Hudson Institute, 1988, p. 27, emphasis added): "The continuing aging of the Federal workforce that will result as large numbers of baby boomers move toward retirement presents a major challenge to managers. . . . Toward the end of the century, *the median age of Federal workers is likely to reach an all-time high.*"

Anticipating the associations of aging with continuous job enrichment does not require great analytic capabilities. If nothing else, boredom often will become a growing problem for the aged and experienced, unless the content of jobs is enhanced. Moreover, longer worklives will perforce require more major shifts in jobs—and, indeed, in careers—and consequently there will be a premium on getting larger numbers of employees acclimated ab initio to job changes as a pervasive requirement, even if technological and product/service innovations abate (which seems unlikely). Insistent attention to more or less continuous job changes and enrichment also will require appropriate adjustments of attitudes. This will be the case especially in connection with learning how to learn, or with "learning organizations" (e.g., Vogt and Murrell, 1990), as contrasted with the learning of a specific skill or job routine that resonates to bureaucratic thoughtways. Perhaps most ominously, successful job enrichment and upskilling constitute the often-unrecognized keys to avoiding social turmoil—if not warfare in the streets—as a consequence of our "sending low-skill jobs overseas" by our various free-trade efforts.

Let us balance the argument a bit, even though the saber-rattling just concluded is appropriate. Efforts at job enrichment and diversity can encompass forces in opposition, as well as complementary and enhancing features. That is, enrichment eliminates many simplified roles into which the organizationally unsophisticated traditionally fit and also jeopardizes many of the overseer positions to which they could aspire. At the same time, job enrichment provides a quick and real-time picture of a person's abilities and attitudes concerning constructively coping with burgeoning interpersonal and cognitive complexities. This potential well suits diversity efforts, for their results must be broadly credible to avoid negative allegations and attributions.

Congenial Structures

These various advantages of job enrichment, extending far beyond cross-training, constitute no simple add-ons to the bureaucratic structure. In central particulars, indeed, the concept implies a negation of the bureaucratic structure, especially in the significant particular of sharply reducing the once huge corps of supervisors and staff required to oversee performance of those in jobs specialized by simplification. Other consequences are more subtle. Thus managements often relied on multiple levels of supervisors and middle managers to induce loyalty as well as to reward it, in both business and public settings (e.g., Marrow, 1974). That costly convenience does not necessarily facilitate work, however, and often simply confounds it. Consequently, new ways with fewer negative effects will have to be found.

The bureaucratic model promises little help in developing the complementarities and even less help in moderating the objective dilemmas. In sum, *absent basic structural change*, job enrichment is heir to the same problems as job rotation, and no doubt in heightened form. Overall, Exhibit 3.1 provides an unsuitable context for job enrichment: for example, no single S-unit can host such an effort, by definition; moreover, the logic of job enlargement is on a collision course with the fundaments of the bureaucratic model—limited span of control, close oversight of performance, and organizing work in terms of parts rather than the wholes emphasized by job enrichment.

Hence, without basic structural change, job enrichment applications can paradoxically fail even as they succeed. For example, one famous application in business succeeded grandly in an experimental setting, only to be embroiled in broader organization politics when it became clearer that many middle management positions would not be required if job enrichment took hold officially (Walton, 1979). Precisely the same situation and consequences occurred in the public sector (e.g., Marrow, 1974, esp. pp. 19–23).

The case for the antipathy between job enrichment and the bureaucratic model is illustrated by a common abortive scenario (e.g., Levinson, 1993). Management becomes convinced of the flexibility and likely increases in productivity that effective job enrichment can bring. The expected great leap forward is announced to a hastily assembled work force, often accustomed to bureaucratic modes as well as to degenerative interaction. These are likely to constitute roadblocks when concerted changes inconsistent with them are attempted. Employees puzzle about what is for real and may be tentative because they do not have relevant skills or attitudes. Management is hurt and often will label employees as ingrates intent only on resistance to change to management progress (e.g., Levinson, 1993).

Worse still, bureaucratic infrastructure can suck the life even from spectacularly successful postbureaucratic innovations such as job enrichment. Consider the well-researched Catch 22 at the Gaines plant in Topeka (Ketchum and Trist, 1992, pp. 25–26). Soon after coming on stream, the Topeka plant was exceeding other units in both productivity and quality, despite its universally acknowledged disadvantages of scale. Great? Quite the opposite.

Bureaucratic features in the Gaines system made real losers out of apparent winners via a policy double whammy. The Topeka plant deliberately rejected a many-layered bureaucracy, but the broader Gaines system was designed with just such a tall and functionally departmentalized structure in mind. Lyman Ketchum and Eric Trist present a vivid description of the self-defeating consequences (1992, pp. 25–26) of that poor fit with job enrichment:

> Corporate policy held that an individual could advance only so many job points at a time. . . . For a team leader, the next step in the Topeka hierarchy was production manager, a jump in job points exceeding that allowed by corporate policy. Promotion in the Topeka system was therefore foreclosed. One

would have to be promoted to a higher-level job in another plant. But here another corporate policy intervened: interplant transfers and promotions were restricted to people in jobs carrying more points than did the team leader job. Therefore, promotion to another plant was foreclosed.

Performance Appraisal

A solid performance appraisal system—including a supporting culture, techniques, and counseling skills—is both helpful and commonly lacking. The case for the broad point of view has been drawn fully elsewhere (e.g., U.S. GAO, 1993a; Golembiewski, 1986a), and aggressive readers can consult the very patchy record of the Civil Service Reform Act, in which difficulties with interaction and structure account for much of the often unenthusiastic reception to its provisions for performance appraisal and bonuses (e.g., Volcker, 1989).

For diversity, specifically, performance appraisal plays an even more crucial and problematic role. To illustrate, the performances of minorities and their evaluation at best will involve numerous serious difficulties. They include (Cox, 1993, pp. 58–102) the common need for nontraditional employees to act unnaturally in workplaces with cultures that may be strange, if not alien; the added complexity of behavioral choices by nontraditional employees; possible loss of a sense of identity in adopting to work cultures; possible or even probable prejudice and discrimination; and very probable negative stereotyping.

If this broad-brushing about the relevance of performance appraisal is reasonably accurate, diversity seems in for an ordeal. Thus we know little about the basic micro-dynamics, especially at the executive level where problems seem to be greatest (e.g., Gioia and Longenecker, 1994). Broadly, directly, and perhaps especially in the public sector, the record of performance appraisal seems shabby. Consider these sources of evidence (U.S. GAO, 1993a, esp. pp. 7, 43): In 1992, a survey of thirty-one thousand federal employees revealed that only 19 percent believed performance appraisals motivated employees to "perform well." In 1989, less than one-third of about thirty-five hundred federal personnel specialists agreed that performance management systems "improved organizational effectiveness." Such evidence is *not* selective, and related effects appear in many places (e.g., Volcker, 1989).

This subsection proposes that such sorry reactions to performance appraisal derive in major ways from the bureaucratic structures under which people work, perhaps especially in the public service. That this crucial and compound generalization typically escapes explicit comment (e.g., U.S. GAO, 1993a) heightens the crucial character of the point.

Let us begin with a flat-footed assertion, which will then be supported by structural interpretations and some empirical research: bureaucratic structures induce little confidence that performance appraisal will be diversity-friendly. Indeed, on very definite balance, that model obfuscates and complicates the appraisal of performance. Basically, perhaps, such structures encourage degenerative interaction—high risk, as well as low openness, owning, and trust. After all, the bureaucratic model rests on basic distrust—in precluding any individual from handling a complete transaction, or in the narrow span of control and the close oversight it not only permits but explicitly intends. This mode of interaction provides an inhospitable context for an effective performance appraisal system (e.g., Gioia and Longenecker, 1994). Such a system profits from, and indeed may require, an environment that emphasizes learning rather than narrow control, trust in opposition to prevailing suspicion, and credibility and commitment rather than coercion or narrow control (e.g., Golembiewski, 1986a).

Traditional structures build around a fixation on the parts of work rather than complete flows and in that basic sense inhibit reasonable judgments about contributions to holistic performance. Performance does *not* inhere in the activities structurally differentiated by the bureaucratic model but derives more basically from their smooth integration in an identifiable flow of work. That integration *can* occur in bureaucratic structures *if* individuals performing separate activities mesh like the proverbial well-oiled machine. But that outcome is usually problematic.

In other words, bureaucratic structures focus on differentiating the parts of a flow of work, while the whole is what counts, for example, in how the combined activities impact a customer or client, or in what qualitative features come to characterize the product or service. The point can be expressed in esoteric ways relevant at both high and low levels of organization, for example, in "differential priority rosters" at upper levels of businesses and governments (Golembiewski, 1983). But the basic point is simple when it comes to judgments about pay and performance. Bureaucratic structures encourage such concerns as, How many As are equal to how many Bs?; or How much more (if any) skill is required to do A than B?

These and related concerns are at least tangential to the holistic issue: How well is $A+B+C$ performed? Commonly, the focus on the separate activities—in both the functional departmentation and the derivative political issues—usually complicates and distorts the basic total judgment and often obfuscates it. Consider only the cost-accounting version of "throwing dead cats in somebody else's backyard," as when it comes to the issue of who is responsible for a glitch in $A+B+C$. Two generalizations apply. Practical realities encourage each separate bureaucratic S-unit to avoid blame and claim success. Whoever wins, the total effect seldom is a happy one for the system.

To put the point in perhaps extreme form, performance appraisal in degenerative systems within bureaucratic structures is more likely to induce narrow loyalty to one's subsystem or S-unit than contribute to a flow of work. The differences can be profound and usually are consequential.

Of course, one can design various surveillance systems—for example, a centralized Quality Control staff—to monitor such subsystemic biases. But that is always costly; it usually results in queuing and handling problems, if not in delays and conflicts; and such devices often raise the level of the artfulness of the convenient (or even necessary) subterfuges by the "line." Most important, such surveillance systems do not relate to the basic causes of the problem. These inhere in the very bureaucratic structure that provides the raison d'être for the usual line-staff distinction (e.g., Golembiewski, 1967), and its fragmenting potential is well known (e.g., Chapple and Sayles, 1961). One can variously damn such features, and that may even help one's disposition on occasion, but basic structural change seems required (e.g., Golembiewski, 1967).

Alternative to structural change, one can pound away at integrative themes like "serving the customer" or "quality is everybody's job." These are often reasonable enough in themselves, given caveats relevant in the public service, where the recipient of services is more an "owner" than a "customer" (e.g., Frederickson, 1992). Fundamentally, however, the problem with such themes is what is missing, as Sherlock Holmes taught us in the *Hound of the Baskervilles*. In plainspeak, the prominence of such integrative themes indicates what is typically missing in bureaucratic structures: their purpose is to create crosswalks between and among the social, psychological, and structural baronies induced or encouraged by the bureaucratic model. Put briefly, the bureaucratic model encourages a pervasive subsystemic bias around the interests of each of the S-units. Hence bureaucratic structures at once explain the common (and even desperate) emphasis on holistic notions like "serving the customer," and bureaucratic structures also simultaneously constitute one of the major impediments to acting on those themes.

This puts the bureaucratic model in the curious position of being the major motivator as well as the most substantial barrier to postbureaucratic innovation—its John the Baptist as well as its Judas, as it were. In Exhibit 3.1, for example, the whole is A+B+C; but no S-unit has responsibility for it. M_{ABC} must struggle against these separatist tides and tendencies, and so must each S, if typically with far less motivation than integrative officials like M_{ABC}.

The basic point has not escaped close observers and even those who shrink from structural change. Illustratively, consider the common aversion to performance appraisals in Total Quality Management variants housed in bureaucratic structures, with TQM aficionados often seeing appraisal as doing little good while inducing tension and threat that are better avoided. Indeed, one might more accurately speak of an antithesis rather than an aversion (e.g., Bowman, 1994).

In any case, TQM directs an all-but-universally constant emphasis on two themes. Quality is everyone's business, and most definitely it is not some "staff"

Quality Control unit's business, as would be encouraged or mandated in bureaucratic structures. Why? The obvious rationale is that a strong QC mandate often has a double meaning in practice—that QC "success" is gained at the expense of others (as in "catching *them* doing something wrong"); and that some "line" successes imply QC "failure" (as in outwitting the controllers or in countering them with greater power).

The point also holds the other way around, as in the good advice to "catch somebody doing something right." That is a way of counterbalancing the inexorable tendencies generated by the bureaucratic model (Peters and Waterman, 1982), but the advice constitutes a band-aid for the symptoms rather than a structural remedy for the causes.

Three summary perspectives
There is no end to such analysis-cum-speculation, but three perspectives serve as a useful in-process summary. For some, the main issue here is, Why should the organization adapt to the workers, as opposed to the workers adapting to it? The working answer has three aspects. Practically, organizations may be a long time waiting on that happy outcome and, particularly where skills and commitment are in short supply, passive organizations will be at a competitive disadvantage. Normatively, moreover, the present focus moves away from "the organization" as the final and sole arbiter. Realistically, there seems to me little probability that "organizational interests" will be seriously neglected in such accommodations to people.

Two additional perspectives apply to employee and management, respectively. From the employee's perspective, it seems clear enough what leads to acceptance of performance appraisal processes. As Lee Gardenswartz and Anita Rowe (1993, pp. 193–96) remind us, this acceptance will increase when employees believe that constructive purposes are being served, as in helping them to do their jobs better and in highlighting useful targets for personal development; that the measurement system will permit assignment of equitable rewards; and that the measurements and rewards rest on acceptable standards. As the discussion above should establish, however, the bureaucratic model provides inadequate service to these bases of acceptance. For example, that traditional model directs attention away from holistic performance, requires a policing apparatus, encourages evasion, and triggers the burgeoning of powerful subsystemic loyalties.

In addition, from management's perspective, bureaucratic structures inhibit acting on two useful generalizations about performance appraisal. Again, Gardenswartz and Rowe (1993, pp. 201–5) direct our attention to these two managerially relevant generalizations about performance appraisal. Thus management is well-advised to move away from traits or personal characteristics as criteria for evaluation and to move toward behaviors directly related to meaningful performance.

The traditional model discourages these movements, and opens evaluations to charges of a "Mickey Mouse" focus on numerous and narrow traits. Moreover, management should also remember that no performance appraisal system is value-free or culture-free. The bureaucratic model infuses its systems with values that are specific to subsystemic interests and is mischievous in that basic sense. Reward subsystemic activities, and that is what will get emphasis. Important "wholes" will tend to be neglected: for example, responsibility for performance on A+B+C; "serving the customer," whether external to the organization or an internal user, as contrasted with serving A or B or C interests; and so on.

Awkward Homogeneous Aggregating

Furthermore, diversity will be served by structural features and approaches that reduce or manage separatisms. Why? The differentiating potential of diverse work forces is inherently great, by definition. For example, as Cox usefully argues (1993, esp. pp. 108–29), cultural differences imply that organizations have to contain— and, ideally, to build around—such major classes of potential fragmenting forces in how people from different cultural backgrounds vary in orientations to space and time, leadership styles, individualism versus collectivism, cooperative versus competitive orientation, locus of control (internal versus external), and communication styles.

Here, again, the prognosis does not favor the bureaucratic model, which is better at seeking to enforce uniformity than at containing diversity. Indeed, it is reasonably accurate to propose that uniformity is an explicit goal of the bureaucratic model. One does not have to read Franz Kafka in the original German to come to that conclusion. Worse still, the bureaucratic approach's pursuit of uniformity creates major divisiveness.

A single example pointedly illustrates the suboptimizing features of the bureaucratic model. Free from the disciplining potential of the measurement of holistic performance, and facing the homogeneous self-interests of mono-specialized employees, individual S-unit supervisors often will take easy (but costly) ways out. Consider the common perversion of performance appraisal in bureaucratic structures. "Even when managers reluctantly follow the process," Larry M. Lane concludes (1993, p. 8), "they typically do so in ways that are not contemplated by the objectives of the system." Consider "rating inflation," which Lane (1993, p. 9) sees as "abundantly present." Here, the goals sought by managers maintain group harmony at the expense of the accuracy of appraisal ratings. As Kevin R. Murphy and Jeanette N. Cleveland (1991, p. 187) describe the suboptimizing induced in the pursuit of uniformity: "The personnel manual may state that accurate performance appraisals are expected, but if this will lead to friction, decreased motivation, and so on, the supervisor who skillfully inflates his or her ratings is acting in the [subunit's] best interest" but probably not in the best interest of the larger organization.

Such wicked double binds help explain why and how performance appraisals in bureaucratic structures "often don't work" (Schneier, Beatty, and Baird, 1988, p. 81). In sum, the traditional system encourages self-defeating dynamics.

Four additional emphases further illustrate aspects of the awkward tendency of the bureaucratic model, in its pursuit of uniformity, to induce vertical fragmentation where horizontal or lateral integration is preferred, or is even required. The broad point was made early on (e.g., Golembiewski, 1962d, 1967), and its salience in recent days has escalated sharply (e.g., Galbraith, 1993a, 1993b; Mohrman, 1993). Here, four reinforcing aspects of the fundamental structural myopia deal with an extended example from workaday levels, a useful theoretical statement, a sense of recent organizational adjustments at executive levels, and a preview of near-future probabilities.

A case at federal operating levels

An extended example illustrates the general point, which comes from an office of the Social Security Administration (SSA) (Rainey and Rainey, 1986a, 1986b). This mini-case sacrifices comprehensiveness to convenience, while preserving the fidelity of the representation. The SSA site was highly bureaucratized, including one S-unit of clerks and another S-unit of claims analysts with somewhat higher grade levels. Both activities required close integration at numerous points, but the separatist prescriptions of the bureaucratic structure nonetheless dominated. That was nothing new, the usual fragmenting tendencies in this case—different attributed status, avoiding the blame for errors in disputes, and so on in several S-units—were exacerbated by another differentiator: race. Broadly, those in the lower-status activity had black skins, and the higher-status unit was white-skinned.

Things being as they often are—at times reflecting favoritism, at times reinforced by differential opportunities, education, and experience—minorities may well find themselves in lower-status activities in a higher proportion of cases than can be justified by equity, their numbers in an organization, or whatever. That is bad enough, but the bureaucratic model's fixation on homogeneous departmentation makes matters worse by grouping high- or low-status activities in *separate* organization units.

Consequently, then, the "normal" fragmentation associated with the bureaucratic model can be rigidified by other differences—in race, or whatever. This potential exacerbates the kind of bureaucratic structural dynamics described at several points above, especially in a diverse work force.

How common are such effects of "awkward homogeneous aggregating" in bureaucratic structures? Quite common, it appears, and with all probable trends angling upward. Consider gender, which has received major recent attention. The traditional view has it that bureaucratic organizations are rational-technical tools for maximizing efficiency, with positions to be filled by the best available candidates. This position is now under serious attack (e.g., Acker, 1990; Cockburn, 1988). As Patricia Martin concludes (1992, p. 208):

> Gender is such a constitutive part of formal organizations that efforts to match *worker with activity* are often efforts to match *gender and activity*: finding men to do men's work, finding women to do women's work. . . . Labor markets, jobs, occupations, organizational hierarchies, work groups, work activities, technology uses, supervisory practices, and procedures for promotion, hiring, and advancement, and so on, are gendered.

Such gendering can occur along a broad spectrum. Thus it can result from direct male collusion to force women into low-paying, dead-end, and unattractive jobs (e.g., Cockburn, 1988), with the genders being clustered in separate work units in bureaucratic contexts. Or the conclusion can occur at a distance, as it were, as differentiating socialization or acculturation tendencies that later may steer the genders toward different activities or jobs.

This proclivity of bureaucratic structures—to departmentalize around single functions or processes, which often are reinforced by other separatisms such as gender, color, and perhaps culture in the SSA example above—stands in marked contrast to what we know in some substantial detail about how to create a balance between differences. The essential prescription is basically the same whether the purpose is to integrate the separate activities in a flow of work like A+B+C, to facilitate communication between people, or to encourage mutually rewarding relationships between the full range of opinional, demographic, skill, or cultural differences. In sum, as the deliberately dated citations below emphasize, we have long known that the integration of differences requires three conditions:

1. Individuals and groups should share superordinate goals or "cooperative interdependencies" (Festinger and Kelly, 1951), while bureaucratic structures encourage fragmenting identifications between S-units and suboptimizing goals within them.
2. Individuals and groups "should experience a good deal of equal-status *contact under rewarding conditions* [for those who] cooperate and develop interdependence" (Fromkin and Sherwood, 1974, p. 211), while bureaucratic structures prescribe mediated contact between S-units as well as encourage win-lose conditions that in the bargain are keyed to subsystemic performance.
3. Individuals and groups should be characterized by qualities such as perceived similarities, familiarity, and personal liking (e.g., McGuire, 1969), which bureaucratic structures tend to discourage between S-units. Such qualities may or

may not exist within an S-unit but, if they do, that probably will serve to exacerbate any conflict between S-units.

The catalog of prescriptions could be extended, but the essential points remain, and they have not changed materially over time (e.g., Zander, 1982, esp. pp. 85–147). In practice, we have made underwhelming use of what we know about the integration of differences.

A casual (but consequential) theoretical formulation

This bureaucratic fixation on homogeneous grouping can be reinforced by many other separatisms, in sum, and that extremism constitutes no virtue, overall. Oppositely, the idea is to integrate the several activities in a flow of work such as A+B+C. Moreover, there will be numerous differentiators, even in the simplest of cases, and our organizational future promises heightened complexity. So why add to the fragmentation, deliberately and structurally?

This fragmenting potential of the bureaucratic model has huge consequences, as a lighthearted theoretical formulation indicates. Consider the Golembiewski First Law of Social Dynamics: That which is easiest, or most convenient, is more likely to occur.

The bureaucratic structure in Exhibit 3.1 promises travail if not trouble in connection with the First Law, as in the matter of who can raise output, or lower it.

Clearly, only all of the S-units, acting collaboratively, can increase output in bureaucratic structures. But any one of those S-units can decrease output, especially S-units at the end, or the beginning, of a flow of work. This may not appear obvious, but brief contemplation suggests the probable dynamics and their significance. Should S_C set in motion forces to reduce output, that will not always be easy to determine or to counteract, especially if S_C is somehow powerful, willful, and skillful at proposing uniquely difficult features of doing C. If S_A and S_B maintain their pace, that may be turned into an indictment concerning their slack resources, so those at A and B may be well-advised to curb their effort. Absent that, in fact, their "excess" resources might be transferred to S_C, who pleads being in deep need. At the very least, S_A and S_B will be vulnerable to charges by S_C that the other two activities are simply easier, require less skill, or whatever.

So what is easier or most convenient? That should be clear enough.

The First Law provides perspective on why it is disingenuous to reinforce or exacerbate the basic fragmenting tendencies in bureaucratic structures. This is precisely what occurred in the SSA thumbnail case, sketched above: differences in race reinforced the separate units departmentalized around the several activities. Although the effect was in part owing to other causes, it remains nonetheless noteworthy that a huge increase in productivity occurred when postbureaucratic structural changes were implemented (Rainey and Rainey, 1986a, 1986b). Many differences could serve as reinforcers or exacerbators of fragmentation—race, local cultures or styles of management, different ways of doing business in the S-units, higher cohesiveness in one of the S-units, and so on.

The First Law of Social Dynamics also encourages in bureaucracies a pervasive bias toward uniformity, between S-units as well as derivatively within them. To make a long story short, one is well-advised to pursue homogeneity in bureaucratic structures, lest *any* differentiating features reinforce the already powerful forces toward fragmentation.

The fixation on homogeneity is neither perverse nor curious. Rather, it merely reflects the poor odds in bureaucratic structures of dealing effectively with almost any differences or individuation. Directly, output or throughput almost always requires horizontal integration—A+B+C, in the present case. But bureaucratic structures encourage vertical fragmentation—A versus B versus C, as it were. Hence the need for homogeneity and narrow control, lest bad come to worse. Hence also the awkward fit of the bureaucratic model and diverse work forces.

A sense of recent adjustments at multiple levels
The fundamental limits of the functional or bureaucratic structure have not escaped attention, of course, but the implications have slowly influenced practice. Overall, for example, close observers have come to a common conclusion (Galbraith, Lawler, and Associates, 1993, p. 85): "The old, hierarchical forms cannot produce the necessary improvements in speed, quality, and productivity. This fact has led to a virtual landslide of ideas about how organizations can operate more effectively with less hierarchy, less overhead, and more participative management."

The stimuli for such revisionism have been building for a half-century and more (e.g., Chandler, 1962), but today clearly represents the flood tide of new strategic initiatives featuring total quality, reduced cycle times, and customer orientations versus self-absorption with internal organizational dynamics. Galbraith (1993a, p. 64) has no reservations about bringing such new or augmented strategic forces to a fine point: "Such initiatives expose the weaknesses of the functional organization, since [those initiatives] require many multifunctional responses and trade-offs. Increasingly, the new information [technologies] will allow greater cross-functional communication and integration, permitting this evolution to continue."

Two basic modes dominate in this fateful transitioning. As Chapter 4 especially details, fundamental structural alternatives to the bureaucratic or functional model have appeared. More commonly, modifications of the basic bureaucratic model have been developed by theorists and practitioners—as in normative or value overlays that seek to integrate the "gaps" in the vertical fragmentation induced by functional structures, in supplementary and often temporary "parallel structures" like those in quality circles, or in various team-building or development activities that seek to bring together what functional structures tend to set in opposition (e.g., Mohrman, 1993), if not in direct conflict.

The so-called super staff functions illustrate efforts to moderate fragmentation at top levels while otherwise retaining the basic functional or bureaucratic model that structurally encourages it. Consider the "product supply system" at Procter & Gamble, which combines under a single authority several previously independent staff activities—purchasing, engineering, manufacturing, and distribution—to provide "materials management" services to division heads, with a counterpart supply unit for each division. A common metric for estimating performance— "total delivered cost"—reinforces the social and psychological identifications of each unit with its mandated division, and this combination is seen as generating useful integrative outcomes—for example, "reducing flow times, reducing inventories, and increasing on-time delivery and quality" (Galbraith, 1993a, esp. p. 53).

A sense of the near future

These first five managerial features do not work well for diversity, viewed broadly, in bureaucratic structures, and clear demographic trends imply the special awkwardness of the bureaucratic model in the fifth particular. To illustrate, consider the probable composition of tomorrow's work force. In 1980, about 25 percent of New York City's population was foreign-born, but the estimate for 2000 is 57 percent. In the city's borough of Queens, even more impressively, it is reported that the students in a single public school speak more than one hundred first languages when at home (Ginzberg, 1992, pp. xvi).

The temptation at work—perhaps even the necessity—will be to assign speakers in different native tongues to separate S-units under the bureaucratic model. That was the dominant pattern in our earlier days of mass immigrations. The consequence will be to add multifaceted fragmenting force to the barriers to the flow of work inherent in bureaucratic structures.

Sophisticated variants on the theme of homogeneous departmentation can do even worse in bureaucratic structures, given sufficient managerial cunning. Employers around the turn of this century often relied on homogeneous staffing—a work unit of Italians, another of Poles, and yet a third of Hungarians—and then management stimulated intergroup competition to induce greater effort. This tended to work, but only until the different ethnic groups got to talking with one another. Then all hell broke loose.

Wrongdoing and Whistle-Blowing

To the degree that this analysis is even approximately correct, organizational wrongdoing and whistle-blowing represent a sixth case of the bureaucratic model not being able to win for losing.

This may seem surprising. Surely, it would seem, intensive developments of the bureaucratic model would emphasize the identification and punishment of any wrongdoers, as a backup in those cases in which rules and regulations plus normal management practices were unsuccessful in inhibiting the malefactors before they got going. Patently, the bureaucratic model is designed to minimize precisely just such errors of commission. (As has long been known—e.g., Gouldner, 1954, pp. 218–24—"mock bureaucratic" variants exist, and may even abound. We here neglect the "mock" variants and focus on high-test exemplars.)

Despite such reasonable intent, however, the association of degenerative interaction with the bureaucratic model seems likely to generate some wicked unanticipated consequences, on balance. To outline this possible or probable chain of effects: wrongdoing might be strongly proscribed and penalized; but whistle-blowing also would be proscribed and punished, as a violation of the chain of command (e.g., Weinstein, 1979) or as an unsanctioned reliance on regenerative interaction. Moreover, since whistle-blowers would be treated unkindly, subsequent reports of wrongdoing understandably might be infrequent and reserved for big-ticket items, although some evidence from controlled field experiments questions this commonsensical view (Miceli, Dozier, and Near, 1991). Indeed, basic perceptual processes might encourage the "systematic neglect" of what should be obvious but is also dangerous to report and hence is better "unseen" or "unheard" (e.g., Blau, 1956, esp. pp. 50–52). Consequently, both whistle-blowing and its underlying perceptual processes might be compromised, and the identification and punishment of wrongdoing and wrongdoers might be inhibited, even as the credibility of accusers was being undermined, especially at the earliest and least troublesome stages.

This chain of effects has a circular and self-heightening character, and it provides a credible explanation of why things are as they often are. Thus one observer notes that many, or even most, organizations reflect "a natural self-sealing mechanism that quashes attempts to question organization policy" (Stanley, 1981, p. 16). Empirical studies do not discourage such a broad view, although they do urge some qualifications on the generalization (e.g., Near, Baucus, and Miceli, 1993).

Supervisory Styles, Attitudes, and Behaviors

Overall, for a seventh and final managerial feature, the bureaucratic model gives but faint hope of generating an organizational leadership that will serve diversity, broadly defined. Consider the issue of "gender displays" (e.g., Martin, 1992, pp. 221–24), for example. The supervisory styles, attitudes, and behaviors consistent with the bureaucratic model—taking control, making decisions, dominating the flow of communication, and so on—fit closely with what some have called "male masculinity displays" and they poorly suit the displays often attributed to women.

The latter, in general, include greater emphasis on building relationships rather than exercising control, on seeking agreement rather than engineering compliance, and so on.

To the degree that the two generalizations apply, obviously, women will be at a clear disadvantage in performance appraisals and promotions in bureaucratic structures.

There is no inevitable determinism at work here. "Male masculinity displays" may be consistent with traditional leadership requirements, but the leadership literature —both now (e.g., Kuhnert, 1993) and way back when (e.g., Golembiewski, 1962c, esp. pp. 208–23)—accords no clear superiority to such displays in practice. Quite the opposite, in fact. With growing diversity, presumably, the disjoint will only widen.

The popularity of leadership concepts and training that imply even a modicum of flexibility from a narrow base (e.g., Hersey and Blanchard, 1969, 1988), for example, implies the perceived mixed consequences of the inexorable homogenizing thrust of the bureaucratic model under which most of us work. The bureaucratic model, it seems, encodes very powerful messages for us, and very early. These messages influence our thoughts and behaviors. This point is nowhere more starkly reflected than in the acceptance by young children of traditional notions about organizing (e.g., Wilcox, 1968), which is consistent with what we know about the less-advanced stages of moral development (e.g., Kohlberg, 1981). Children tend to operate at those moral levels which feature unmediated stimulus —> response chains, and these developmental niches seem to be at once reinforced by, as well as to gain power from, the encoded messages in the children's environment about legitimate ways to behave in collective settings. These messages come from family relationships, schools, and so on (e.g., Verba, 1961).

If it will come from anywhere, however, the respect for diversity will come from the more advanced levels of moral development, and the bureaucratic model provides mostly negative contributions toward such development. Hypothetically, the bureaucratic model encourages fixation at lower levels (e.g., Argyris, 1957), and this may induce frustration or dissatisfaction in persons who are sensitive to cross-purposes between organizational demands and developmental imperatives. Consider the inhospitality of many work settings for broad ranges of differences, such as those between central tendencies in the attitudes and behaviors of men and women toward supervision (e.g., Cahoon and Rowney, 1993, esp. pp. 341–46). Bureaucratic contexts seem to inhibit accepting such differences, let alone exploiting them as mutual growth opportunities.

Such features lead to a wisecrack of mine: "Wherever people learn about organizing, that somewhere especially includes their parents' knees and other low joints." Witness our son, at about age four, who resisted efforts to get him to sit in the chair his father normally occupied at dinner, as a gentle exercise in role flexibility. "No," this savant explained firmly, "there can only be one boss."

But wisecracks suffice no more here than anywhere. Three sections provide some detailed support for the introductory comments above. To begin, attention gets directed at how the bureaucratic model inclines management toward degenerative interaction as well as associated leadership practices that poorly serve diversity. Brief illustrations in two following sections outline cases for both particulars. Discussion frames these leadership features as "transactional" and also suggests diversity-unfriendly effects. See also the section in Chapter 4 on transformational as contrasted with transactional leadership.

Bureaucratic ideation and interaction with authority

Structures like those in Exhibit 3.1 are nested in an ideational context that inhibits regenerative interaction, and this better serves autocratic figures than it does partners in interaction. For example, bureaucratic contexts explicitly prescribe restrictions on interaction between authority figures and others: impersonality in relations between organization members and formal authorities, as well as between them and their clients, and a system of procedures and rules for dealing with all contingencies at work, which system reinforces the reporting insularity of each S-unit by providing a narrow self-interest as a focus for all formal authorities beneath M_{ABC}.

Quite directly, at both interpersonal and organizational levels, such prescriptions incline more toward reducing trust and increasing risk than toward their regenerative counterparts. Similarly, tendencies to limit openness and owning also exist. Such probabilities discourage the regenerative interaction that is at the heart of a sensitivity that at once affirms diversities and provides a sound basis for beginning to deal with them.

Bureaucratic structures and operating biases

Exhibit 3.1 structures also encourage leadership behaviors that may be labeled as "authoritarian" or "directive." That is, no matter what the preferences of people in them, bureaucratic structures encourage and even require primary attention to such activities, among others: direct control so as to minimize errors of commission and to assign responsibility for them when they do occur, as reflected in one-to-one supervision and in a narrow span of control; "doing things right, the first time, and from the top"; restricting the flow of communication, both formally because of the specialized responsibilities of individual S-units, and informally to maintain power and leverage for bargaining between S-units and with M_{ABC}; and an emphasis on loyalty or, if that fails, on obedience via socialization or coercion to the total organization, if possible, but more likely to the individual S-unit.

In sum, these operating biases assume centrality because bureaucratic structures imply very high costs of slippage at any point in the flow of work. Most graphically, absent costly band-aids such as large volumes of in-process work in inventory, a single obstreperous S-unit can reduce output to zero. That is the most ominous sense of the First Law of Social Dynamics, as applied to bureaucracies.

In various ways, such "directive" leadership activities do not well serve diversity. For example, clearly, job rotation and job enrichment are poorly served by the operating biases of authority roles consistent with the bureaucratic model. Evidence as well as common sense supports the diversity-friendliness of both job rotation and job enrichment, as the next chapter details.

Bureaucratic structures and transactional leadership
Paramountly, authority figures in Exhibit 3.1 structures are encouraged to be "transactional," in the common parlance (Bass, 1985; Bass and Avolio, 1990), and this also has diversity-unfriendly effects, on balance. To be sure, this boundary may be transcended consistently by some of those in formal positions of bureaucratic authority and episodically by many more, but these two possibilities can hardly be credited to the bureaucratic model. In brief, transactional leadership (Golembiewski and Kuhnert, 1992, pp. 4–7)

> works within an organization culture and its associated goals and systems, as they exist: it does not preoccupy itself with questioning formal goals
>
> is responsive to immediate self-interests at lower stages of human development (e.g., Kohlberg, 1981), if they can be met while doing the prescribed work
>
> is oriented toward top-level planning in a one best way or a few best ways and then toward tying immediate self-interests to an existing organization's infrastructure, its culture, goals, and systems
>
> basically motivates by exchanging rewards, or promises of rewards, for services rendered
>
> encourages degenerative interaction—the focus is "on compromise, intrigue and control. Because they focus on the process, as contrasted with the substance of issues, [transactional] managers are seen as inscrutable, detached, or even manipulative" (Golembiewski and Kuhnert, 1994, p. 5).

Repeat: the bureaucratic structure encourages formal authorities in a transactional direction.

This does not mean, however, that managerial elites always want their minions to perform transactionally. Indeed, many managements devote time and resources to mitigating transactional effects (e.g., Hersey and Blanchard, 1969, 1988). Moreover, taste-makers in such matters are ballyhooing the virtues of a polar opposite of the transactional model (Burns, 1978; Bennis and Nanus, 1985). The concluding sections of the next chapter give some attention to this polar opposite.

This much seems defensible, at least, given what we know. Unless replaced or fundamentally qualified, the bureaucratic structure variously limits the scope of authority figures at multiple levels. Moreover, even if it does not induce basically transactional leadership, the fundamental bureaucratic thrust requires that all would-be transformationalists swim against very strong organizational currents.

How can this point be reinforced economically? More will be said about transactional leadership in the last section of the next chapter, but here discussion focuses on the crucial theme that, as Bernard M. Bass and Bruce J. Avolio emphasize (1993, p. 112), an "organization's culture develops in large part from its leadership," although reciprocal effects also will occur.

Transactional leadership misses many bets in regard to the development of a culture appropriate for diversity, as can be suggested by an introductory contrast that anticipates in outline the discussion in a closing part of the next chapter. Thus in highly innovative and satisfying organization cultures, which reasonably can be viewed as diversity-friendly, Bass and Avolio see transformational leaders in such terms (1993, p. 113):

> [They] build on assumptions such as: people are trustworthy and purposeful; everyone has a unique contribution to make; and complex problems are handled at the lowest level possible. Leaders who build such cultures and articulate them to followers typically exhibit a sense of vision and empower others to take greater responsibility for achieving the vision. . . . They foster a culture of creative change and growth. . . . They take personal responsibility for the development of their followers [who participate in developing] their full potential.

The reader can play the mind game required to complete the contrast if suitably prepared by the previous discussion and if empowered to want to do so. Basically, does the bureaucratic structure encourage transformational behaviors and attitudes in building such cultures? The associated queries about bureaucratic structures are obvious. For example, Do they encourage growth and development? Do they assume employees are trustworthy and should be treated in trusting ways? Do they encourage dealing with problems at the lowest possible levels?

If the reader's answers are negative, and no essential doubt should exist about that, they provide concluding—and powerful—perspective on why and how bureaucratic structures poorly serve diversity.

A Concluding Note

To some, there may appear in this analysis to be an irony related to employment discrimination. To put a perhaps too fine point on the issue, litigation may seem the result of this effort to foster diversity by emphasizing its incompatibility with traditional bureaucracy. As one reader of these Ransone Lectures observed: "Employers are most vulnerable in discrimination suits when they do not adhere to job descriptions, formal structures, and other aspects of traditional bureaucracy."

That is true, but job descriptions *will not disappear* in a postbureaucratic infrastructure, as succeeding chapters suggest and establish. But, again for example, postbureaucratic job descriptions *will differ*. To illustrate, their focus will be on cross-training or enriched jobs rather than on narrow specialization, with more attention to group as well as individual contributions and with more attention to personal growth and accumulated competencies than to what a person happens to be doing, to how much of it is done, or for how long.

This transformation in managerial infrastructure will get detailed attention later, but the present line of argument clearly undercuts the rationale for much of what passes as personnel management, especially in the public sector. Succeeding chapters will highlight several of these incompatibilities but without resolving them. Fortunately, there is an ongoing ferment about the kind of personnel management infrastructure that can at once contribute to this analysis and capitalize on it (e.g., U.S. Office of Personnel Management, 1992).

Notes

1 An earlier version of this chapter was part of "Diversity and Organization Structure," a paper delivered at the 1993 Berkeley Symposium on Public Management Research, University of California at Berkeley, July 19, by this author and William A. Osuna.

2 For an early analysis of how traditional "staff" concepts exacerbate the fragmenting tendencies, consult such sources as my work (e.g., Golembiewski, 1967). Updated views require no basic modifications of such analysis, as is clear from a reading of a useful survey of "staff" dynamics in business (Lawler and Galbraith, 1993).

3 Each managerial perspective is supported by a substantial literature. Here, see Campion, Cheraskin, and Stevens (1994).

4 MOVING TOWARD DIVERSITY-FRIENDLY SYSTEMS, I: ATTRACTIONS OF AN ALTERNATIVE STRUCTURE

Well-known structural arrangements can accommodate diversity far better than does the bureaucratic model, and even the single illustration here makes the point adequately, for several reasons. Most important, the alternative model used here has a substantial and growing presence. Indeed, of all nonbureaucratic variants, this exemplar is the most broadly distributed. Specific incidences are not known, and horseback estimates have little to recommend them. For those who insist, perhaps 20 percent of the organizations I see have some properties like the exemplar of interest here, at both high and low levels, as well as those in between, and mostly in business.

Motivators of Structural Embeddedness

The present insistence on embedding diversity in a congenial structure has generic motivators. Broadly, and perhaps especially in government (e.g., Laudicina, 1993, p. 30), organizations making progress on managing diversity often have prior histories of experience with postbureaucratic forms. Illustrations must suffice here: thus NASA was an early leader in integrative "matrix" structures (Sayles and Chandler, 1992); and the Metropolitan Atlanta Rapid Transit Authority, or MARTA, was a state authority whose legislative mandate deliberately made it free of many typical restrictions on government organizations (Golembiewski and Kiepper, 1988).

Moreover, and perhaps penultimately, organizational life may be considered holographic. That is, each feature represents not only a particular but also embodies a sense of the whole. Hence the common mixed experience with add-ons or overlays to basic bureaucratic structures. Ultimately, one has to change all of it to change any of it. Incremental changes will tend to be temporary—to fade out if not reinforced; to be co-opted in practice by the sense of the whole in features not targeted for change or opaque to it; or to create unanticipated hitches between the sense of the whole associated with the new features and the surviving infrastructure. Phillip Selznick (1949) drew early attention to such effects, and they also nicely frame the core dilemma of our national health care debate (Mueller, 1992).

In narrow particulars, moreover, the focus on structural embeddedness is followed by the review in Chapter 5 of alternative whys and hows for diversity-friendly contexts. These examples will be limited, but still useful, in those highly probable cases in which change in the bureaucratic model is deliberately limited.

Other factors strengthen the rationale for emphasis on the present structural exemplar. Thus flow-of-work structures are no contemporary fad. Their earliest beachhead was gained at the highest levels in business organizations, beginning in the 1920s and gaining momentum in the 1960s (e.g., Chandler, 1962). Public sector applications also exist at high levels (e.g., Carew et al., 1977). At lower levels of organization, the broad diffusion of the alternative structure is substantially a contemporary phenomenon (e.g., Golembiewski, 1993a), although its roots go back to reflections on post–World War II experiences (e.g., Drucker, 1954, pp. 193–226, 262–72) and especially to the theorizing to which those experiences gave impetus (e.g., Argyris, 1957).

In sum, then, the illustrated alternative applies at both executive and operating levels. This is a powerful attraction and permits the analysis below to be protean—sometimes referring to senior levels, then to workaday levels, and in most cases being pitched at a generic level.

Despite such motivators of attention, the present approach satisfices rather than maximizes: it illustrates for a single alternative exemplar what Chapter 3 demonstrates for the bureaucratic model. In sum, structural variants have significant implications for success in valuing diversity as well as in managing it, although the diversity <—> structure interface is typically neglected. For example, Harry Triandis, Lois Kurowski, and Michele Gelfand (1994, p. 778) devote only one paragraph to "task structure" and neglect other structural features altogether in their otherwise exhaustive review of workplace diversity.

Some Missing Features in This Analysis

Even though it addresses a critical shortfall, this analysis does not do it all. What is missing in this chapter? Six emphases, especially, still will require attention when this chapter has had its full say.

For comprehensive demonstrations about how postbureaucratic exemplars affect diversity, broader arrays of structural alternatives are required. Thus Galbraith (1993b, pp. 23–26) identifies six basic types of businesses, along with numerous subtypes. Henry Mintzberg (1979) details five types of structures; Golembiewski (1987) focuses on four; while Danny Miller and Peter H. Friesen (1984) require twelve organizational archetypes. Moreover, much is now known about fine-tuning the specific structural model used here for illustrative purposes. Those details do not much affect this analysis, but they have been attended to elsewhere (e.g., Golembiewski, 1993c). In addition, exciting evidence suggests that our organizational evolution does not stop with the model of choice here (e.g., O'Toole and Bennis, 1992), but that does not deter even as it intrigues.

In addition, second, this chapter must be selective in its coverage. As Mohrman notes (1993, p. 128), structure alone does not suffice to generate the required horizontal or lateral relationships. To be "fully effective," integrative structures also require mission, strategy, and values for overall guidance; objectives and budgets to guide operations; information systems that connect relevant individuals and subsystems; development profiles and career paths that contribute to the ability of individuals to function in integrative organizations; and performance-management practices that encourage the effectiveness of individuals, teams, and systems, as well as facilitate valid and reliable estimates of effectiveness. This analysis does not attend exhaustively to any of these systemic reinforcers of lateral relationships. But it does seek to provide a useful framework for such a full analysis, along with revealing illustrations of the character of that analysis.

Here, then, we seek a reasonable next step rather than an end of the road. The illustrative focus here is on a flow-of-work model that captures the essential qualities of real-life structures at two extreme levels of organization. At the higher levels of organization, variants of the structure typically are called division or M structures, which William G. Ouchi (1984) has elaborated into a model of society. At lower levels of organization, analogues focus on organizing around autonomous teams, enlarged jobs, or discrete subassemblies (e.g., Cummings, 1992).

Third, this discussion does not give much attention to transitions or transformations, but this lack should not be taken to imply that it will be easy to change bureaucratic structures and their associated policies and practices. Although success rates are substantial (e.g., Golembiewski and Sun, 1993), changeovers can be tough, especially when degenerative interaction exists and no concerted efforts are made to change that condition. For example, the mixed results of one federal effort to unbundle or unbuckle policies and procedures, long and firmly bureaucratized, are amenable to just such an interpretation (e.g., Dutcher, Hayashida, Sheposh, and Dickson, 1992, esp. pp. vii–viii, 126–28).

On the other hand, these real limitations do not mean that this chapter hunts only small game. Thus increasing numbers of organizations are adopting flow-of-work properties (e.g., Golembiewski, 1995, chaps. 7 and 8). So there is a momentum on which this analysis can build and toward which it may contribute. Moreover, we now have burgeoning batches of detailed reports of successful changeovers and of the conditions underlying them (e.g., Rainey and Rainey, 1986a, 1986b). Meta-analyses of large batches of change programs reveal that a proportionate share occur in the public sector, where results compare favorably to the very high success rates attributed to business sector programs (e.g., Golembiewski, Proehl, and Sink, 1981, 1982; Golembiewski and Sun, 1993).

Fourth, this analysis rests on a growing but still incomplete literature. The effects of flow-of-work structures are documented most fully for smaller, integrative clusters of employees—for example, autonomous groups or sociotechnical interventions (e.g., Pasmore, 1988). For large aggregations, the lack of explicit research attention to sociological and psychological dynamics has not prevented the diffusion of the model to most of our larger business enterprises, in large part because the case for superior performance of adopting firms seems relatively secure (e.g., Dess and Davis, 1984). Fortunately, major additions to our knowledge have become available in recent years, both in business (e.g., Galbraith, Lawler, and Associates, 1993), and in government (e.g., Barzelay, 1992).

What follows, then, is an analytic amalgam. The discussion rests on the available literature, which it cites selectively. Informed judgment, based on thirty years of consultation in business and government, at times fills in the inevitable linkages not established by replicated research.

Fifth, no attention here goes to the boundary conditions of the flow-of-work model. These are well enough known to be available in summary form (e.g., Golembiewski, 1995, esp. chap. 7) and in any case do not essentially modify the analysis that follows.

Sixth and last on this short list of what is missing in this chapter, consider its opening words: Well-known structural arrangements can accommodate diversity far better than does the bureaucratic model.

The words were chosen carefully. Thus they do not mean to say that bureaucratic organizations—absolutely, positively—cannot deal with diversity. That would be false to such realities as this one: the armed services have made substantial inroads into issues of diversity; indeed, they are in the front-line legions; and in times of peace, those services often rely on powerful bureaucratic infrastructures. No doubt, also, their rule-making and coercive powers have played a role in such progress. Wisely, however, the armed services have applied huge resources to what Chapter 2 labels "valuing diversity," when it became manifestly obvious that acting on "augmented affirmative action" could not be sustained by rule-making or coercion, even in what are far more "closed systems" than are normally tolerated in businesses or in government. Refer back to the unfortunate history of the U.S. Navy sketched in Chapter 2. Disaffection, destruction of property, and even violence became the bills that had to be paid for early military efforts toward diversity in an unrelievedly bureaucratic mode.

Let me put the present argument in straightforward terms. As useful as it has been, and will continue to be, "valuing diversity" will not suffice (e.g., Egan, 1993). That emphasis must be extended to "managing diversity." Moving determinedly into this fifth strategy distinguished in Chapter 2 will require moving away from the bureaucratic model, whose basic animus is toward uniformity rather than diversity. Trying to manage diversity within bureaucratic contexts has Sisyphian qualities, in short, for reasons that include the sampler considered in this chapter.[1]

To be sure, also, it is often convenient or even necessary to live with the bureaucratic model or with modifications that help that old-fashioned structural medicine go down a bit better. How far and how fast reformation effects will progress still remain issues of great relevance, indeed, of statesmanship proportions. Whatever those balance points of retaining the old while moving toward the new, this chapter sketches real associated costs of vestigial remains of the bureaucratic model and also implies substantial limits on the ability to approach in bureaucratic contexts the fifth strategy detailed in Chapter 2—managing diversity.

Fortunately, this analysis can go beyond pointing with alarm when and where bureaucratic forms remain, as they in most cases certainly will—at least in substantial form and for some indefinite time. Chapter 5 provides numerous illustrations of the kinds of policies and programs that lean toward postbureaucratic forms, as it were, but nonetheless modify rather than dismantle the existing bureaucratic infrastructure.

Postbureaucratic Models and Diversity: Variants at Executive and Operating Levels

Exhibit 4.1 presents a schema of one common postbureaucratic model for the activities A+B+C which yield some product, service, or discrete subassembly. The differences between this structure and that in Exhibit 3.1 may seem minor, but they are profound. Basically, in Exhibit 4.1, each S-unit performs the same complete flow of work, and hence S-unit performance may be compared directly. Where S-units perform different complete flows of work, the standard of comparison often involves return on investment or some relative measurements such as percentage of market share, percentage of recidivism, and so on. Basically, as a result, each S-unit will tend to generate social and psychological forces that contribute to the effectiveness and integration of its complete flow of work, which wholism stands in marked contrast to the fragmentation of S-units in the bureaucratic mode.

Of perhaps even greater relevance in flow-of-work structures, judgments about the performance of A, B, and C will be subject to broadly political processes that encourage their integration. The reader might well remember that similar influences in bureaucratic structures tended to fragment a flow of work. Basically, the within-S-unit emphasis will tend to emphasize problem-solving about any difficulties, largely because all contributors share responsibility for that S-unit's performance. Relatedly, between-S-unit comparisons in flow-of-work structures will be focused on productivity and quality at the lowest comparative cost. This contrasts sharply with between-S-unit bureaucratic dynamics, where competition

Exhibit 4.1 A Postbureaucratic Structural Model

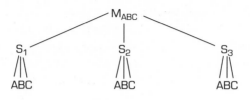

Properties

Basic departmentation puts *related activities* together in an S-unit—flows of work, discrete subassemblies, products, strategic operating areas or units, and so on.

Integration of related activities helps minimize errors of omission and also encourages cross-training, job enrichment, as well as in-process setups and inspection.

Authority and responsibility are both vertical and horizontal in each S-unit—following the chain of command and also building around personal as well as group loyalties and commitment integrating the several contributions to an immediate flow of work. Hence control is pervasively both "up" the chain of command and "across" it in each S-unit, due to shared social and psychological membership.

The span of control can be very wide, or narrow, given the ease of measuring holistic performance.

The primacy is on holistic performance relative to a good or service for which all S-unit members share responsibility, which reduces transfer costs and moderates jurisdictional issues as it locates them within each S-unit rather than between two or more S-units.

focuses on relative budget shares, and success in obtaining them reflects a broad range of situational determinants beyond performance on a flow of work. Moreover, enriched jobs are compatible with Exhibit 4.1 structures, and this also will help locate responsibility for performance at action levels.

These general comments will receive reinforcement and elaboration in two ways. First, and generically, the alternative model highlights the growing prominence of lateral or horizontal integration, as contrasted with the vertical fragmentation induced by the bureaucratic or functional model. Postbureaucratic structural forms vary in their response to the same basic urgency: divisional models got major attention over the past few decades; then, matrix variants attained prominence (e.g., Davis and Lawrence, 1977); "smaller" often has been touted as "better" or even "beautiful" (e.g., Gilder, 1989); we live in the era of "total quality management," of course; and most recently reduced cycle time has gone to the head of the line, in the analytic (e.g., Stalk and Hout, 1990) as well as the popular literatures (Goldratt and Cox, 1992). In different ways, these variants attempt to facilitate horizontal or lateral integration. That is the key factor shared by all the examples above as they deal with growing complexity and pressures to perform (e.g., Mohrman, 1993).

Second, detailed comparisons will develop a range of differences between Exhibit 3.1 and 4.1 structures. Again, the focus will be on the seven managerially relevant features considered in Chapter 3, but this time with reference to how they relate to one postbureaucratic structure—a flow-of-work model.

Necessarily, the narrative will be illustrative rather than exhaustive. Ample discussions are available elsewhere, in both research (e.g., Golembiewski, 1987, 1994) and popular media (e.g., *Raleigh* [N.C.] *News and Observer*, 1993).

1. *Regenerative Interaction.* Significantly and perhaps paramountly, the flow-of-work structure helps avoid the critical effects on interaction characteristic of the bureaucratic model. Each S-unit will tend to be characterized by regenerative interaction (see Exhibit 4.2), and this will encourage communication within each S-unit that is valid, reliable, and focuses on mutual solving of problems while minimizing the creation of other or greater issues. Interaction between S-units is difficult to predict, but the quality of that interaction is of less moment than in bureaucratic structures. In sum, the flow-of-work S-units are not linked sequentially, and hence relationships between S-units might be variously competitive without marked negative effects on production and quality. Indeed, competition between S-units may exist naturally, as it were, with energizing effects.

How can one be sure about these central conclusions? Consider two ways of building a convincing rationale—one generic and the other targeted to specific political dynamics.

Generic Case for Regenerative Interaction

Exhibit 4.1 structures basically reflect a philosophic stance that encourages marshaling strong psychological commitment within each S-unit, with the practical consequences of lowering risk, as well as heightening trust, openness, and owning. This stance might be conveniently labeled as growth-oriented versus control-oriented and gets support from various early theoretical perspectives such as Theory Y versus Theory X (McGregor, 1960), the dimensions for self-actualization (e.g., Argyris, 1957), and so on. There is no need to develop a detailed proof here, for that has been done elsewhere (e.g., Golembiewski, 1993c). Illustratively, Argyris

Exhibit 4.2   Regenerative Interaction and Some Major Consequences

Regenerative Interaction

HI	Openness
HI	Owning
LO	Risk
HI	Trust

Some Consequences of Regenerative Interaction

Relevant issues, ideas, and feelings will tend to be raised.

Decision making will tend to rest on high degrees of consensus, moving toward long-lasting solutions that relate to real problems.

Psychological success will tend to be high.

Energy levels will tend to be high, although at times they may be expressed in high degrees of conflict as new issues are raised and worked on.

Over time, energy levels will tend to remain high and levels of conflict will vary depending on new problems to be confronted, as well as on experience with regenerative interaction and confidence of unit members in one another.

(1957) proposes that individuals have predispositions for development from a limited repertoire of activities to an expanding set, from a short time perspective to a lengthening one, from dependence to growing independence and interdependence, and so on.

A bold contrast can be made. Flow-of-work structures permit such growth-oriented movement, as subsequent discussion will detail. In contrast, bureaucratic structures inhibit this movement, as the previous chapter shows. Different sets of consequences—mode of interaction, degrees of frustration, and so on—are thus engaged by the two alternative structures. For example, a growth-oriented structure should encourage regenerative interaction by reducing the risk people experience; heightening trust in each S-unit; and curbing defensiveness and fixated behavior, thereby increasing openness and owning. Broadly, also, regenerative interaction should serve to reduce the frustration people feel at work. Reinforcing such forces, members of S-units in Exhibit 4.1 structures will tend to share psychological commitments which are induced by, as well as add force to, the comparative measurement of performance facilitated by flow-of-work structures.

The bold contrast having been made, let us pull back a little—but without qualifications that reduce the basic point to a triviality. Thus regenerative interaction is not always structurally induced. Shared experiences may bond even strange bedfellows; personal liking or "chemistry" may dominate; and so on. Moreover, individuals usually prefer regenerative interaction, and this preference can at times become a shared value that overrides the degenerative urgencies consistent with the bureaucratic model. These conditions in bureaucratic structures may occur either within an S-unit or between S-units, but they will be deviant cases.

But don't bet on the persistence of such deviant cases in bureaucratic structures. Typically, even successful efforts to develop shared values have to be periodically reinforced in bureaucratic structures, so pervasive are its inducements to degenerative interaction and to fragmenting behaviors and attitudes (e.g., Golembiewski and Kiepper, 1988, esp. pp. 61–144). A recent attempt in a federal agency to graft postbureaucratic elements onto a traditional structure illustrates the point. The application seems to have had effects in the expected directions, in general, but they were nonetheless underwhelming. This was apparently owing to low levels of trust (Dutcher, Hayashida, Sheposh, and Dickson, 1992) that were not confronted, as well as to the use of managerial innovations as "Christmas tree ornaments." The basic structure was maintained and only decorated with add-ons, in a manner of speaking.

The basic point escapes few observers, but not many of them follow through to the structural implications. Total Quality Management, or TQM, so much in the managerial air nowadays, stands as a case in point. Its aficionados such as W. Edward Deming (1982) typically highlight the need for effective interaction as a necessary precondition but do not prescribe a structure congenial to that precondition. Hence TQM's common difficulties (e.g., Golembiewski, 1995, chaps. 6–9) because the bureaucratic model usually dominates in places where TQM is applied.

Requiring regenerative interaction, and then doing nothing to reinforce it structurally, reminds me of the Polish recipe for chicken goulash. It begins: Steal four chickens. Such recommendations simply posit the crucial condition, rather than detail what to do and how to do it.

Special Case for Regenerative Interaction

In a second sense, even fewer qualifications hedge the association of structure with mode of interaction. Directly, a powerful motivation for regenerative interaction inheres in flow-of-work structures because they highlight any performance differences between S-units. Or to say much the same thing, the presence of degenerative interaction in flow-of-work structures will tend to be reflected in the inadequate performance of individual S-units, and the responsibility for that is hard to avoid. Hence, at least within each S-unit, problem-solving will tend to dominate over defensiveness when glitches occur.

The key point can be made by way of a simple but meaningful contrast, which again involves the First Law of Social Dynamics, introduced earlier. In the bureaucratic model, any single S-unit can independently serve to reduce output or quality and can possibly even stop the sequential flow between S-units; but only all S-units acting together can serve to increase them. In an Exhibit 4.1 structure, in significant contrast, any single S-unit can raise output or quality; but only all of the units acting collusively can serve to reduce output or quality. This identifies a major difference between the two structures, which powerfully affects choices of the balance point between local discretion and overhead control when one structure or the other dominates.

There is no doubt about which alternative is easier or more convenient in flow-of-work structures. That elemental fact underlies the greater wriggle room possible in that structure. Details follow.

The political dynamics in the two basic structures also differ substantially, and so will their consequences. In a Social Security Administration application of the flow-of-work structure, for example, sharp increases in productivity were observed during the movement away from the bureaucratic model (Rainey and Rainey, 1986a, 1986b). The phenomenon is not unusual. Experience suggests that a 10 to 15 percent initial effect on reduced costs or heightened productivity accompanies basic change toward flow-of-work structures (e.g., Golembiewski, 1979, 2:309–30). Others report similar effects, even when they wished they would not occur (e.g., Macy, 1978, p. 20).

What explains such effects? They suggest forces made available for performance on task, rather than forces bound up in defensiveness or resistance.

Basically, continuous reinforcers for each S-unit to innovate and improve are built into the flow-of-work structure. In gross terms, no mystery exists about what is going on. In general, S-units in bureaucratic structures labor politically to achieve the greatest possible slack in their individual budgets. In flow-of-work structures, in general opposition, each S-unit strives to reduce its costs for comparable quality and quantity. The difference is profound.

Let us put the point in another way. Exhibit 4.1 structures encourage continuous improvement, in part because any one S-unit may stimulate it, as well as gain credit for it. In contrast, bureaucratic structures often are characterized by "straight-line production curves," which imply a shared norm maintaining or restricting output. Under the bureaucratic model, this seems a reasonable outcome—perhaps even the desirable outcome, when judged against the high conflict potential of S-units higgling and piggling to put themselves in a favorable position concerning their particularistic contributions. Hence S_C might well belittle performance increments at S_A and S_B by proposing that this merely establishes that A and B are "easier" than C and, hence, that S_C needs more resources. Indeed, the very anticipation of such an argument likely will curb efforts at A or B to do better or faster. Tellingly, their success would (in effect) reward C while relatively depriving A and B. That is, bureaucratic structures tend to level down, all other things being more or less equal.

In sum, the association of the flow-of-work model and regenerative interaction rests on an incomplete literature, especially at high levels of organization, but the pattern depicted here remains robust (e.g., Golembiewski, 1987, 1989b). Thus that association dominates in both research and consulting experience, as reflected in the ongoing search for various postbureaucratic structures to ease communication at senior levels (e.g., Johnson, 1992, p. 22) and throughout the organizations (e.g., Galbraith, Lawler, and Associates, 1993; and especially Cohen, 1993).

Consider the effects of structural change on interaction in one state agency—from the bureaucratic model to a direct form of Exhibit 4.1—which had the expected effects. A few snippets from before and after comparisons suggest the movement from degenerative to regenerative interaction (Carew et al., 1977, esp. pp. 327–29, 335–37):

Before Condition (Bureaucratic and degenerative)	*After Condition* (Flow of work and regenerative)
Functional specialization dominated, and no work unit "was responsible for a particular youth; hence service flow was often inconsistent and haphazard"	Several Youth Service Teams now provide "continuity of services" for specific batches of clients
Communications were "often strained and hostile"	"Collaborative problem solving" comes to dominate over "circumvention"
Interaction was "mistrustful"	A survey indicates the system is more "trustful, flexible, facing problems, sharing decisions, cooperative . . . and participative"

Where structural changes do not occur, interventions can be characterized as "patches" that attempt to link the activities fragmented by the bureaucratic model. In such cases, typically, periodic reinforcing experiences are necessary to inhibit the decay of effects (e.g., Golembiewski and Kiepper, 1988, esp. pp. 30–94).

Regenerative Interaction and Diversity

Generalizing from personal experience and the sparse observations of others, regenerative interaction also seems important in coming to grips with diversity. Indeed, this may understate the probable reality. Absent ameliorative and effective communication, that is, much abrasion can be expected as organizations seek to deal with the full range of differences at work in gender, race, age, preferences about management styles and issues, and so on. Put directly, such differences often imply formidable barriers to communication. This confounds problem-solving and decision making which, in turn, both contribute to as well as rest on the character and quality of the relationships between people and groups.

Even these few comments imply the centrality of regenerative interaction in determined programs that aim at valuing differences; and that centrality is even greater for organizations intent on managing diversity. Absent regenerative interaction, "difference" implies "distance," and that encourages trouble. It is trite but true to observe that only effective communication stands any chance of bridging the numerous gaps across which diversity programs seek to build, whether their focus is largely on interpersonal relationships or aspires to be truly organizational.

Indeed, dealing with diversity literally can bend the language. Thus organization planners will need all the help they can get, if only for the taxonomic effort required to assess eligibility for preferred treatment in group-entitlement concepts of diversity. For example, we grievously simplify in speaking of cultural differences between "native white" and "Hispanic-Americans" that will have to be accommodated in programs of valuing diversity. The U.S. Census needs four categories to differentiate those of Spanish origin, and a full sixteen are required to differentiate the former category (Jackson and Associates, 1992, p. 22). Even those variegated categories used by the Census Bureau grossly oversimplify. As William A. Osuna (1993) challenges, concerning those of Spanish origin like himself:

> Do we become simply "Mexicans–Puerto Ricans–Cubans–Central Americans"? People ignore the fact that Latin American countries can be highly diverse, especially Argentina and Mexico. Do Cuban Jews, Brazilian Germans, or Belizean Palestinians and Syrians become "Hispanic-Americans"? Do we include European Spaniards as "Hispanic-Americans"? What about the Portuguese? Are people of pure Meso-American blood "Hispanic," too? Do we group by

language group and/or generalized regional origins, or is ethnicity controlling? We definitely live in interesting times.

Living cooperatively with diversity in organizations will require far more than taxonomic dexterity, of course. Indeed, that emphasis no doubt will complicate living together, as some argue persuasively (e.g., Klein, 1993). Hence, again, the relevance of regenerative interaction. Usefully viewed, systems of interaction constitute alternative "fields," and (as in physics) differences between fields can be profound. Consequently, the same stimulus seen as "refreshing candor" in a regenerative system can become "unbearable insensitivity" in a degenerative system. High levels of trust, especially, seem both a social glue and a lubricant, and they (of course) characterize regenerative interaction which, in turn, is favored by flow-of-work structures. Numerous recent encounters concerning race and gender suggest not only the practical relevance of the point but imply that things are getting worse.

Moreover, a broad view of "diversity" also heightens the salience of regenerative interaction. For example, what may be called "technology transfer" will have a growing prominence, and that typically involves broad ranges of stakeholders in all stages from design through implementation—encompassing many specialties normally separated by formidable barriers within and between organizations. In large part, timely success here depends on regenerative interaction. As one high-technology executive observes (Bylinski, 1990, p. 73): "You delude yourself if you think that the emphasis . . . is on technology. It's a humanistic task." A similar point also applies to related phenomena that will fill our future and raise issues about dealing with diversity at many levels and in many guises. For example, consider integrating temporary multifunctional teams of many varieties; merging two or more previously separate organizational cultures, or subcultures, perhaps embedded in two or more social cultures; unbuckling or spinning-off subsystems having grown beyond optimal size; and bringing together organizational "generations" who differ in life experiences, training, and so on. As Table 3.1 shows, regenerative interaction seems facilitative of and perhaps even required for the development of those competencies most frequently rated as "very important" in culturally diverse organizations.

This diversity-friendliness of regenerative interaction also can be highlighted by brief considerations of three themes. They relate to gender, to a pair of cultural prototypes, as well as to the issue of the stand-alone capability of regenerative interaction.

Flow-of-work structures, regenerative interaction, and gender
Many observers in a somewhat earlier time predicted that a profound organizational transformation was under way. Simply, the larger numbers of women entering the work force would change the definition of what constitutes good management,

with the once popular androgynous approach of Alice G. Sargent (1981) even attempting to integrate the strengths of both traditional "male" and "female" roles. As Allan R. Cahoon and Julie Rowney express the sense of this transformation (1993, p. 345):

> There was to be a shift from the male model as characterized by rugged individualism, autonomy, and independence to a more feminine model that focused on interdependence, mutuality, networking, and teams. The objective of this new management was to capitalize on the necessary male characteristics: dominance; independence; orientation on achievement; rational, analytical decision making; forceful communication; and competition. But these would be blended with the effective female traits: concern for people; attention to the nonverbal cues; increased interpersonal sensitivity and awareness; creative, intuitive decision-making; and empowering leadership.

This transformation does not seem to have occurred at the expected rate, either in this country or abroad (Cahoon and Rowney, 1993, pp. 345–46), perhaps for two basic reasons. Thus the penetration of women into decision-making roles has been steady, as noted in Chapter 2, but it hardly rates as spectacular. Moreover, the predictions seem to have grossly underestimated the staying power of bureaucratic concepts that, as it were, keep sending "male"-oriented messages. In any case, research does indicate a substantial stability about attitudes among men toward women and "female" roles (e.g., Brenner, Tomkiewicz, and Schein, 1989).

The issues here are tortuously complex, but at least a few points seem reasonably certain about structure, interaction, and gender in today's organizations. First, flow-of-work structures admit far more flexibility than bureaucratic structures, and the former do not clearly prescribe traditionally "male" roles and attitudes. See also the section below on leadership. Hence, at least, there seems no derivative need for women in flow-of-work structures to adopt "male" models. That adoption does not seem to work as a basic strategy for females (e.g., Cohen, 1989), but the research required to support a firm conclusion implies great difficulties of measurement and operational definition.

Second, postbureaucratic structures and practices continue to show steady and even substantial diffusion throughout business and government (e.g., Hall and Parker, 1993; Mirvis, forthcoming). This presumes a continuing challenge to, and probably the dilution of, any sex stereotyping built into models about organizing and managing. It also implies the emergence of models with a greater balance —of directiveness moderated by sensitivity, of assertiveness mellowed by cooperation, and so on (e.g., Korabik and Ayman, 1989).

Third, regenerative interaction seems one reasonable antidote to sex stereotypy, as by increasing the capacity to build and maintain relationships in fluid or even turbulent environments. Women have been widely reported to have a special sensitivity toward relationships (e.g., Hoy, 1990). But whatever that case, and irrespective of gender, the salience of relationship building seems to be growing in both business and government. This trend encourages getting all hands aboard in responding to a substantial departure from the command-and-obey mode consistent with the bureaucratic model.

Flow-of-work structures, regenerative interaction, and cultures

It does not do violence to the comparative descriptions above and in Chapter 3 to extend them into substantially opposed organization cultures associated with the bureaucratic and flow-of-work structures. Cox (1993) gives us a convenient comparison to bend to present purposes—at once building on his distinctions between "high-prescription" and "low-prescription" cultures, while also extending them in Exhibit 4.3.

As Cox also concludes, low-prescription cultures can be diversity-friendly, while high-prescription cultures imply serious barriers to diversity. In the latter cultures, in sum, diversity does not represent strengths to be built around. Rather, diversity represents a "lumpiness" in a bureaucratic organization's approach to the ideal of a smooth and homogeneous mix of persons and skills.

Stand-alone capacity of regenerative interaction?

One question may remain left open for some readers, to conclude this brief review. Can degenerative interaction have a stand-alone character, as it were, in the face of a bureaucratic structure?

The answer is yes, but.

Ample evidence supports the "yes" component. The value-laden behaviors associated with high openness, owning, and trust as well as with low risk can exist spontaneously in bureaucratic organizations, but not commonly; and well-known learning designs also can induce regenerative behaviors there, at least for a time. This is no news and has been supported in both laboratory settings (e.g., Boss, 1978) and in the field (e.g., Golembiewski and Carrigan, 1970; Golembiewski and Kiepper, 1988). In short, most people prefer regenerative value-loaded behaviors and attitudes; at times, those preferences au naturel can be so pronounced as to blunt or significantly diminish the degenerative press of bureaucratic structures; and quite commonly, in recent years, planned efforts have sought to reduce degenerative consequences of bureaucratic structures. On the last point, well-known learning designs have high success rates in sensitizing people in organizations to their preferences, in inducing shared commitment to try to act on those preferences, as well as in developing appropriate skills.

Why the "but," then? Typically, periodic reinforcements of such learning will be required where bureaucratic concepts dominate. Even if individuals prefer

Exhibit 4.3 Two Kinds of Cultural Types

High-Prescription Culture	Major Dimensions	Low-Prescription Culture
Do both at the top, once, do them right, and be consistent: "tight" systems that are centralized	Policy-making and implementation mix	Within policy and mission constraints, implementation can proceed in many styles and at various paces: "tight/loose" systems can permit broad delegation
Narrow	View of "right" or "good" behaviors or styles	Broad, except for core values like quality
Quick to express evaluations, especially negative and punitive ones	Orientation to judgmental behavior	Evaluations follow attempts to encourage expression of the full range of ideas as well as exploration of their sense and connotations
Risk-aversive	Orientation to risk	Calculated risks are accepted and even encouraged, as necessary for learning and innovation
Intolerance of and focus on, even to the detriment of positive contributions	Reaction to mistakes	Equal or greater status of positive contributions and even a view of mistakes as unexpected learning opportunities
Tends to be degenerative	System of interaction	Tends to be regenerative
Must be based on comparisons of different activities	Measurement of performance	Can be based on comparisons of similar activities
Loyalty, which may be reinforced by coercion or conformity	Basic identification	Commitment to shared goals and missions, which imply local empowerment and a narrower sense of "management prerogatives"
On parts: e.g., roles and jurisdictions	Basic focus	On wholes: e.g., flows of work, customers

From Cox (1993), esp. pp. 169–70, and extended from that source.

regenerative interaction, bureaucratic models continue to encourage degenerative features, within S-units but perhaps especially between them. Hence structurally induced dilemmas typically wear down even strong normative agreement about preferences to avoid degenerative interaction.

2. *Job Rotation.* Exhibit 4.1 structures minimize, when they do not totally avoid, the problems associated with this useful managerial technique. An outline provides the required contrast, using as a framework the five points of conflict and contention discussed at some length in Chapter 3. In contrast with the bureaucratic model, job rotation in flow-of-work structures faces such attractive life prospects:

> Only one S-unit need participate, which eases start-up costs and reduces the temptation to resort to overhead coercion or manipulation to induce reluctant buy-in.
>
> Costs will be localized to the appropriate S-unit and so will any derivative advantages from a successful rotation program.
>
> Candidates for rotation are known to those involved in providing the rotation experience.
>
> Rotatees can remain in their organization units, with reduced socialization costs although at a possible loss of positive networking.
>
> Rotatees can directly apply any knowledge, skills, or relationships gained in rotation and cross-training with minimum costs and dislocations.

Job rotation and cross-training will be valuable adjuncts in diversification efforts, and any leverage inherent in structural arrangements consequently will be helpful. In the long run, individual flow-of-work units can encompass jobs of narrow scope for beginners as well as enriched jobs suitable for motivating growth and development. See also the discussion below of job enrichment. Such arrangements provide useful, and perhaps even critical, flexibility for the nontraditional employees looming so large in our future work forces. Recall that earlier discussion highlights the growing proportions in our work forces not only of the young and recent immigrants but also of growing numbers of older employees. All can profit from working under various flexible arrangements, while their employing organizations also can gain strategic as well as tactical advantages—a cross-trained work force, an organization culture that targets as well as facilitates learning, and so on (e.g., Hall and Parker, 1993). Narrowly, flow-of-work structures also will in several senses make life easier for rotatees as well as for their managers. As one indicator, supervisors of S-units in flow-of-work structures need not fear that valued successful rotatees will not return.

3. *Job Enrichment.* Many managements move beyond job rotation and cross-training in separate activities and go on to aggregate bundles of once separate

activities in enriched jobs. In the case above, one can envision three classes of operatives in each S-unit, with appropriate differences in compensation: Class I operators: competencies in A, B, and C; Class II operators: competencies in A+B, or A+C, or B+C; and Class III operators: competency in A or B or C. Such mini-career ladders can provide a sense of mobility and progress, without requiring the reliance on tall structures.

Such arrangements are beyond the bureaucratic model's tolerance, and this is a great and growing liability. Indeed, technological change often will leave no reasonable alternative and, beyond that formidable elemental, three other points deserve brief mention. First, individuals in flow-of-work structures can face the challenge and reward of a mini-career ladder, which offers a sense of progress while preserving immediate contacts and relationships. This will be especially useful in the case of older workers who are not promoted, as well as for those who are content to remain in their S-unit. The implied bundle of opportunities—relief from boredom, greater competencies, enhanced mastery over a set of operations, and so on—are less available to the successful graduate of a job rotation effort in a bureaucratic structure. There, indeed, the rotatee may be restricted to aspiring to a supervisory (S) job. In turn, this reality may be a major factor in diminishing the enthusiasm of Ss in bureaucratic structures for job rotation programs.

Second, individuals successful in progressively enriched jobs will experience a sense of psychological growth as well as of earned movement toward S status. This developmental potential can have a high salience, not only in the sense of specific competencies gained but, even more so, in terms of a demonstrated capacity to learn how to learn continuously. That seems to be one of tomorrow's very large demands, as in the growing attention to "learning organizations" (e.g., Garvin, 1993).

Third, problem-solving can be encouraged via job enrichment, which reduces the need for formal order-givers and direct overseers of performance, while more closely approaching the realization of the goal that performance is what matters. Typically, for example, inspection, problem-solving, and even job setup responsibilities can be bundled together, which provides scope for employees as well as simplifies what had become complex tangles of line and staff responsibilities pregnant with frustrating potential for disruption.

In other versions of the approach, operators can have "automatic responsibility" whenever they see something that needs doing. This was the case in the early NASA. Employees do the something that they observe needs doing, if they have the requisite competence and if what they observe has a higher priority than the activities in which they are currently involved. Otherwise, their responsibility lasts until they bring the matter to the attention of someone who does have the requisite knowledge and skills. Employees obviously need to be alert and informed, at a minimum. Direct supervision roles will be reduced and on many occasions will become unnecessary, with consequent reduction in personnel costs. This both contributes to, and is required by, the "flat" flow-of-work structure.

Other attractions of job enrichment also deserve note. The flexibility permitted contrasts sharply with the role-boundedness characteristic of bureaucratic organizations, as well as with the narrow sense of loyalty in traditional organizations to S-unit special interests. There, the primary goals often involve getting credit for any successes and avoiding blame for all failures. In flow-of-work structures, the primary and contrasting urgency is to solve the problem and only secondarily to assign responsibility for failure—if that is required, or is desirable. Often, it will be enough to get the job done and to learn from any performance glitches so that all may avoid them in the future. In the ideal case, indeed, there are no "errors," only "unexpected learning opportunities." Exhibit 4.3 makes that point, among others, in contrasting high- versus low-prescription organization cultures.

The flexibility of job enrichment also minimizes the personnel adjustments required by absences, sickness, or turnover. This flexibility often will be a useful feature for nontraditional employees, as when a single parent must see to the emergency health needs of a child.

Not at all incidentally, the success rates of job enrichment applications are substantial (e.g., Alber, 1978; Nicholas, 1982, esp. p. 535), and so is the record for extensions of the approach such as the reliance on autonomous teams (e.g., Cummings, 1992).

Failures do occur, of course (e.g., Levinson, 1993). Typically, however, they occur for reasons that are quite well-known (e.g., Pasmore, 1988) and hence often can be anticipated and minimized by planning and policies. For example, a guarantee that no one will lose employment due to a successful enrichment effort can remove an often stout barrier to change. Nowadays, such a guarantee is largely pro forma, but it was not always so. Indeed, some observers still do not in practice appreciate the irony of why resistance to job enrichment by employees sometimes makes far more sense than taking the risk that they will enrich themselves right into unemployment.

Using "Involvement" as a Lens

Just as is the case with prescription glasses, the conceptual lenses through which one views organizational phenomena will influence, if not determine, what one sees and how clearly. Consider as one such lens three degrees of employee involvement (Lawler, 1988):

Suggestion involvement has employees propose changes but stops short of granting them the power to make changes and to be responsible for them.

Job involvement encompasses changes in the design of work that permit employees more workaday control over their jobs. Typically, but not always (e.g.,

Ford, 1969), employees are granted an enlarged or enriched job or membership in an autonomous group by management, and that grant redefines a greater but still limited scope for control.

High involvement far surpasses the second type by building a potential for broadening influence over the job by operators and lower organizational ranks—by power sharing, broad dissemination of strategic and tactical information, skill building, and broad involvement in what are typically "management prerogatives"—selection, training, and the like.

These three categories help frame a paradox. Involvement, and especially its two more advanced forms, is not adopted in anywhere near the volume that the record of success seems to justify. Given clear cases of limited success, internal studies by three giants of American industry report that their high-involvement plants are 20 to 40 percent more productive than low-involvement but otherwise comparable plants (Ledford, 1993, p. 149). Similarly, but astoundingly, a study of ninety-six high-involvement plants showed that three out of four far surpassed industrial averages on a variety of measures. Various comparisons pegged these advantages in the range of several hundred percent (Ledford, Cummings, and Wright, 1992).

Why this apparent paradox? And what can be done about it?

The paradox of overall success and incommensurate diffusion of high-involvement structures and principles has a direct working answer. That is, the bureaucratic model has a long record of acceptance, it prescribes narrow control, and it supports a broad concept of managerial prerogatives. In addition, there are startup costs in time, dollars, and knowledge in moving away from the bureaucratic model. Moreover, penetration into service areas has been limited, with most applications occurring in manufacturing. The service sector not only contains many possible sites for applications, but growth is greatest there. Finally, until recently, sufficient satisfaction often has existed with bureaucratic forms that changeovers were not motivated by a sense of urgent necessity.

Then was then, and now is later. From an important perspective, the rate of diffusion can be expected to increase as the knowledge base grows and as the urgencies burgeon, and both seem likely. Survey data support this speculation (e.g., Lawler, Mohrman, and Ledford, 1992). This incrementalism is reasonable, if disheartening to maximizers. Few saw the bureaucratic model as "broken" until recently; hence the moderate rate of diffusions of postbureaucratic structures, and especially the more advanced forms of them.

4. *Performance Appraisal.* This activity often has been a troublesome one in organizations—indeed, so much so that well-placed observers have at times heatedly debated about whether anything constructive can be done. Some observers opt, flatly, to eliminate appraisals. This particular brand of human resource war-

fare has been going on for decades, with prominents arrayed on both sides of the argument. The contention started early (e.g., McGregor, 1957; Mayfield, 1960), and still remains with us (e.g., Perry, 1991).

At least as far as these 1993 Ransone Lectures are concerned, no great mystery surrounds this debate. The present view has four features: the case for *some* form of performance appraisal is convincing; in practice, the conventional form of appraisal often creates more confusion and fear than motivation to work effectively and efficiently (e.g., Deming, 1986); that disjoint between ideal and real often can be traced in convincing ways to the bureaucratic structure dominating in both government and business, as well as to the degenerative interaction associated with that model; but that structural connection typically remains unrecognized or underappreciated, even in sources hell-bent on reform (e.g., U.S. GAO, 1993a, pp. 28–29).

This section attempts to improve on this prevailing state of affairs by detailing the appraisal-relevant features of a structure alternative to the bureaucratic model. Flow-of-work structures like that in Exhibit 4.1 promise no magic bullet in connection with performance appraisal. But they can facilitate performance appraisal in several major senses and thus contribute to managing central differences and difficulties in performance. Moreover, flow-of-work structures also can serve as a valuable context for efforts to value and manage diversity (Jackson and Associates, 1992, p. 253) which, admittedly, is a theme the reader has seen before but gets reemphasized nevertheless.

Consider only four points in the broader brief that can be made for performance appraisal in a flow-of-work structure.

First, and primarily, decisions about performance will occur in the context of immediate contributions to a complete flow of work—perhaps a product or a service or a discrete subassembly or subroutine. In effect, this groundedness constitutes a major discipliner of judgments. Moreover, even if contention exists, it is usually within an S-unit, and the common good encourages the sprightly resolution of disputes and, if possible, mutually learning from them. In contrast, appraisals in bureaucratic structures will tend to reflect greater loadings of other factors such as loyalty to an S-unit, or conflicts between two or more S-units which may be beside the point of contributing to holistic performance and all too often are directly antagonistic to it. For example, in a traditional structure, an S-unit's power status may distort judgments about subsystemic shares of the responsibility for holistic performance.

Second, the greater incidence of regenerative interaction in flow-of-work structures creates a congenial force field for making decisions about performance. For example, high trust will influence how judgments about performance are made as well as received. A sense of equity seems more likely under regenerative interaction (e.g., Golembiewski, 1986a). Patently, this potential provides puny support for bureaucratic structures.

Third, ideally, performance appraisal in Exhibit 4.1 structures emphasizes the enhancement of present as well as future contributions to performance by those who share immediate responsibility. The associated tendency is to place performance appraisal in a helpful and communal context. This contrasts with the biases in bureaucratic structures toward individual sink or swim, as well as toward rewards or punishments for particularistic activities that are imprecisely linked to holistic performance. To illustrate, flow-of-work structures often involve S-unit peers in training and appraisal activities (e.g., Perkins, Nieva, and Lawler, 1983). A rising tide of competence can raise everyone's boat in a single flow-of-work S-unit, while serving as a possible win-win model for other S-units.

Fourth, Exhibit 4.1 structures are congenial to group rewards for performance (e.g., Golembiewski, 1986a). This is especially the case in the structural variant relying on forms of autonomous groups, but other approaches to the same end are available (e.g., Lawler, 1992; Doherty and McAdams, 1993). Here, as in gain sharing, each S-unit becomes the unit of compensation as well as the focus of loyalty, with individuals sharing in their S-unit's fate as a derivative of comparative common performance in a flow of work. Consequently, appraisal becomes a facilitator of cooperative effort or an indicator of skills or attitudes that can improve the lot of all in each S-unit. This contrasts sharply with judgments about individual strengths and weaknesses in particularistic activities that require reward or punishment, as bureaucratic structures typically do.

Features like these four will help moderate the numerous pitfalls and pratfalls associated with performance appraisal, and such enhancements also should help in proactively dealing with diversity. Perhaps basically, the failure in appraisals to create the reality of equity, as well as its appearance, only reinforces and exacerbates any tendencies toward divisiveness—to reject adverse personnel actions against self as "just prejudice" or to dismiss positive personnel actions for others as "just favoritism."

If anything, indeed, the value of performance appraisal in our organizational future will escalate. The point applies perhaps most forcefully to aging work forces and especially so given the reasonable goal of avoiding a flood of litigation. Frequently, in my earlier consulting practice, performance appraisal was given a very low priority for older workers, on the convenient rationale that "Joan (or John) will soon be gone to retirement." This view was heard at various ages—sometimes even when employees were only fifty and many times by their late fifties or early sixties. Given what has already occurred with respect to increasing retirement ages, this view now has a precious as well as self-defeating character. If reasonably probable increases in "normal" retirement age also occur, the once dominant view will become downright silly. The age of retirement has increased for all but selected occupations—fire fighters and airline pilots, for example—and probably will continue to do so.

A Summary Perspective

The selective considerations above contribute toward, as well as derive context from, two summary perspectives on performance evaluation. In turn, those perspectives deal with several generalizations and then with a specific state—fear.

Generalizations about performance appraisal
The first focus here is on four generalizations related to employees and then systems. First, we know much about the conditions under which employees will respond positively to evaluation processes. According to Gardenswartz and Rowe (1993, pp. 193–96), several conditions especially encourage positive reactions: the perception that constructive purposes are being served, as in helping the employee to do better and in highlighting areas of personal improvement; confidence that the measuring system will generate equitable rewards; and belief that measurements and rewards rest on acceptable standards.

Second, flow-of-work structures contribute to generating and maintaining such conditions. The key element is that each S-unit can develop shared values that relate to a whole—a product or service or a discrete subassembly. These provide an immediate context for defining and providing working answers to the central questions in evaluation: How "good" did I/we do? What represents "better" and what behaviors or attitudes will help achieve it? Moreover, these sets of S-unit values are tested, and to a degree validated, by multiple comparisons in flow-of-work structures and in that sense transcend the internal-only standards characteristic of the bureaucratic model.

This discipline of S-unit norms serves the three conditions above. The associated dynamics contribute to the shared perception that constructive purposes are being served by evaluation, to the confidence that evaluation processes will generate just rewards, and to the credibility of the belief that acceptable standards underlie evaluation processes.

Third, although the details are far beyond present purposes, good models exist for how such attractions related to performance appraisal in flow-of-work structures can be built into a compatible framework for career development and performance management systems. For example, Diana Elliott and Daniel Stolle (1993) detail one consistent approach for meeting developmental needs for individuals and their organizations.

Fourth, and last on this catalog of generalizations about performance appraisal, two generic motivators dominate in explaining attention to it as well as to the structure in which it is embedded. They are distinguished as narrow and broad, respectively.

The narrow motivator merely needs reemphasis, for the theme has been voiced more than once. Directly, the absence of structures that encourage convenient as well as valid estimates of performance runs the risk of the equivalent of organizational hernias—of defensive alliances, often reinforced by demographic similarities, that constrict or can choke a flow of work. These choke points are usefully minimized, at the very least.

Broadly, managing diversity is usefully reinforced by reward-and-punishment systems responsive to progress on diversity within units whose performance also can be assessed validly and reliably. The issue goes beyond making line managers and supervisors responsible for diversity initiatives, then, as useful as that is in moving toward managing diversity (e.g., Laudicina, 1993, p. 26). Merely reporting statistics on the hiring, firing, or promoting of protected groups can proceed independent of performance, or might even be inimical to it. This encourages diversity by the numbers and does not manage diversity, but merely indulges it.

Indeed, failure to link performance with diversity may breed cynicism and distrust about the sense of the organization as a moral and ethical endeavor which employees can join to transcend their clear limitations as individuals. The evidence suggests that the consequences of sham diversity are bad enough, especially as a few nontraditional employees are parachuted into once all-male and all-white bastions. In contrast, when a small proportion of males enter a "female" profession (e.g., Ott, 1989), the effects seem a bit more benign, if far from ideal. Complicating such early dynamics by condescension about performance risks a potentially explosive mixture.

Fear, performance appraisal, and TQM

The four major sections of discussion above—beginning with regenerative interaction and leading to the new performance appraisal possible under an alternative structural model—share considerable common and underappreciated ground with those who wish to drive fear from the workplace. No doubt foremost among these advocates is the late W. Edward Deming (e.g., 1986), who leads the major contingent of those forces preaching the gospel of Total Quality Management, or TQM.

The TQM position is especially clear with regard to performance appraisal, and that explains the selective focus below. The argument could easily be extended as well to job rotation and job enrichment, but that extension will not have priority here.

The sense of Deming's advocacy can be put in a conceptual nutshell, as by Exhibit 4.4. Basically, Deming encourages an emphasis on understanding systems rather than blaming individuals. Traditional performance appraisal inclines toward the latter and creates "management by fear." This is doubly disadvantageous, if not disastrous. Thus it encourages a widespread hunkering down, taking a low profile: the work force becomes "reluctant to accept risk, to contribute new ideas, to get involved, and to be willing to accept responsibility" (Lowe and McBean, 1989, p. 31).

Exhibit 4.4   Two Approaches to 11 Aspects of Performance Appraisal

Aspect of Performance Appraisal	Traditional Management	Total Quality Management
Basic orientation	Individual as conforming to the dictates of the macro-system	Work group as participating in continuous improvement of both micro- and macro-system
Core responsibility	The key variance in performance is due to individual differences, which management must isolate and reward or punish after designing the "perfect system"	The key variance in performance is due to system inadequacies, which are to be dealt with by management substituting continuous improvement for perfectionism, as well as by fostering the conditions which increase the desire of many/all employees to contribute with both their hands and minds
Primary goals	Narrow control and its documentation	Problem-solving that gets reflected in personal and organizational development
Guiding motto	"Do it right, once, beginning at the top"	"Do it better each time, and especially at the operating levels"
Managerial role	Supervisor as judge	Supervisor as teacher/coach, facilitator
Managerial style	Directive, evaluative, often punitive ("find someone doing something wrong, and stop it")	Facilitative, rewarding ("find someone doing something right, and help spread it through the system, as appropriate")
Frequency of appraisal	Episodic, periodic	Real time, or at least frequent
Degree of formality	High	Low
Target of rewards	Individuals	Groups
Basic assumption	It is impossible for everyone to meet standards, so scarce resources have to be allocated to the few who do so	All or almost all can meet standards, given a responsive system and effective managerial efforts to recruit, train, and induce collaborative conditions
Basic method	To personify the search for inadequate performers, which "freezes feelings" in defense against management and stifles upward feedback	To objectify the discussion of processes and productivity by the use of statistical and analytic tools, which will serve to "unfreeze feelings," thus reducing defenses and enriching upward feedback

From Waldman and Kenett (1990), p. 67; Bowman (1993), p. 39; and many other sources.

Perhaps worse still, in addition—at least to Deming—traditional performance appraisal misdirects attention to the individual and away from the system. This is grievous because Deming assigns over 90 percent of the variability in work to systemic causes. In this view, traditional performance appraisal is not only wrong, but it is an evasion of the key managerial responsibility. As Deming observes (quoted in Moen, 1989, p. 63): "Basically what is wrong is that performance appraisal or merit rating focuses on the end product . . . not on leadership to help people [collaborate at work]."

What Deming and like-minded observers want to avoid seems clear enough. Inter alia, they would like to avoid

> Extrinsic motivation "by constantly judging people" (Deming, as quoted by Michaelson, 1990, p. 44); this should be replaced by "intrinsic motivation, self-esteem, dignity, and eagerness to learn"

> Distancing employees from each other and from their collectivity by fear and by competition for scarce resources; these should be replaced by cooperation and sharing information to improve processes on a continuing basis

> Traditional performance appraisal as individually oriented, focused on separate activities or functions, and judgmental; these should be replaced by versions that are systemic, have a holistic focus, and are developmental in orientation

> Reliance on performance ratings; this will free up those many officials—largely "staff"—who "now make, study, revise, justify, administer, regulate, appeal, and adjudicate these systems" (Bowman, 1993, pp. 29–30)

Broadly, when asked how he would make judgments about compensating people, Deming answered: "I would consider anything but ranking" (as quoted in Neave, 1990, p. 388). Deming apparently favors skill-based seniority systems, as reinforced by long-term consensus about those who have demonstrated leadership at work (Bowman, 1993, pp. 28–29).

It is not clear in TQM theory, however, how all these (and more) things to avoid can be realized within traditional structures and networks of interaction. Curiously, that is, Deming and his followers encourage doing away with conventional performance appraisal; but TQM devotees generally are soft, or obscure, or merely neglectful of the two pillars of the fear associated with conventional appraisal—what are here called the bureaucratic model of organization structure and degenerative interaction. For example, James S. Bowman (1993, p. 20) at one point flatly announces: "The Weberian [bureaucratic] model is the predominant method of management [but the] last two decades, most notably the 1980s, demonstrated that this entrenched, top-down style of management is no longer sustainable." Bowman adds about the bureaucratic model that "it was developed . . . to discipline and control an illiterate workforce. It separated thinkers and doers; once management defined the optimal systems, the role of the worker was to follow them. Variations were seen as the failure to perform according to job specifications, and performance appraisals rated accordingly."

Such insights, however, essentially disappear from the specifics of subsequent discussion. Relatedly, Deming (e.g., 1986) and others generally call for a pattern of relationships like that here labeled "regenerative," lest the good gospel of TQM get devalued by the ways people distance themselves from one another. But the interaction between degenerative interaction and bureaucratic structure does not receive emphasis, and Deming and other TQMers are either silent or vague about how the required transformation in interaction systems can be attained.

These shortfalls of attention are notable. First, TQMers fail to emphasize that the bureaucratic structure provides pervasive and continuous support for degenerative interaction, as well as for conventional performance appraisal, even as they fail to emphasize an alternative to that model. Second, TQMers provide neither a theory nor technology for organizational learning about regenerative interaction, or anything like it. Organization Development and Quality of Working Life (QWL), in sharp contrast, not only provide both a theory and technology for change, but extensive surveys also establish high success rates of change in appropriate directions (e.g., Golembiewski, Proehl, and Sink, 1981, 1982; Golembiewski and Sun, 1993; Nicholas, 1982).

These shortfalls represent two serious omissions in the TQM case—indeed, they constitute glaring oversights. In opposition to the bureaucratic model, both the flow-of-work model and regenerative interaction are diversity-friendly as well as hospitable to TQM. Clearly, we need more of this combination. Charles Handy well presents the brief for quality in our emerging globally competitive world (1990, p. 145): "Organizations will only survive if they can guarantee quality in their goods or their services. Short-term profit at the expense of quality will lead to short-term lives. In that sense, quality is, to my mind, the organizational equivalent of truth. Quality like truth will count, in the end. No one, and no organization, can live a lie for long. Hard to define, impossible to legislate, quality like truth is an attitude of mind."

5. *Facilitative Aggregation.* Basically, flow-of-work structures reflect a commitment to heterogeneous departmentation, and this promises to serve diversity in narrow as well as broad senses. Consider only one example of each.

Narrowly, the Social Security Administration mini-case described in the previous chapter has features largely unique to bureaucratic organizations and could not occur in the same form in flow-of-work structures. There, the fragmenting tendencies between functionally specialized S-units were exacerbated by the fact that blacks performed certain lower-status tasks in one S-unit while whites in another S-unit handled higher-status tasks. The clear potential was realized: the bureaucratic model's focus on S-unit functional homogeneity was reinforced by racial differences, which contributed to problems in the necessary linking of the contributions of the several S-units.

In flow-of-work structures, each S-unit includes all related activities. Hence whether or not minorities perform some low-status activities in any S-unit, all those in each flow share a common identification, which, more often than not, will encourage effective problem-solving in each S-unit. A kind of fail-safe feature also is at work. That is, even if such problem-solving does *not* occur, this shortfall will serve to spotlight an ineffective S-unit. Hence primary self-interest also will help reduce any fragmenting tendencies internal to an S-unit, including race. Moreover, sooner rather than later, convenient job rotation and job enlargement opportunities in flow-of-work structures also would presumably serve to reduce any pigeonholing or type-casting.

Broadly, heterogeneous departmentation also seems diversity-friendly in many other regards. Consider only one contrast, which has substantial support in theory as well as in practice. Overall, the emphasis on homogeneity in traditional structures encourages loyalty to an S-unit, a mixed blessing in the absence of reliable measures of comparative performance on a flow of work. This structural license for behavioral control can easily get out of hand, resulting in various organizational inflexibilities, neuroticisms, and even pathologies—in particularistic conformity, in narrow groupthink, or in "going to Abilene" because of a stultifying "crisis of agreement" (Harvey, 1988).

Overall, in contrast, the heterogeneity around which flow-of-work structures are organized encourages a preoccupation associated with behavioral control but—a very critical difference—that kind concerned with problem-solving by a whole rather than with protectionism by each of several structurally differentiated parts. This encourages the expression of broad ranges of opinion and a zest for innovation, while constructively subjecting them to the discipline of the comparative measurement of performance. The implied differences can be profound for valuing or managing diversity as well as for many particularisms related to both task and maintenance.

This description, necessarily dense at times, highlights a stark comparison. In short, loyalty to subunits in bureaucratic structures can be troublesome. In contrast, such loyalty in flow-of-work structures can reinforce norms for high quality and performance.

These general comments will get useful reinforcement from several particular senses in which flow-of-work structures can serve diversity, broadly conceived. Four examples cover the range from behavioral diversity to different styles and climates, with the last of the sections dealing with functionally integrative teams. A significant caveat by way of clarification—or vice versa—closes this summary of how and why flow-of-work structures serve the needs of diversity.

Diverse Behaviors and Personal Profiles

Both within and especially between S-units, flow-of-work structures imply both theoretical and practical support for behavioral diversity—whether the issue relates to the degrees of authoritarianism of employees or to their personality profiles.

The argument is clearest between units, given that each unit is organized around its own flow of work. The lack of the need for close linkage between the S-units, because they are autonomous in sequential and temporal senses, implies less turbulence caused by within-unit differences. Consequently, differences between S-units may exist in flow-of-work structures. My mind's eye locks in on several product manager groups, each charged with marketing a different product, yet comparatively assessed in terms of relative market share. They all did it in their own wondrous ways. Thus a peanut butter group adopted the sense and nonsense of its basic customers, complete with beanies sporting whirling propeller blades. The reader can conjure up her or his own view of the cake-mix crowd—its contrasting gender, culture, artifacts, vocabulary, and so on. Similar contrasts have developed in public agencies, perhaps especially between special-purpose versus traditional units in the military (e.g., Ogburn, 1959).

In addition, within-S-unit differences in flow-of-work structures would, if not somehow satisfactorily accommodated, show up in poorer comparative performance. Hence continuing motivation for conflict resolution is built into Exhibit 4.1 structures. Moreover, many have proposed that any within-unit differences in attitudes and orientations, on balance, would positively contribute to useful innovation and experimentation. The argument has often been made, especially at macro-levels—for city-states, cultures, or even nation-states (e.g., Cleveland, 1993, esp. pp. 16–30). The argument for diversity as stimulus to effort and creativity at the organization level has never been made more economically than by Satoru Tsujimoto, an executive of Mitsubishi Motors, when he emphasized that diversity positively heightens employees' perceptions of workplace equity, and this in turn positively influences innovation, as others have noted (e.g., Di Tomaso, Thompson, and Blake, 1988, p. 22). Tsujimoto said (as quoted in Andersen, 1991): "The Southern California area . . . there are so many different races. From these [come] different values. So there are many different [auto] designs."

In contrast, under the bureaucratic model, close and even subtle sequential and temporal linkages between the S-units are required, and this elemental provides both practical and theoretical motivation for minimizing all possible sources of turbulence, even from minor differences. Hence the common quest in such structures is for homogeneity and uniformity, as illustrated most vividly by the early vogue of personality testing so as to cull the different and the deviant (e.g., Whyte, 1956). If often done in unreasonable ways, then, the quest for standardization—not only of outcomes but also of processes and even people—does have strong motivation where bureaucratic models dominate.

The present point also can be approached by well-known generalizations from group dynamics. Consider the bare notion that contact is often associated with a mutual improvement in attitudes (e.g., Deutsch and Collins, 1951), and this is clearly what the flow-of-work structure intends: to reinforce the integration of activities in a flow of work by departmentalizing around the full set of activities so as to build positive attitudes among all contributors to that common flow.

This generalization reflects a probability statement, of course, because we know that personal contact—although it typically has marked effects on attitudes and behaviors—does not induce unidirectional effects (e.g., Webster, 1961). The flow-of-work model encourages generally benign outcomes via shared goals within S-units, as well as via the convenient estimates of comparative performance between S-units. The probable chains of effects need only be suggested. Within individual S-units, individuals will tend to find and build on perceived similarities between members, to develop familiarities, and even to generate personal likings for one another. These are common reinforcers of effective relationships between people (e.g., McGuire, 1969; Zand, 1972), as noted in Chapter 3. Hence, operationally, the burgeoning tendency to involve members of flow-of-work structures deeply in the selection, training, and evaluation of co-workers (e.g., Perkins, Nieva, and Lawler, 1983).

In bureaucratic structures, similar dynamics also will build strong relationships in S-units. But the homogeneous departmentalization is likely to mobilize such relationships awkwardly, for example, in defensiveness and protectionism against other particularistic S-units. It is that simple and that profound.

These elaborations of a basic point could be continued, but let us rise above the details to bring this major comparison to a conclusion by illustration, and one that is not too fine. The bureaucratic model has a strong bias toward requiring adaptation to a basic homogeneity. Hence, in that traditional model, the common sense of a "melting pot" approach to diversity—if not its necessity.

In sharp contrast, affirming and managing diversity fit far more comfortably with other metaphors. As Pomerleau (1993) reviews for us, attempts to embody a multiculturalist perspective have been couched in metaphors understandably reflecting heterogeneity, as in a "mulligan stew" (Thomas, 1990, p. 112), a "mosaic" (Rieff, 1991, p. 176), a "quilt" (Jesse Jackson, as quoted in Loden and Rosener, 1991, p. 137), and "immigrants and their hosts would not so much assimilate as leak into one another like flavors when you cook" (Salmon Rushdie, as quoted in Pomerleau, 1993, p. 17).

Diverse Processes and Routines

Exhibit 4.1 structures have a substantial potential to serve the richness suggested by such metaphors. For example, given that some standardization often will be useful or necessary as to outcomes or products, individual S-units in flow-of-work structures can accommodate differences and even idiosyncracies—various mixes of personal skills or experiences, organizational histories, cultures, and so on. Moreover, the differences reasonably encompassed by flow-of-work structures also can stimulate continuous improvement.

One case comes to mind, forcefully. A public agency was built around flow-of-work principles, and great public attention was focused on the comparative performance of S-units. At midyear, an auction was held. Other S-units could bid in dollars of budget to gain access to effort-saving processes or routines developed by the clearly successful. All bids could be declined but, at year's end, a "tell all" banquet was held. There, both successes and failures were detailed for their contributions to common learning and for future use without charge.

The total sense of this example seems clear enough. An Exhibit 4.1 structure admits diverse interests, experiences, and skills, but critically leavened by easy comparative estimates of performance. Each S-unit also has a continuing self-interest in improving processes and routines, if only because any one of the other S-units might be so inclined. Moreover, each S-unit could profit from any self-generated improvements, but not forever. Increments in self-esteem and even in dollars of budget—to be spent as the innovative S-unit decided, within very wide constraints—encouraged taking advantage of the structure's flexibility in compound senses.

Diverse Styles, Climates, Cultures

Again, no practical or theoretical reasons inhibit an S-unit in a flow-of-work structure from developing a distinctive style, climate, or culture. People being people, such differentiation often will occur, whatever the basic structural model, as Charles T. Goodsell correctly reminds us is true even of bureaucratic structures (1985, esp. pp. 38–42). The basic principle is equifinality: typically, numerous routes can take one from A to B.

So why fight nature? A very practical reason, even a compulsion, exists in bureaucratic structures. There, differentiation often will complicate or even disrupt the sequencing of separate activities. Consequently, most managers in such structures will keep as tight a rein on differentiation as they can (e.g., Ogburn, 1959). Whether it involves prima donnas or premier performers, goes the common concern, differentiation between S-units can cause problems in bureaucratic structures. Why? At a maximum, output could be reduced to zero by turbulence between S-units in bureaucratic structures.

In contrast, no possibility of such a collision of differences reducing output to zero exists in flow-of-work structures. There, each S-unit is organized around a total flow, which permits relatively unambiguous estimates of performance and also encourages resolution of any differences between those S-unit colleagues performing activities A, B, and C. Quite the opposite motivation characterizes bureaucratic structures. There, separatist tendencies (if anything) encourage getting the other guys before they get you.

Neither practice nor principle suggests, let alone requires, that flow-of-work S-units cannot each develop differently in culture, artifacts, vocabulary, and so on. Quite the opposite, in fact. In practice, this diversity-friendly individuation has often occurred—perhaps most dramatically in the product manager structures common in industry—and such individuation is commonly associated with superior performance (Golembiewski and Kiepper, 1988, pp. 8–11). The supporting evidence derives largely from smaller groups and collectivities, but the argument for macro-system effectiveness in divisional structures also impresses (e.g., Dess and Davis, 1984).

This happy concordance should, by this time, not be surprising. Briefly, flow-of-work S-units can respond to their specific and even idiosyncratic causal textures—immediate environments, personal features of members, their stages of life and career, and so on—and this massive fact should facilitate adjustments to changing conditions as well as contribute to a sense of real mastery of the local environment. This even *sounds* diversity-friendly.

Both practice and principle, in contrast, discourage differences between S-units in bureaucratic structures, which could well impede the smoothness of the total flow of work to which each of the particularistic S-units contributes. Metaphors like the "melting pot" are no more likely to work in organizations than in twentieth-century America, and such probabilities add to the growing case for the diversity-unfriendliness of bureaucratic structures.

Is structural change really needed for such changes in styles, climates, and cultures? The major alternative relies on a specific cathartic stimulus when a social system is "stuck"—the coming of an appropriately charismatic leader with the required vision (e.g., Bennis and Nanus, 1985). The view here is not entirely opposed but proposes that the devil is in the details. Even the appropriate "great person" would find the pathway to diversity eased by structural change, and the rest of us would find such change very desirable, if not absolutely necessary.

Functionally Integrative Teams

As a final and most powerful perspective here on how Exhibit 4.1 structures can facilitate integration of a flow of work, Exhibit 4.5 describes several varieties of teams that are evolving in response to the increasingly obvious problems with functional or bureaucratic structures. Commonly, if at different levels of complexity and scope, the four exemplars of teams in Exhibit 4.5 all seek to integrate sets of activities to facilitate a flow of work. Among many other sources, Susan G. Cohen (1993) provides especially useful overview and descriptive detail.

Here, our summary purposes will have to be satisfied by three points related to

Exhibit 4.5. First, the four exemplars of integrative teams are arrayed in terms of progressive scope and complexity, but numerous other types might be inserted at various points in that progression.

Second, these useful integrative team structures are also progressively incompatible with bureaucratic structures because they more comprehensively seek to induce lateral relationships. Parallel structures constitute the best fit with traditional structures; networks are clearly in a different realm; and autonomous teams clearly reject bureaucratic principles.

In contrast, the fit between the exemplars and Exhibit 4.1 structures is much more comfortable. Most directly, S-units in flow-of-work structures can themselves be autonomous teams and project or development teams. Commonly, Exhibit 4.1 structures as well as the exemplars in Exhibit 4.5 share the sense of "rugged groupism" that Xerox and others have adopted for success. The Xerox philosophy deserves extensive quotation (Watkins and Marsick, 1993, p. 97):

> We [at Xerox] believe in the values of bringing things together to create work units or teams responsible for a whole set of activities. This concept, of course, rests on faith in the human spirit and intellect. It assumes that a diverse group of people . . . can do a better job in today's world of constant change than any set of "formal procedures," methods, or controls administered by a remote, centralized management. It assumes that group learning is possible and . . . is more than the sum of the individuals.

Third, the literature is nowhere near exhaustive nor methodologically impeccable, but both research and experience suggest the usefulness—indeed, on occasion more the necessity—of integrative teams. The research on self-managing teams supports such conclusions:

> Studies of individual applications have produced attractive results, on balance, on both self-report and objective measures (e.g., Walton, 1972, 1979).

> Comprehensive cost-benefit analyses are rare (Cohen, 1993, p. 217).

> Adoption rates are substantial and growing, based on general agreement that such integrative teams usually "work" and, consequently, that "rigorous research" is a luxury.

> Comparisons of multiple settings indicate a range of effects on productivity and broader measures of effectiveness that include costs, quality, and safety, with a range of effects from modest (e.g., Goodman, Devadas, and Hughson, 1988) to substantial (e.g., Cohen and Ledford, 1990).

> Comparisons of multiple sites indicate general improvements in attitudes about work (e.g., Cohen, 1993, pp. 216–17).

> Concern with quality tends to be high.

Exhibit 4.5 Selected Integrative Teams and Their Features

Types of Integrative Teams	General Features
Parallel structures (e.g., Bushe and Shani, 1991)	Supplement existing structures in general, recommend or advise only Typically temporary and/or part-time Easy to set up; require no changes in authority, power, or structure Can develop unique norms for problem-solving vs. steady-state operations Substantial evidence of usefulness in limited spheres
Self-managing teams (e.g., Herbst, 1962; Hanna, 1988)	Encompass activities in a total flow of work or discrete subassembly Usually small, N = 10–15 Responsible for many/all functions—from operations through inspection, compensation, and even selection/training Basically shift authority/power downward Reduce cycle times: action level is often the decision level Generate social and psychological forces that reinforce integration of activities required by task Substantial success rates
Project and development teams (e.g., National Industrial Conference Board, 1965; Stewart, 1965; Loo, 1992)	Collections of resources, often white-collar and professional, who deliver some product or service to a client Often combine home base in a functional department and one or more project assignments; multiple loyalties must be managed Can be large—in the hundreds or more Have extended time horizon, but end point is quite definite Ad hocracies, with substantial potential for flexibility Often a useful if not necessary form, with well-known advantages and costs and with numerous applications
Networks (e.g., Drucker, 1988; Savage, 1990)	At times hailed as the team structure of the future Membership is diverse and changing Composed of individuals or groups who share an evolving set of interdependencies

Examples

Quality circles, task forces, productivity improvement teams

Limitations

May find it difficult to gain legitimacy
Members may be on short leashes from home units
Are the "shallowest" of integrative exemplars and have the most modest potential for returns on investments

Autonomous groups, self-designing teams

Face resistance from functional or processual units—e.g., due to shifts in authority/power
Reduce need for middle management and hence may generate conflict
Bureaucratic infrastructures limit applicability in traditional organizations

Various start-up operations (e.g., new plants or refineries, launching a product or service)
Research and development ventures
A weapon system

Can generate strong resistance in traditional organizations, especially where budgets are controlled by functional departments
Tension levels often are high

Investment banks (e.g., Eccles and Crane, 1987)
In Digital's view of self as an organization with a "networked design"—with a "core of 40–50 people in fourteen locations, with several thousand more participating indirectly, having firm agreement on the goal and a distributed leadership structure" (Cohen, 1993, p. 199)

Little data about incidence or effectiveness

Absenteeism and turnover seem to vary in industrial studies (e.g., Cohen and Ledford, 1990), but most observers expect reductions in both, based on early studies (e.g., Herbst, 1962, esp. pp. 64–81).

A Significant Caveat/Clarification

The research literature on heterogeneity versus homogeneity in work groups remains far from complete, but two generalizations seem apt. Directly, first, solid reasons imply that associated effects will be powerfully influenced by whether the organization context is bureaucratic or has dominant flow-of-work features. Quite consistently, to explain, heterogeneity seems associated with benefits on tasks requiring creativity and judgment (e.g., Jackson, 1991), and this suggests that the most positive effects of diversity will be reflected in postbureaucratic structures. Here, similarity-attraction theory may apply (e.g., Bryne, 1971), but its effects are diminished because of the probably shared objective of maintaining performance in flow-of-work structures, which, moreover, facilitate reliable and valid estimates of performance are facilitated by the basic structure.

Consistently, the evidence inclines to the view that heterogeneity at times may reduce cohesiveness and attachment to the organization (Tsiu, Egan, and O'Reilly, 1992, pp. 570–75), and this analysis supports the hypothesis that such effects are more characteristic of bureaucratic organizations. There, on the present accounting, pressures toward uniformity are greater whether the employees are in work groups that are supportive of management or whether (if for different reasons) the employees are in work groups adopting aggressive or hostile postures toward management. There, also, similarity-attraction theory explains such resistance quite directly.

Such a possibility or probability helps explain some contrary findings in the literature. Thus, with complications far beyond present purposes, one study associates heterogeneity with *lower* levels of personal attachment to firms (Tsiu, Egan, and O'Reilly, 1992). This would not be surprising in a bureaucratic structure, but in an otherwise exemplary study, the researchers note only that their data come from the "lowest-level operating units." On average, bureaucratic structures dominate there, but that remains speculative in the case at issue.

Second, the available literature is tethered short in an important particular. The strong but qualified tendency in major sources is to focus on the favorable reactions of minorities to heterogeneity (e.g., Kanter, 1977), but that seems clearly inadequate (e.g., Tsiu, Egan, and O'Reilly, 1992, esp. pp. 570–71). A true cost-benefit analysis must factor in the reactions of *both* majorities and minorities.

6. *Wrongdoing and Whistle-Blowing.* A credible case in principle can be made for the usefulness of flow-of-work structures in connection with wrongdoing and ethical resisting, a.k.a. whistle-blowing. Basically, given the advantages in the comparative measurement of performance by each S-unit, wrongdoing takes di-

rectly from the shared bottom line, and this would seem to encourage whistle-blowing, particularly within an S-unit where the earliest preventive measures can be taken. Presumably, for related reasons, it also would be hard to conceal wrong-doing within a flow-of-work S-unit, even though the higher cohesiveness attributable to each unit might support defensive reactions by an S-unit against outside authorities. Moreover, if this analysis is reasonably correct about the common association of regenerative interaction with flow-of-work structures, that reinforces the general argument just sketched.

Despite some support in the available literature, direct tests of the present position have not yet been attempted. Some research does associate high degrees of ethical resistance with a "high supportive and low defensive organization climate" (Keenan, 1988, p. 250), and no conceptual strain is required to locate comfortably this description within the conceptual territory staked out here for regenerative interaction. Overall, however, research in this area is plagued by major conceptual and operational issues (e.g., Near, Baucus, and Miceli, 1993, esp. pp. 217–22). So it seems most appropriate to leave the conceptual argument as is—that is, attractive but speculative.

7. *Supervisory Styles, Attitudes, and Behaviors.* Overall, flow-of-work structures will admit a broad range of supervisory styles, with no reasons in principle or practice prohibiting each S-unit from responding differentially to its own unique blend of diversities. This is convenient because all of us are developmentally unique, and the differences can be profound as well as pedestrian.

This possibility suggests useful flexibility and leverage for diversity, perhaps especially in the case of the often-remarked differences in central tendencies in the behavior and attitudes of nontraditional employees in the roles of supervisor as well as of supervised. People come to their work with different developmental profiles, for example, with respect to motivations or concerning orientations toward "tough" and "tender" feelings. Differences in motivations, predispositions, or values definitely exist; and whether a person is (for example) a woman or man may help anticipate and explain some part of these differences, but plenty of variance will remain as unexplained or unique (e.g., Golembiewski, 1977a, 1977b).

Structures need to provide room for such interacting differences. This is not the place for details, although aspects of such differences are well enough known, as in the case of racioethnicity (e.g., Cox and Nkomo, 1993, esp. pp. 211–16) and in gender (e.g., Cahoon and Rowney, 1993, esp. pp. 341–43, 346–51). So we know what differences may appear when diversity is taken into real management account; and we can even assign some part of explanations of those differences to specific variables. Broadly, flow-of-work structures provide a context within which such explained as well as unique variances can be worked on under the discipline of a shared responsibility for performance assignable to specific S-units.

Beyond these introductory comments, discussion will zero in on two facets of leadership associated with flow-of-work structures. Specifically, the two following sections deal with leadership seen as supportive or participative and transformational.

Supportive or Participative Leadership

As it were, flow-of-work structures permit switch-hitting when it comes to the leadership style of formal authorities while, as suggested in the previous chapter, bureaucratic structures incline markedly toward a directive or authoritarian style. To explain, an autocratic style may be enacted in flow-of-work structures, but that style is neither required nor recommended. As they will, authorities in Exhibit 4.1 structures also can opt for the attributes of the supportive style that the literature associates with higher productivity and especially with higher satisfaction. A supportive style has such features:

> Supervision by one to many, with an emphasis on encouraging the cohesiveness of the work group.
>
> A deemphasis on close oversight and punitiveness.
>
> Substantial autonomy in task, which is permitted by the facility of measuring and recognizing performance, especially for enriched jobs.
>
> Wide dissemination of job-relevant information, which is often required as well as convenient in flow-of-work structures.
>
> Substantial participation in decisions regarding work and delegation of decision making within the framework of general criteria provided by vision, cultural, and mission statements.

Several traditions of inquiry establish the linkages of such features to high satisfaction and productivity, especially to the former (e.g., Miller and Monge, 1986). Consider the research with "consideration" and "structure," following the early work of Edwin A. Fleishman (1962) and its various extensions (e.g., Likert, 1967, esp. pp. 47–80). The former (Con) refers to an ability to develop "mutual trust, respect, and a certain warmth between the supervisor and [her or his] group," while "structure" (Str) indicates a "supervisory role largely conceived in terms of assigning tasks, planning to get work done, and pushing for production" (Golembiewski, 1989a, p. 181). Broadly, HiCon managers are responded to more favorably than LoCon or HiStr, with a HiHi profile apparently being best of all.

Exhibit 4.1 structures incline toward HiCon and also provide a context within which HiStr/HiCon can influence a total flow of work. HiCon can exist in bureaucratic structures, but that usually will reflect strong personal qualities rather than a responsiveness to the urgings of that model. HiStr represents what bureaucratic structures and concepts encourage, if not require; but HiStr in such settings will perforce be directed at particularisms rather than at a flow of work, and hence supervisory control may drift toward pickiness, if not arbitrariness.

As noted, flow-of-work structures also can admit directive or autocratic leadership but, unlike bureaucratic structures, do not encourage or require such a style. Directive leadership might be relied on in special circumstances—as for a very young work unit just learning elemental tasks, for a work unit dominated by individuals with strong authoritarian preferences, or for employees sharing a view of work as responsive to only a narrow range of their needs. Such circumstances do occur although, to judge from the literature, neither commonly nor for an indefinite time. Flow-of-work structures permit flexible responses to what comes and what goes.

Transformational Leadership

Exhibit 4.1 structures also seem compatible with transformational leadership, which—first in historical analyses (e.g., Burns, 1978), then in popularizations (e.g., Bennis and Nanus, 1985), and more recently in detailed experimental work (e.g., Bass and Avolio, 1993)—has gained a very high profile. It is commonly contrasted with transactional leadership, which received some attention at the end of the previous chapter. Broadly, transformational leadership is seen as useful by many and as absolutely necessary by some under conditions of complexity and change.

All of the major linkages of transformational leadership (TFL) with specific structural arrangements have not yet been established by concerted research, but the presumptive case seems strong (e.g., Bass and Avolio, 1993). Here, the case will be sketched for the compatibility of TFL with the flow-of-work exemplar of postbureaucratic structures. Chapter 3 sketches some of the linkages of transactional leadership (TAL) with the bureaucratic model.

Conveniently, let us begin with a stark contrast. Basically, TFL attempts to raise consciousness about issues of consequence to organizations and their members, while TAL seeks to adapt employees' needs to what is already defined as consequential. In outline (Golembiewski and Kuhnert, 1992, pp. 4–7), although definitions can differ substantially (e.g., Yukl and Van Fleet, 1992, pp. 173–77), it is safe to note that TFL

> Uses authority and power to help radically reshape the social and physical environment, thus helping destroy the old way of life and making way for a new one.

> Urges a broadening perspective on organizational experiences and on their value systems, especially by relying on end values to guide cooperative behavior of superiors and subordinates. In contrast, TAL leads through bargains concerning instrumental values or roles.

Approaches this broadening via a basic change in an organization's culture, which can be approached in several related ways (Bass, 1985):
- by raising levels of individual awareness about what they need to function more fully, by expanding consciousness about the limited range and value of common outcomes in their workaday organizations, as well as by enlarging the sense of ways to act on that awareness and consciousness
- by getting individuals to transcend immediate self-interests for the sake of the team, organization, or larger polity
- by expanding an individual's portfolio of needs and wants or, relatedly, by raising individual aspirations about expected or desired levels of need-satisfaction

Uses a decision-making approach that contrasts with that of the transactional style.
- TFL emphasizes the broad range of need-satisfaction inherent in developing an expanded consciousness of the idealized possible, as well as in working under it; TAL emphasizes the specific payoffs to be given for complying with the existing and prescribed consciousness.

Uses a framework for construing and evaluating reality that differs in two basic senses from TAL, building on the work of Lawrence Kohlberg (e.g., 1981).
- Transformational leadership (TFL) develops more comprehensive "frames of reference" at progressive stages of adult development (e.g., toward personal growth and self-realization); TAL remains fixated at lower levels of development (e.g., pay and fringes).
- For TFL, richness of choice is the hallmark of healthy individuals and systems at high levels of development; TAL emphasizes one basic choice—complying or not complying.

The temptation waxes strong to gild two particular lilies: about how transformational leadership is compatible with flow-of-work structures and about how TFL can variously serve the valuing or managing of diversity in the organizations of our near future.

But that temptation will be resisted, at least in the main. A dialogue will be largely allowed to happen, between the eyes of readers and the ears of listeners to these 1993 Ransone Lectures. Nonetheless, two illustrations will help prepare the reader's mind for the opportunity to do his or her own thing.

Structure and transformational leadership
On the basic issue of wriggle room for first-line supervisors and middle-level managers, especially, far less exists in bureaucratic structures than in flow-of-work structures. TFL consequently permits only narrow applications in bureaucracies,

to which TAL is better suited. This seems crystal clear, in concept (e.g., Yukl and Van Fleet, 1992, esp. pp. 173–77).

The only practical issue involves the need for TFL. At least for the foreseeable future, that need seems great at all organization levels. Why? Generally, consider only the challenges to expand effective consciousness about global competition, tighten budgets, and reflect on the permanence of change when it comes to both requisite skills as well as required products and services.

Patently, these highly likely challenges imply transformational leadership. And that, in turn encourages basic structural change to accommodate TFL.

At the level of more specific research, however, much remains to be done before fine-grained generalizations are substantially hazard-free. Empirical research is in its early stages, with Bass's (1985) Multifactor Leadership Questionnaire getting the lion's share of attention. As Gary Yukl and David D. Van Fleet (1992, p. 176) summarize the sense of that emerging research, it "usually finds a correlation between transformational leadership and various criteria of leader effectiveness."

Transformational leadership and diversity

TFL seems more compatible with diversity than is transactional leadership, especially with the fourth and fifth approaches to diversity distinguished above. These two approaches relate to valuing differences, as well as to managing for diversity, or organizing around it. TAL might suffice for the other three approaches and seems dominant in the first approach to diversity.

Indeed, given the descriptions above, this conclusion has a tautological character. For example, truly affirming diversity requires an expanded sense of consciousness as well as high stages of adult development, which are prominent elements in any description of transformational leadership. In contrast, TAL is oriented toward preserving the status quo, which implies no urgency when it comes to progress on diversity. In addition, perhaps, TAL also might be useful for the fourth strategy described above—valuing diversity—but even then only in that variant which rests on an underlying concept of adaptation or a melting pot. In this variant, diversity is to be explicated and understood for basic reasons: from the white male perspective, as a way of indicating the extent of the emerging challenges to adaptation and to the melting pot; and from the perspectives of minorities as well as white males, as a demonstration of management's good intentions in allowing the fuller expression of diversity, but only or largely during that indefinite but limited period within which adaptation *better occur*.

Summary

The contrasting generalizations in this and the previous chapter imply very different life chances for efforts to value or manage differences in organizations, given alternative structural forms. In sum, two structural models seem to imply very different costs and opportunities in dealing constructively with diversity. The bureaucratic model implies a range of inflexibilities and difficulties in association with style of interaction, job rotation, job enrichment, performance appraisal, orientation to departmentation, wrongdoing as well as its polar partner ethical resisting, and leadership. The flow-of-work model promises a higher potential for easing the challenges of diversity, again as viewed in the context of seven managerially relevant factors.

The analysis above has a limited reach, to be sure. That is, structure is not everything; and bureaucratic along with flow-of-work structures do not exhaust the available alternatives.

Nonetheless, this analysis has a relatively firm grasp. The two illustrative exemplars do represent important structural variations in organizations; and the two different structures have broad ranges of contrasting consequences for interaction, culture, styles of supervision, and so on. Much of the analysis relates to entrance or low levels of organization, but the sense of the discussion also extends (if more tentatively) to all levels of organization (Golembiewski, 1993a), especially in connection with interaction, leadership, and the basic question of structural types.

This relatively certain knowledge inspires no undiluted optimism about action, however. Consider only three caveats. First, the widespread adoption in the public sector of flow-of-work structures would constitute a real revolution, but, necessary as that appears to be, even such thoroughgoing change will leave public management still short by a revolution, or even two. Specifically, clear experience in business implies the need to fine-tune flow-of-work structures, and that recognition constitutes an organizational revolution in its own right (e.g., Golembiewski, 1995, esp. chap. 3). Despite this need, there seems no way to avoid the nuanced learning experiences associated with getting Exhibit 4.1 structures to work. Perhaps, at best, these unavoidable learning experiences will constitute less of a surprise in the public sector, based on the accumulated experience in business.

Second, part of the public sector experience with flow-of-work structures has been bad, at least to some observers. In Britain, for example, that model at times gets confused with—and is even inextricably linked to—zesty efforts to whittle away at the public service or perhaps even to hollow it (e.g., Pollitt, 1990). This confusion or linkage seems incautious, in the present view. At least, it confuses a means (the structure) with an end. Let us be clear about the present end: to facilitate via structural change the ability of the public service to perform its historic and new missions with effectiveness and with a special focus on diversity. Both are required to protect the public service against efforts to whittle away at it or to hollow it.

Third, even absolutely unqualified and convincing evidence might not lead to replacement of bureaucratic structures. This implies an irony or a paradox, given the growing chorus of energetic pleas for basic change (e.g., Osborne and Gaebler, 1992). In sum, diversity implies threat and even fear; and both these features in the past have been powerful motivators of a heightened reliance on the bureaucratic model.

Probable or not, this knee-jerk reaction has a high cost: rigidity will be the price of the spurious security of traditional ways and means. To suggest the point, consider only three kinds of employees: new entrants into the work force, or persons new to a particular job, who at first may find sufficient challenge in a narrow or even routinized job; those relieved to have *any* job under conditions of more or less chronic unemployment; and those who prefer routinized jobs that permit (or even require) fantasizing or daydreaming—for example, some of those approaching retirement, those alienated from work, or those expecting only episodic or short-lived worklives.

The bureaucratic model accommodates to such employees, but only on entrance; and managements have to beware thereafter. Practically, many jobs—and a sharply growing proportion of them—now demand more of the employee, and these demands almost certainly will burgeon. Moreover, employees can, and do, and should, develop and change during their worklives. Thus, even employees in the three classes above may gain experience or age and come to expect greater variety and challenge in their work. They may find frustration escalating because of need-depriving work, which could prove troublesome to employees and management as economic conditions improve. Thus intent to quit may grow, with diminished commitment and greater difficulty of "putting in a day"; later, large numbers of experienced employees suddenly may leave as soon as economic conditions permit, or adversarial collective bargaining relationships may develop. Or people may learn either that their needs and expectations about work are changing or that available jobs require different and even "higher" needs and expectations.

Only a little reflection is necessary to establish that flow-of-work structures are more able to accommodate this broad range of conditions encountered at work. In particular, such structures permit the more need-satisfying work that most individuals seem to need, most of the time. Moreover, Exhibit 4.1 structures also can encompass the special situations illustrated above—for example, narrower jobs when employees begin to gain experience and then enlarged jobs, in the same locus and for the same people, when sufficient development occurs.

The bureaucratic model tends toward one size fits all. That applies inconsistently to socks and even worse in life or work.

Existing workplaces have made use of the flexibilities of alternative structural models—at times, very comprehensive use (e.g., Perkins, Nieva, and Lawler, 1983; Lawler, 1992)—and growing attention to the two structures emphasized in this chapter seems a definite part of our future in ways both strategic and superficial. Often, indeed, elements of both models may appear cheek by jowl, as it were. In one setting, for example, employees can opt for one of two compensation tracks: a premium-pay track that rewards individuals for continuous development of cross-training competencies on a large number of activities and skills; or a normal-pay track for those who are "tapped-out" or who are satisfied with their present portfolio of competencies as well as with the associated compensation. Individuals on the premium-pay track are paid for what they can come to do and to be, that is, for their willingness and ability to build growing repertoires of skills and competencies. Employees on the premium track are not paid for the conventional reasons: what they happen to be doing, how much of it they do, or how long they have been doing it. These latter guides for compensation had their day but now relate more to history than to today's scene.

This may understate the probabilities, in fact: diversity may be destined to lead, and the evidence definitely inclines to the view that this cannot go either very far or very fast without broad-based structural change beyond the bureaucratic model. Increasingly, for example, the issue at work is getting through today in ways that—if they do not facilitate dealing with our fast-approaching tomorrows—at least will not overly complicate dealing with them. There seems plenty of evidence that both public and business employers face growing pressures to begin to follow diversity strategies. To put the point directly, many businesses are just now learning the ropes about global competition for customers as an adjunct to, or even as a replacement for, long-acknowledged competition about technology. And most governments will face continuing challenges to do more with less and to justify more convincingly what they do. This reflects their newly competitive environment.

Moreover, both sectors probably will increasingly face the need to compete for employees—always to get the best of those with high potential and increasingly to get their share of skills in short supply. Shortages already exist in many job classes for perhaps 50 percent of U.S. employers, and forecasts call for more of the same (Hudson Institute, 1988; Towers Perrin & Hudson Institute, 1990). Such scarcities, if and when they occur, will only exacerbate our future of escalating differences and diversity. The problem will become one of attracting and retaining scarce resources, and that usually includes greater tolerance of differences as well as greater attention to a quality of working life that provides more scope for differences.

Note

1 An earlier version of this chapter was part of "Diversity and Organization Structure," a paper delivered at the 1993 Berkeley Symposium on Public Management Research, University of California at Berkeley, July 19, by this author and William A. Osuna.

As the two previous chapters reflect, developing a managerial approach to diversity does not have to be a case of virtue being its own reward. Far from it, in matters great and small, diversity has long had its compensating and even rewarding features.

I vividly recall a day in the early 1970s when I was working with government officials following a series of grisly killings in public parklands. A few rogue bears were the culprits, and their targets often were women. A task force was working on a warning sign, and its all-male and middle-aged members were having a tough time with one aspect of female hygiene that seemed involved in the attacks. The best they could do was self-conscious and elliptical, beginning, "There will be days during each month," and ending after more than one hundred words with a warning that there would be far better times to go hiking or backpacking.

The committee members were doubtful, but they finally responded to their consultant's periodic reminders that they were an all-male group dealing with unfamiliar material whereas not more than ten or twenty feet beyond the walls of the conference room were numerous resources who could provide female perspective on the warning. So a group of office personnel were invited in and shown the committee's product, which had squeezed so many words on a sheet of newsprint in such small type that people had to cluster around the easel to see the draft.

Diversity triumphed and not for the first or last time. The women quickly agreed: "We see what you're getting at, but it's really very wordy." Could they give the warning their personal attention, now? "Why, of course." A few minutes later, the ad hoc rewrite group emerged with the warning that got distributed throughout government parks. It read: "When you're having your period, don't go in the wilderness areas."

Beyond adding skills and numbers to augmenting traditional (and usually white male) perspectives, approaches to diversity can have a range of useful effects. Successfully valuing and managing diversity also are necessary in philosophic, moral, political, and practical terms.

1. *What Have We Learned about Infrastructure?* In addition to basic structural change to encourage diversity-friendly work sites, what else can be done to develop a facilitative infrastructure? The issue is consequential, for basic change in bureaucratic concepts will be uneven and slow in coming.[1] In the United States, for example, various postbureaucratic innovations such as job enrichment have been widely adopted and more extensively ballyhooed. Yet the basic bureaucratic ideation often still lurks in the background, if it does not have a place up front and centerstage.

Hence the significance of the question, What can be done about infrastructure, given the probable backing and filling about basic bureaucratic notions? Possible targets include policies, procedures, and practices, as well as cultural features. Experience has been somewhat fruitful, and a few exemplars at once illustrate what has been done while they also suggest what needs doing.

The organizational commitments associated with possible diversity-friendly exemplars vary widely, but the focus here will be on low- to mid-scale exemplars, applicable in both public and business sectors. Other small-scale commitments deal, for example, with providing convenient phone access to parents with latchkey children, of whom there may be 4 to 7 million or more (Cookson, Seligson, and Garbarino, 1986). Such facilitated contact may ease the "three o'-clock syndrome" for concerned parents. Big-ticket items include child care, in which organizations may play various roles (Friedman and Galinsky, 1992, pp. 181–87): providing a center for their employees' children; making payments directly or through employees; arranging for discounts from private vendors; helping create needed services; and providing referrals.

An introductory sense of the useful targets for such diversity-friendly infrastructure can be provided with a pleasing economy of words. In sum, the focus will be on common barriers to managing diversity, as well as on how the illustrations below deal with them. Specifically, considering nontraditional managers only, Morrison (1992) reported that interviews with 196 managers revealed a "remarkable consensus" about the dominance of the following six barriers: prejudice, especially in the form of treating differences as weaknesses; inadequate career planning; loneliness in hostile and supportive work settings; lack of savvy by nontraditional managers, in part because of being out of networks and loops; greater comfort in "dealing with one's own kind," despite the need to operate substantially in many less comfortable settings; and ineffective balancing of the needs of family, job, and career.

The several exemplars below relate to these consensual barriers. For example, the "range rider" or "shadow consultant" can help all managers and perhaps especially so in connection with the second, third, and fourth barriers above. Cases also can be made for the relevance of this single diversity-friendly exemplar to the other three barriers, but those cases involve more of a reach.

Another curious consensus also is emerging, which in effect constitutes an amalgam that suggests hardheadedness, a lack of vision, and even a certain refractory quality if not meanness, in business but especially in government (e.g., Gard, 1994, p. 1). Thus too little is being done with reference to diversity, as Willa Bruce and Christine Reed (1994) note with respect to the "simplicity" of federal theories and training at the supervisory level. Moreover, and especially in the public sector, relevant learning seems to be of the hardball variety. Again relying on Bruce and Reed (1994, esp. p. 39), much of the learning about "family friendly organizations is confined to specific economic sectors and is driven primarily by the forces of labor supply and demand" rather than by compassion or by normative concerns.

This consensus motivates this chapter in major ways. The present purposes include an intensification of interest, and proactive attention is still possible. Those purposes also urge that diversity-friendly efforts do not necessarily imply large investments and can also have very attractive cost-benefit ratios. In many cases, that is, significant developmental resources already have been invested—both in diversity-friendly programs and in ways of implementing them. In other cases, moreover, only will is necessary to engage a diversity-friendly strategy.

2. *Adding a Strategic Push.* Immediately, however, the text will emphasize its strategic as well as summary objectives. That such a summary chapter can be written implies that diversity-friendly things have been going on, and this chapter will, I hope, add more zip and variety to similar efforts in the future. The present ambitions, however, extend beyond adding sense and substance to these two generalizations.

Further, the discussion places diversity-friendliness in a strategic context. Specifically, that is, most of the exemplars below began as programmatic responses to specific problems and particular target groups, with local champions playing roles in adoptions. This is the first phase or stage in moving toward what Dana E. Friedman and Ellen Galinsky (1992, pp. 195–203) see as a mature recognition by management of work and family concerns. The other two stages may be described as *integrated*, in which executive commitment expands, policies and procedures are set in place, and a broadening range of concerns are addressed; and *mainstreaming*, in which an organization's norms and culture also change, as reinforcers of proliferating policies, procedures, and structures. Useful details are available (Galinsky, Friedman, and Hernandez, 1991), but a sketch suffices here.

Despite their basically programmatic origins, the goal here is to stimulate movement toward mainstreaming by providing some sense of how diversity-friendly adoptions might be begun and extended. Three generalizations provide useful direction for this movement. First, mainstreaming an issue typically involves suitable framing or reframing. Consider child care, which was at first seen as a "woman's issue." Framing the issue that way was false to insistently emerging realities: single parenting was a growing issue and not only for females; dual-career families were increasing and often had child care concerns; and even traditional families often increasingly had two breadwinners in a nuclear home and faced child-rearing issues.

Consequently, child care is better framed as a mainstream human resources concern and even more specifically as a diversity-friendly issue. Such reframing has been attempted in many work settings. Specifically, as of a few years ago, perhaps four thousand to fifty-six hundred U.S. employers provided some form of child care support (Friedman, 1990; Kossek, 1990, p. 769).

Second, mainstreaming often highlights a growing disjoint in today's management: "equal treatment" does not always mean "equity" and in many cases can imply inequity. Providing everyone with insurance coverage for maternity or even orthodonture may be inequitable to various constituencies. Put another way, different innovations attract different constituencies, and increasingly diverse work forces imply burgeoning constituencies that challenge "equal treatment." Empirical research supports this line of thought (e.g., Kossek, 1989).

Third, a careful needs assessment should—but often does not—precede the choice among diversity-friendly alternatives (e.g., Friedman, 1988; Kossek, 1990). The causal textures of specific organizations—their dominant culture, if any; their subcultures; features of the work force; and development histories, among many other factors—should influence, if not determine, such choices. For example, opinions in national samples often are divided about the attractiveness of specific diversity-friendly policies or programs such as day care (e.g., Fernandez, 1986, pp. 152–63).

It could hardly be otherwise, for we are a diverse nation; but it will frequently be the case that specific organizations or loci will present specific needs. My own university, having grown explosively in a decade or less, is now growing old. After a furious spurt, the university provided a good home for many, and recruits stayed over the long run. Consequently, an alarmingly large cohort is now approaching retirement in a telescoped interval, and that gives a specific flavor to our issues of diversity. Similarly, and for reasons that seem obvious on the face of it, businesses now giving the most attention to family <——> work interfaces tend to fit one profile (Kraut, 1992, pp. 223–35). They are scientific and high-technology; are coping with labor shortages; have younger work forces; have high proportions of female employees; are located in "progressive" communities that are diversity-friendly; are nonunion, or largely so; have a concern with employees' well-being; and serve consumer markets and hence are more likely to be responsive to the needs of many stakeholders, including employees. By and large, the attention to work <——> family in such firms is understandable. Organizations with other profiles can select other diversity-friendly infrastructures.

3. *Immediate Flow of Analysis.* So how will this chapter proceed in reflecting a strategic orientation toward the adoption of diversity-friendly infrastructure? The

flow here will be simple. In order, attention goes to diversity-friendly policies; then diversity-friendly representational vehicles are illustrated; later, what will be called diversity-friendly supports are introduced; and, finally, approaches to diversity-friendly decision making are sampled.

In each of the classes of exemplars, attention will be given to three features. Building on the previous two chapters, the structural implications of each exemplar will be sketched. Typically, the diversity-friendly exemplars developed because of the often awkward consequences of bureaucratic structures. Ironically but understandably, traditional structures at once need diversity-friendly innovations and yet complicate or confound their application.

Building on the previous two chapters, again, all exemplars will be viewed with an eye to the dominant interaction style that gives them the most zip. Here, the earlier discussions of regenerative and degenerative interaction will have a definite and significant place.

Finally, each exemplar of a diversity-friendly infrastructure also will be associated briefly with the organization level or levels at which the greatest impact can be expected.

Diversity-Friendly Policies

Organizational policies constitute a central feature of any management infrastructure, but policies in bureaucratic structures typically are insensitive to diversity when they are not downright diversity-unfriendly. That does not have to be the case, at any level of the hierarchy. Experience illustrates how and why.

Even federal public policy is beginning "to get it" regarding diversity-friendly initiatives. Thus the Family and Medical Leave Act went into effect in early August 1993, even if long after many business firms had adopted similar or even more far-reaching policies. That legislation will give an estimated 2.5 million covered employees per year the right to take up to twelve weeks of unpaid leave without fear of adverse personnel actions—to care for a newborn or for the ill, or to attend to their own health needs. Apparently employees are skeptical whether this will be a breakthrough or more of the same old fast-shuffle (Ezell, 1993, pp. E-1, E-4).

Here, five exemplars of diversity-friendly policies are discussed, and they all have substantial histories that suggest how much can be done if we put our minds to work. (The pun *is* intended.) These five exemplars are: flexible work hours; flexi-place or telecommuting; Management by Objectives; cafeteria benefits; and job posting. These five suffice to make the point that many diversity-friendly policies already exist and are successful.

This review is highly selective, and other exemplars cover a broad range. These possibilities include job sharing, about which very little is known in a systematic way (Meier, 1979; Lee, 1982) but which has strong diversity-friendly features. The

Exhibit 5.1 Components of a Flexible Workday

Flexible hours, e.g., 7–10 AM	Core hours, including lunch, e.g., 10 AM–2 PM	Flexible hours, e.g., 2–7 PM

range of exemplars also includes various approaches to personal development, for example, assessment centers, career development, and so on, about which so much has been written as to make a summary here both redundant and impossibly unspecific. Many sources, both early (e.g., Golembiewski, 1979, 1:203–33) and more contemporary (e.g., Hall, 1986), can be consulted by eager seekers after other diversity-friendly exemplars.

1. *Flexible Work Hours.* Unless you were there at the creation, as it were, it may seem strange that flexible work hours (henceforth, often FWH) did not always exist. FWH seems obvious and is now broadly applied, with perhaps 20 percent of our work forces operating under one variant or another at the latest comprehensive reckoning (e.g., Ronen, 1981, pp. 171–74). After a three-year study, the federal government took no definitive overall action concerning FWH, but many agencies or subunits exercise a local option to make FWH available to their work forces. Businesses have been more aggressive. Over three-quarters of a selected population of business firms recently reported they make FWH available to at least some of their employees (Mirvis, forthcoming, as reported in Hall and Parker, 1993, p. 10).

What hit organizations like a rushing wind and now has achieved substantial acceptance? The FWH concept is simple, as Exhibit 5.1 suggests. Basically, all FWH employees work each day; and certain "core hours" exist in FWH programs when everyone is to be at work; but certain portions of the workday permit "flexing" one's times of arrival and/or departure on an individual and even spontaneous basis. Depending on legislation and organizational policies, some employees may be able to "bank" extra hours worked one day to be applied as credits against time obligations for the week or the month.

Why the rushing wind? There seems little doubt about that. Paramountly, FWH almost always "works," and is well received in both business (e.g., Golembiewski and Proehl, 1980) and government (e.g., Golembiewski and Proehl, 1978).

Today's reader, again unless she or he was there at the creation, may be surprised that anyone ever doubted that FWH has a range of positive effects and at modest cost. Then, however, common early reactions to FWH featured suspicion, if not overt hostility. So let us risk a bit of overkill on the chance that early reactions persist among some observers.

FWH variants can be permissive, although the details will not long delay us. For example, the longer the total FWH workday, obviously, the greater the discretion available to employees. FWH days may be ten hours long, and some organizations have found it useful to go to as many as fourteen to sixteen hours or more. Similarly, flexibility increases as the periods for flexing are longer. And "banking" privileges may vary from none to "saving" excess hours worked in one day so that they can be applied to reduce work in the same week, the current month, or even year.

Flexible work hours programs have broad-spectrum applications to human needs or conveniences. Thus the plan could be used by single parents who need time to arrange help for a sick child; anyone who decides to sleep a bit longer (or less) than normal; a harried commuter who wishes to avoid traffic problems coming or going to work; a determined fun-lover intent on getting an early start on a weekend or on getting a bit more relief from the weekend just passed; and both "day people" and especially "night people" who can make better accommodations to FWH than to normal work hours, with diurnal and circadian rhythms suggesting major differences between optimal working times for people (e.g., Patkai, Petterson, and Akerstedt, 1973); and so on.

The needs for flexibility in managing time seem ubiquitous and are growing. For example, survey data make it abundantly clear that all employees—and especially nontraditional employees—have great difficulties scheduling regular family business, not to mention special events (e.g., Fernandez, 1986, pp. 84–93). Many people are working longer, if nothing else, and having longer commutes.

In an elemental sense, then, flexible work hour plans are inherently diversity-friendly. They can be applied throughout most organizations in response to numerous situational differences beyond these Ransone Lectures but nonetheless otherwise quite well-known (e.g., Ronen, 1981). In practice, FWH plans most affect those at low or mid-organization levels.

The broader picture for FWH also has a very positive character. Here, it is possible only to illustrate, but the sampling of positive effects more than makes the point. Thus, typically, 90-plus percent and more of employees like the program, although supervisors and managers can require a bit of experience with FWH to reach such staggering levels of acceptance. FWH programs almost all survive start-up, and the subsequent failure rate is a percent or two over a three-to-five year period, by all accounts (e.g., Golembiewski and Proehl, 1978, 1980). Beyond that, the literature is replete with positive cases in point. For example, close observers (e.g., Golembiewski, Hilles, and Kagno, 1974; Golembiewski, 1979, 2:215–52; Ronen, 1981) report that, inter alia, flexing commuters can save large chunks of time, while decreasing urban traffic congestion as well as the costs of operating transit systems; family life improves for flexing parents, on balance;

reductions occur in absenteeism, turnover, and tardiness (Pierce, Newstrom, Dunham, and Barber, 1989); and increases in productivity, or at least no decreases, have been associated with most flexible work hour installations (e.g., Schein, Maurer, and Novak, 1977). Perhaps surprisingly to some, increases seem to be *more* characteristic in the public sector (e.g., Golembiewski, 1980). Above all, the programs seem to work even for those who do not much use them. Apparently, the option of use is powerful enough for many employees, much of the time (e.g., Golembiewski, Hilles, and Kagno, 1974, p. 527).

The case for FWH being diversity-friendly is also easy to make. Indeed, our early research and applications intended that FWH deal with what Morrison (1992, p. 51) called the great and growing "difficulty in balancing career and family" for women, who often face the dilemma of parenting during that life stage when career strides are most possible. FWH makes the dilemma a bit less challenging, permitting some flexibility in scheduling family affairs, providing for a suddenly sick child, and so on.

What is true for women also holds for a broad range of employees—single-parent minorities, African-American women suffering from a double dose of prejudice that limits educational and job opportunities, as well as dual breadwinners from traditional family-centered cultural backgrounds. Consider only the numerous hassles that develop about being late under normal working hours. That problem fades to obscurity with FWH. Moreover, it is probable that "different" employees are the most likely to be hassled about being late, with nontraditional employees being more vulnerable to supervisory scrupulousness or pure pique.

This catalog of positives should not be misunderstood, however. FWH cannot work miracles, nor is it responsive to all that ails our workplaces. For example, the technique will not settle all that troubles a two-breadwinner family with a new addition (e.g., Bohen and Viveros-Long, 1981). But FWH clearly makes a contribution to improving the quality of working life as well as an organization's diversity-friendliness.

The complex dynamics of why and how flexible work hours programs work have not been satisfactorily established by rigorous research (e.g, Golembiewski, 1990, esp. pp. 179–93), but that fact has not rained on the technique's parade. Adoptions not only persist but seem to be spreading (e.g., Cregar, 1988; Christensen, 1989). Useful research continues (e.g., Kossek, Barber, and Winters, 1993) and may require modifications of what now seems obvious, but the positive reception of the technique is credibly explained by various well-known behavioral theories. Thus FWH applications meet human needs—both anticipated and spontaneous. And that can reduce frustration, clearly. In turn, that might reduce the motivation to see the workplace as dissatisfying, or even as an enemy, and this would leave available energies that could—*but might not*—get directed into more efficient and effective work.

But, as I say, such views might seem reasonable enough now. But in flexible work hours' early days, all hell often broke loose. Why? Brief considerations of structural and interaction considerations provide perspective on why, to many, the now often obvious seemed highly dubious.

Degenerative Interaction

Perhaps the basic source of concern about FWH inheres in the commonly degenerative nature of interaction between people and groups in bureaucratic organizations. It occurred early to many supervisors and managers, for example, that FWH requires work settings with some trust and that "some" was "more" than a substantial proportion of managers believed did or could exist.

That expectation about trust underlying flexible work hours was (and is) correct; and adoptions clearly seem affected by employees' estimates of their trust in the intent of management (e.g., Kossek, Barber, and Winters, 1993). Nonetheless, the results of FWH applications suggest two points: that enough trust does exist or can be developed and that the attractions of FWH override any residual concerns for employees and (at times, after some positive experience) for supervisors as well. That regularity characterized the early applications (e.g., Golembiewski, Hilles, and Kagno, 1974), and more recent experience requires no basic modification of these expectations. Recessionary times do not seem to have encouraged managements in any number to play hardball with FWH applications, but that possibility requires monitoring.

Some ideas die very hard, however. So it was that, in a follow-up study about four years after an otherwise successful FWH installation, we found many basically satisfied employees but also a few very tired supervisors and managers (Golembiewski, Fox, and Proehl, 1979). In fact, the pooped-out contingent constituted about 4 or 5 percent of all managers. In a few words, they had never been able to *trust* their flexing employees, and they felt too much *risk* to be sufficiently *open* and *owning* about that to their employees or to overhead management, both overtly pleased with FWH. Under the goad of degenerative interaction, the tired remnant chose the difficult path: not trusting, they tried to be at work to directly observe flexing employees during most or all of the total FWH workday—twelve hours, no less!

Our consulting practice honors the criticality of the quality of interaction in two basic ways. First, when contemplating a FWH application, at whatever level, the prescription urges movement toward regenerative interaction as a prerequisite. If nothing else, the supervisor might announce to his first reports: "I hear you like flexible work hours. So let's start talking straight. If too many things fall between the cracks, critics may attribute that to the program—to people being unavailable, and so on. So don't jeopardize what you like."

Second, the significance of regenerative interaction is obvious in the way we approached some of the earliest applied research on flexible work hours (e.g.,

Exhibit 5.2   Schema of an Organizationwide Flexible Work Hours Application

R&D representatives meet with consultant-researcher (C-R) to learn of flexible work hour features, as well as to select from options—length of core hours, "banking" privileges, and so on—for one unit of about one hundred employees

R&D representatives choose indicators of success or failure of "pilot study" installation; C-R designs research

Based on research results, R&D representatives will determine whether to extend the application

Positive results motivate the extension in R&D, whose experience also attracts corporate officials who wish to extend flexible work hours throughout the firm, by fiat

C-R urged, rather, that corporate officials announce guidelines for acceptable FWH variants so that each of forty-some managerial units could choose its own specific variant or decide not to implement because of perceived local poor fits of work requirements to the FWH policy template

Corporate officials agreed, reluctantly: they wanted all but universal diffusion of the immensely popular pilot program but settled for modestly permissive boundary conditions, i.e., a thirteen-hour day, two large bands of flexing time, no notice required by an employee intending to flex, and "banking" of excess hours only in a current week

About 80 percent of the forty-plus eligible units adopted *some* flexible work hours variant suitable to local needs and resources, with consulting help to tailor applications to local settings and work forces. The common focus of the consulting was on norm-setting, e.g., about appropriate behaviors that would minimize local trouble spots, about ad hoc rules of the game, or "FWH etiquette," and so on

C-R encouraged adopting units to hold periodic evaluations, for example, at one and three to five years, using brief surveys or randomly chosen "sensing groups." Results would be fed back to all unit members

About one-third of the managerial units evaluated their programs periodically: fine-tuning occurred on occasion, but no unit discountinued its FWH variant over the subsequent decade.

Golembiewski, Hilles, and Kagno, 1974). The most economical way of elaborating the present point is via a long list, but so be it. The total cycle began with an R&D unit that wanted to improve the quality of working life for its employees at low cost. Exhibit 5.2 highlights the major features of the total implementation effort— from a pilot study in an R&D unit of about seventy-five to installations in many managerial units at a location with several thousand employees.

Exhibit 5.2 reflects many attempts to induce regenerative interaction and, when that was not possible, at least to try to inhibit degenerative interaction. Basically, this occurred in two ways. In an implementing mode, regenerative elements seem clear enough. For example, consultants-researchers sought to induce trust in various particulars, as in involving R&D personnel in the detailed design of a survey to assess FWH effects. Similarly, the approach also encouraged local option in decisions about diffusion—in a yes, no decision, but especially in the many details concerning which specific FWH variant was best suited for individual work settings. This insistence was directly contrary to top management's initial felt urge, after reviewing the results of the FWH pilot, to extend the innovation throughout the organization by fiat. On the consultant's advice, management subsequently authorized a set of FWH maximum boundary conditions, which local management could approach to the degree deemed appropriate at individual sites.

Moreover, in a broader sense, regenerative interaction was encouraged as a prime vehicle for guarding against the possible loss of a valued benefit. Recall the common supervisory admonition: "Let's keep talking." That implies regenerative interaction, which provides useful—indeed, sometimes necessary—support for dealing with any emerging problems under FWH. In effect, this ties an aspect of employee self-interest to regenerative interaction.

Bureaucratic Structures

Traditional structures do not accept FWH variants with open arms, as it were, and the dominance of traditional structures motivated much early concern about FWH applications. For example, cross-training and job enlargement patently would contribute to the smoothness of adaptations to spontaneously different arrival times, often day-by-day choices, as people could cover for one another, no matter what the demands of work at a particular time. As Chapter 3 develops in detail, however, bureaucratic structures are not likely to oblige in this regard. Diversity-unfriendly concomitants of traditional structures often surface in FWH applications, as in concerns about the loss of close supervisory control during the extended FWH workday. Moreover, permissive FWH variants can encounter technologically based resistance when the several separate bureaucratic activities (A, B, and C, in the terms of Chapter 3) are closely linked, as in sequential operations under tight time constraints or when (as in some police and security work) certain minimum staffing requirements exist.

The record of the success of FWH applications implies that workable accommodations usually are made, and some standard ways of mitigating resistance seem clear. Why? Primarily, many bureaucratic structures depart from the ideal, as in Alvin W. Gouldner's (1954) well-known "mock bureaucracies," and this provides wriggle room. Consider several features of Exhibit 5.2, which refers to a basically bureaucratic but nonetheless loosely linked organization. FWH worked there, in part, because many employees did not have to mesh their activities in a close sequence of operations. Hence late or early arrivals did not play havoc with a smooth flow between work stations. Moreover, it often is possible to reorient supervisory control to rely on consented-to norms and goals, as contrasted with attempted close oversight or by suppression of "negative attitudes." The fragmentation of work in closely linked bureaucratic structures constitutes a real barrier to such reorientations, of course, as is alluded to in Exhibit 5.2.

The "other case" has never been documented by rigorous research, at least as far as I know. But the presumptions seem both clear and positive. This "other case" involves FWH variants in flow-of-work structures.

Generally, flexible work hours should receive a better reception in nonbureaucratic structures like those in Exhibit 4.1. Thus immediate supervisors manage a related set of activities, and this facilitates both goal-setting and measurement of performance at the lowest levels. In addition, the social and psychological identifications with each S-unit also will encourage consensus about goals and norms, and the implied self-regulation will reduce the need for close and autocratic oversight by supervisors and overhead management. Enriched jobs and cross-training also ease adjustments to FWH.

2. *Flexi-Place.* Here, consider the bounded but real difference which a few classes of employees have experienced for years—choice about the specific location of doing their work. Especially with the revolution in electronic communication, substantial and increasing use is being made of "flexi-place" (henceforth, usually F-P). Individuals at many levels of organization—often professionals, but not necessarily so, and usually those without supervisory responsibilities—can in various combinations work either out of traditional offices, convenient satellite settings, or their homes. The affected jobs include those of attorneys, computer programmers and developers of various forms of software, some librarians, secretaries, writers and editors, and, generally, the growing cadre of telecommuters armed with computer and modem.

One distinction will not long delay us, although it can be significant in practice. F-P is not necessarily reserved for those who are fully electronic, as it were. So not all F-P is telecommuting via computer, modem, and perhaps fax machine. But most of it is, and that difference will be disregarded for present purposes.

A decade or so ago, F-P was seen as the answer to many needs. Thus futuristic human resource planners anticipated telecommuting impacts at multiple levels: individual and familial, in responding to the issues associated with great and growing proportions in the workplace of females and single heads of households; organizational, in reducing central office space and associated costs; urban, in reducing commuting time, decreasing accidents, and reducing time away from home; and social, in countering the alienation between home and work that many see as a prime result of classical industrialization.

Boas Shamir (1992, p. 275) gets to the heart of F-P's perceived leverage. He observes: "Here was an opportunity to rectify [major problems], achieve a reintegration and reduce some of the tension attributed to the organization of work in industrial society." That possible leverage encourages expansive thought. Shamir adds (1992, p. 275): "It was believed that working at home would 'free work from the constraints of time and location', to use a phrase coined by Bailyn (1988), and increase the quality of working life."

Despite its Johnny-come-lately status compared to business and entrepreneurial applications (e.g., Fleming, 1990; Mills, 1993), let us concentrate on a federal F-P initiative launched in January 1990 as a pilot study. Federal F-P may be described as (Joice, 1993, p. i; emphasis added): "a Government wide, nationwide project which allows Federal employees to work at home *or* at geographically convenient satellite offices *for part of the workweek*. . . . FP was established to improve the government's ability to recruit and retain capable employees, to improve employee quality of life, and to reduce Federal operating costs."

It requires no special insight to see how F-P could serve several diverse populations. From the start, F-P was seen as helpful in placing disabled employees (e.g., *Newsweek*, 1993a), who constitute a subpopulation of that far larger cohort of employees having problems with urban transportation. Other probable users include single parents, notably women with young and especially nursing children; those who want to vary their routines; and those who provide home-based care for the aged or ill or for other dependents.

F-P also is responsive to a very large subpopulation—the 43 percent of surveyed federal employees who reported that their most productive periods occurred outside of normal working hours (Joice, 1993, p. iii). This is consistent with the long-known fact that not all people have similar circadian rhythms (e.g., Patkai, Petterson, and Akerstedt, 1973). In short, there seem to be "day people" and "night people."

High performers also got special recognition in the federal pilot program. Participants were carefully selected, and care was taken to safeguard the interests of the several agencies, the employees, and any labor union or professional associations.

Business or entrepreneurial F-P applications have been ongoing for a decade and more and have a similar profile, motivations, and outcomes.

The setup costs for F-P seem manageable, even easily so. Estimates for a full-scale home office are about $5,000 for computer, printer, phone and modem, as well as fax machine (Mills, 1993). In the federal service pilot project, however, the costs of supporting start-up for a single F-P employee seem to be substantially less than $1,000 (Joice, 1993, pp. 31–32), apparently because employees use their own equipment and furniture, rely on otherwise unused computers as well as ancillary equipment, and so on.

In any case, then, high start-up costs seem no deterrent, and hence F-P can economically serve various policy initiatives. For example, the Americans with Disabilities Act requires accommodations by employers if they are not overly difficult or expensive. Flexi-place can provide a reasonable way to meet these legal requirements, while retaining a valued employee and easing the rigors of coming and going to work.

What about the bottom line? The available evidence, though necessarily tentative, seems to meet reasonable expectations. Exhibit 5.3 conveniently abstracts some major results, relying only on the federal pilot study. Here, a questionnaire survey employed three waves of responses: a pretest six months before start-up, a short posttest at six months after start-up, and a long posttest after a year. In addition, multiple data-gathering approaches were used at the three points in time.

Other evidence from the broader telecommuting research also contributes to a generally positive picture of cost benefits. Thus F-P can be a tonic for many employees, while serving organizational and broader social purposes. Early findings indicate that F-P variants have effects much like those reported in the federal study (Joice, 1993, p. 49):

> Measures in areas such as job performance, motivation, quality of life, and cost indications . . . show that Flexi-Place, using employees with proven performance, was a success. Flexi-Place shows promise as an effective mechanism for national efforts regarding work/family, transportation, and energy issues. . . .
>
> Most participating organizations spent very little money on pilot programs. . . .
>
> Indications of improved job performance (productivity), reduced usage of sick leave (benefits), improved health (health care) and reduced vehicle usage (transportation/energy issues) for a significant proportion of the participant group suggest long run reductions in costs.

The federal experience seems to be broadly representative of F-P effects. For example, Lis Fleming (1990) highlights these covariants: increased productivity; reduced costs of office space, even for larger staff; and decreased absenteeism. And Phillip E. Mahfood balances a case or so of failed F-P with a huge list of benefits (1992, pp. 10–30), as well as with recaps of results like those from a four-month study in San Diego County. Among other effects, Mahfood (1992, pp. 119–22)

Exhibit 5.3 Some Major Features of Flexi-Place Applications in Federal Government

About 90 percent of all surveyed supervisors and 95 percent of all participants indicated their performance was either unchanged or improved, with some variation for different aspects of performance. Since 84 percent of participants had prior job ratings of either "outstanding" or "exceeds fully successful," the F-P record is noteworthy (Joice, 1993, pp. iii–iv, 12, 16–19, 21)

Disability of either participant or a disabled dependent was characteristic of 12 percent of all cases surveyed

Twenty percent of federal participants had preschool children living at home (Joice, 1993, p. 11). Nearly half (46 percent) of all federal participants had twenty or more years of work experience, and an additional 38 percent had eleven to nineteen years (Joice, 1993, p. 12)

Some supervisors—but no more than 2.5 percent in the federal pilot study—were concerned about their control over job performance of employees on F-P (Joice, 1993, p. 19)

Depending on the facet of personal life, between 12 and 77 percent of respondents reported "improved" with no more than 3 percent reporting "decline" on any facet (Joice, 1993, pp. 23–24)

Adequacy of and access to materials and equipment was seen as having "declined" for about a third of federal participants, which is no surprise given the low cost per employee (Joice, 1993, pp. 25–26)

Sick leave usage was lower for over 40 percent of the participants and stayed the same in about 45 percent of the cases (Joice, 1993, p. 28)

About 80 percent of supervisors saw F-P as desirable in cases with minimal refinement, and virtually all participants had a positive reaction (Joice, 1993, p. 32)

Nonparticipating federal employees had manageable problems with F-P (Joice, 1993, p. 34)

A full cost-effectiveness estimate of the federal F-P pilot is not yet available (Joice, 1993, p. 41), despite favorable indications re recruitment, retention, and sick leave reports that the county saved $1,440 per year in the costs of office space alone for every telecommuter working at home two or more days per week, productivity increases were up to 40 percent, and participants saved 3,300 vehicle miles of travel during the 120-day study.

Despite high expectations and the record sketched above, however, F-P diffusion has not been as rapid or as thoroughgoing as some had expected—or perhaps hoped is the better word. No reasonable estimates of F-P incidence are available. Although it appears that nearly 8.5 million people worked at home at least eight hours per week during the mid-1980s, most of them were not telecommuting in the full sense (Shamir, 1992, p. 280).

Anecdotal evidence must suffice in the absence of data on F-P incidence. Some researchers have identified substantial F-P populations (e.g., Christensen, 1988b); many observers are aware of firms like the F. I. Group, which grew from two employees in 1964 to some eleven hundred in 1988 and does perhaps 70 percent of its work in nontraditional sites (Kinsmon, 1987); a few see F-P as spreading like wildfire (e.g., Mahfood, 1992); and about a dozen projects in state and local governments also are under way (Desky, 1993b, p. 1). Nevertheless, some researchers even question whether the genre is sufficiently diffused to warrant serious study (Olson, 1987). Illustratively, one observer reports that only ninety of nineteen thousand eligibles elected an F-P option (Perin, 1990); and, similarly, Aetna had forty-five thousand employees, of whom 70 percent were women, and we are told only that "hundreds telecommute from their homes" (Hymowitz, 1990).

What accounts for this apparently limited diffusion? Two points provide useful perspective.

Situational Facilitators or Inhibitors

F-P exists in a kind of force field: certain factors facilitate its implementation with attractive effects; and certain features limit its reach. Both sets may be classified under five major rubrics—individual, the work, organization, career, and family. Exhibit 5.4 illustrates the fuller schema suggested by available research, conflating tendencies from several sources (e.g., Hall, 1990; Joice, 1993; Kanter, 1989; Shamir, 1992). Generally, the illustrations support Shamir's conclusion (1992, p. 276): "It appears that neither the quality of work life nor the quality of home life is automatically improved by home work." But the effects trend strongly in a positive direction.

In sum, F-P can provide a useful and convenient piece of the infrastructure for diversity-friendly organizations. (The concept also can apply to home-based businesses, perhaps even more widely, but that is not the present focus.) F-P seems at least a low-cost program, with positive consequences as well as with a substantial potential for further diffusion. Available evidence also supports, but does not yet establish, major cost-effective features.

To be sure, limits will always be with us. Who and how many employees can participate, and especially for extensive home versus office balances of time? With experience, those limitations seem to be decreasing, and that trend will probably continue. In some senses, F-P is a secret too well-kept. Thus the federal government is in the midst of a three-year pilot study involving about a thousand employees, but the vast majority of federal employees did not know the option was open to them when the pilot stage was already well advanced (Joice, 1993, pp. 45–46).

In sum, F-P seems useful but clearly is no all-purpose remedy. Basically, it extends neither to every job nor to all those performing jobs with a good fit for F-P. In the federal pilot study, for example, the option seems to have been a reward for past effective service. Extensions are justified as convenient measures of performance exist or reasonable goals can be negotiated. Adopting organizations also will have to consider various legal liabilities (e.g., Mahfood, 1992, pp. 99–116), which are real but do not seem onerous. Moreover, the supporting research impresses in neither sum nor substance. Virtually all F-P organizations appear basically interested in getting on board rather than adding to scientific knowledge. Finally, F-P effects seem very sensitive to the number of permitted home days. A "little dab" does not seem to do, in short (Ramsower, 1985, pp. 57–70).

Interaction and Structure as Inhibitive/Facilitative

Additional perspective on limited F-P applicability also comes from a focus on interaction and structure, in turn, which concludes this section on flexi-place. Of course, these emphases have characterized all of this analysis; and they also serve to highlight aspects of Exhibit 5.4.

Interaction

The character of interaction seems a major factor in the successful adoption of F-P variants and may be critical. Under degenerative interaction—where trust is low and risk is already high—management and supervisory resistance is understandable, and not only to flexi-place. Hence the easy recommendation that efforts to increase regenerative interaction—with their high success rates (e.g., Golembiewski, Proehl, and Sink, 1981, 1982; Nicholas, 1982)—should be conscious prework for any organization seeking to move beyond bureaucratic ways and means, as by adopting flexi-place.

This advice does not seem to be followed generally, at least in the federal F-P. The apparent hope seems to be that the success of demonstration efforts will motivate diffusion, but the prognosis for this hope is not positive, based on broad experience with programs of change (e.g., Rogers, 1962). In any case, reasonably, federal sources

Exhibit 5.4   **Five Domains of Selected Features Facilitating F-P Applications**

Individual	*Work*	*Organization*
Low needs for affiliation and support or willingness to moderate them	Jobs feature chunks of related activities rather than separate and sequentially interdependent activities in different jobs	Culture features trust in employees as well as between them and managers
High need for autonomy		Focuses on objectives and results
Record of solid prior performance	If in bureaucratic structures, jobs are loosely linked	Recruits and socializes supportive supervisors, able to monitor out-of-sight employees
Substantial need for balance between home and work demands	Permits time at home as well as at a "normal" workplace	Does not use piece rates, at least in a coercive mode
Low need for upward mobility, at least for a period of time	Is high on motivators vs. satisfiers (Herzberg, Snyderman, and Mausner, 1959)	Recognizes dual ladders—managerial as well as technical/ professional
A self-starter	Permits reasonable security for data sets	

discourage coercion concerning F-P adoptions (as reported in Desky, 1993b, p. 16). Coercion probably would only heighten any existing degenerative tendencies.

More broadly, cases exist in which degenerative interaction obviously dominated in F-P applications. For example, one business organization decided that all F-Pers were independent contractors, which, among other features, would "save" the employing organization the substantial fringe benefits due to all employees. The F-Pers complained that the reclassification came as news to them, and they successfully sued the employer (Mahfood, 1992, pp. 151–55). Needless to say, F-P had a restricted life in this organization.

Organization structure
Bureaucratic concepts do not provide ideal structural fit for flexi-place, and this bare fact inspires management resistance. A key concern centers around the failure to appreciate how one can monitor someone who cannot be seen (Desky, 1993b, p. 16),

Career	Family
Willing not to be on management track, at least for a time	No preschool children, or adequate child care, constitutes the simplest case
Strong technical orientation	
Willing about, and capable of, functioning with reduced access to informal networks and schmoozing	Where preschool children live at home (20 percent in federal pilot study), or where participant or dependent is disabled (12 percent in federal pilot study), no pattern of adverse consequences was reported, but presumably these constitute possible risk factors that can be compensated for by care concerning other features
"Comfortably plateaued," at least for the F-P interim; doing well and content to keep doing it	
Willing about, and capable of, development in professional and/or entrepreneurial ways, as contrasted with reliance on bureaucratic promotions	
	Family is supportive and understanding about separating some work/home domains, while integrating others
	Adequate space and conditions for worksite at residence

an obvious kissing cousin of the close oversight of performance prescribed by bureaucratic structures. Thus Constance Perin (1990) notes that the "principle of continuous visibility" is powerful in the bureaucratic model. In addition, control exercised over how others move and how they allocate their time helps some people to symbolically define their status and authority. In addition, since that control may variously contribute to performance as well as complicate it, F-P opponents have some reasonable grounds for their counterargument. From bureaucratic perspectives, Perin observes (1990, p. 22), managers can see F-P as a "repudiation of their inspectional and disciplinary rights."

Looked at from the other side of the coin, resistant managers appear uncomfortable in helping to set goals and norms that will enable them subsequently to manage as an alternative to close oversight. Typically, management by outcomes versus details takes off only after cross-training and job enrichment, which is to say, after some experience with postbureaucratic structures and concepts. Such practices free supervisors from hovering at the employee's elbow, as it were. Training in goal- and norm-setting also is more consistent with flow-of-work structures, as the discussions of transactional versus transformational leadership in Chapters 3 and 4 help establish.

Several of the observations made with respect to FWH also apply here. For example, substantial cross-training or job enrichment can be very helpful at both loci of F-P work—at home, as well as at the office. That individuals can be in touch electronically reduces the need for any piece of work to be done at a specific site, but training in flexibility as well as enriched jobs are needed to limit the supervision of details. Bureaucratic structures do not help here.

For such reasons and others, close observers of F-P do not hesitate. Shamir (1992, pp. 281–82) sees the bureaucratic structure as the main impediment to F-P applications. Refining this basic point, M. H. Olson (1988, emphasis added) concludes that the traditional model is "a major barrier *even when* technology is available and cost-effective." And cases exist in which some F-P applications have been bureaucratized to death, as by attempts at electronic surveillance of the micro-productivity of keyboard operators (e.g., Shamir, 1992, pp. 282–83).

3. *Management by Objectives.* Although the flood tide seems to have passed for MBO, the concept has appeal both generally in relation to diversity and specifically as facilitative of such elements of diversity-friendly infrastructure as flexible work hours and flexi-place. Harold Levinson puts those attractions nicely in an article that was prominent in the early criticism of MBO. He wrote (1970, p. 125): "The intent of clarifying job obligations and measuring performance against [one's] goals seems reasonable enough. The concern for having both superior and subordinate consider the same matters in reviewing the performance of the latter is eminently sensible. The effort to come to common agreement on what constitutes the subordinate's job is highly desirable."

Basically, MBO focuses on outcomes, especially measurable ones, whenever possible. This replaces the bureaucratic fixation on inputs, specific processes, or routines. In broadest compass, then, MBO is oriented toward the holistic and integrative rather than the particularistic and fragmenting. Overall, MBO also contributes to "loose, tight" systems of management and in so doing seeks to focus on unities in ways that facilitate reasonable responses to ubiquitous diversities. The "tight" inheres in agreed-upon objectives, typically of some breadth but in principle applicable at all levels of organization (e.g., Locke and Latham, 1984). The "loose" of the system relates to how the objectives are accomplished and varies with subcultures at work, specific local histories and traditions, as well as the developmental stages of specific work forces and other multitudinous localisms at (ideally) all levels of organization. "Loose" is also limited (for example) by applicable laws and organization policies, as well as by macro-environmental features such as the state of the economy.

Degenerative Interaction

There seems no doubt that even the best-intended MBO often sinks on the shoals of poor communication, and it seems especially vulnerable to low trust and openness (e.g., Muczyk, 1979). The associated game-playing is common, debilitating (e.g., Golembiewski, Nethery, Hilles, and Shepherd, 1992a), and known well enough to require no further comment here, except to underscore the paradoxically infrequent attention in MBO programs to training and norm-setting about appropriate interaction (e.g., McConkie, 1979).

For reasons that also should be obvious, then, especially given the discussion in Chapters 3 and 4, regenerative interaction is a good fit with MBO. Indeed, regenerative interaction seems all but necessary.

Why the reservation "all but necessary"? Two points suggest the broader answer. Thus the associated goal-setting processes can be powerful per se (Kanfer, 1990, esp. pp. 126–39; Locke and Latham, 1984) and may induce participants to transcend middling levels of degenerative interaction. In addition, successful experience with MBO variants can—although no one knows how often—induce the building of trust and the lowering of risk associated with regenerative interaction (e.g., Golembiewski, Nethery, Hilles, and Shepherd, 1992b).

Bureaucratic Structures

Traditional structures at once need but also confound, if they do not preclude, the kind of "cross-walks" intended by MBO. Elementally, for example, MBO seeks the glue of agreed-upon objectives to overcome the fragmenting tendencies of typical structural arrangements. But the achievement of many important objectives—let us say, of S_A in bureaucratic structures—may be affected seriously by others—let us say, again, by S_B and S_C.

Hence the usefulness of one accommodation, in both public and business arenas (e.g., Golembiewski and Kiepper, 1988, esp. pp. 61–94). Heads of S-units in traditional structures develop their individual MBO plans, but a critical step in their review involves presentations in public sessions involving all other S-units as well as the integrating executive (e.g., Golembiewski and Kiepper, 1988, pp. 61–94). Here, usually in two to three days, all MBO plans are "cross-walked" for informational purposes, at least; to tease out implications for all S-units; to isolate interdependencies, as required; and to restructure individual MBO plans or even to agree to "shared goals" as necessary.

In addition, this MBO variant—like almost all others that develop integrative linkages—applies *up* the organization to the integrating executive, as well as *down* from that executive to subordinates. The executive's draft of goals, earlier developed in consultation with individual subordinates or clusters of them, might be variously massaged in such sessions. In contrast, the typical MBO application in a bureaucratic structure has a unilateral and downward flow, as is clear in Levinson's quote that opens this subsection.

Basic structural change would highlight and strengthen such cross-walks: in sum, flow-of-work structures simplify MBO-ing. Directly, because each S-unit in our Chapter 4 illustration encompasses a separate but similar flow, cross-walks are within-unit rather than between units. This simplifies organizational life and also fixes responsibility while allowing heads of the several S-units to concentrate on how their diverse mixes of people and processes can be maximized in contributing to performance.

Although far beyond our present purposes, other structural arrangements also may be applicable. Such alternatives include project management (e.g., Loo, 1992) and matrix structures (e.g., Davis and Lawrence, 1977). Critical synthesis of such alternative structural designs is conveniently available elsewhere (e.g., Golembiewski, 1987, 1995).

4. *Cafeteria Benefits.* Some diversity-friendly policies are simple in principle but imply major problems in implementation. So it seemed with "cafeteria benefits," or CB; but that was then.

That CB responds to numerous diversities is transparent, in principle. Simply, employees can help design their own benefits packages, given various constraints like the legal ones that so many dollars must go to FICA and income tax withholding. As I explained early in the history of this innovation (Golembiewski, 1979, 2:279): "X dollars go for this coverage, Y dollars for vacations, and so on. Such plans . . . clearly imply a movement toward greater employee choice and freedom. Moreover, such programs also rest on a responsiveness to different stages of human or career development. . . . Thus, employees with children might seek greater dental insurance coverage; those approaching retirement might opt for larger coverage for catastrophic illness, and so on." The Dependent Care Assistance Program is one of the popular CB options recently made available to employees (Friedman, 1990).

Initially, however, CB implied huge operational problems to most observers, and not only those committed to lockstep uniformity. Estimates of start-up costs assumed huge proportions, for one thing, in the earliest CB days which go back a quarter of a century, in my experience. Flexible programming was not a strong suit of earlier human resources data-processing packages.

Today, the operational problems are well in hand, and even traditional managements have grown accustomed to granting a degree of choice in their menus of benefits. Indeed, one source identifies 150 varieties of comprehensive CB programs (Ford Foundation, 1989, pp. 26–27), and this by itself implies great attractions in the suitability of CB variants for many different needs—even idiosyncratic ones— of both individuals and families. In addition, advertisements alert interested users that comprehensive data-processing packages can encompass diverse CB plans.

The packages, in effect, distinguish the "fixed" elements of the typical benefits package from those items that are "variable" and hence might be included in individual CB packages. The problems of dealing with once-bewildering combinations of benefits have now been substantially tamed by available software.

No convenient estimates of CB adoptions are known to me. Only a few firms have gone public about their CB offerings (e.g., Tavernier, 1980); and perhaps 10 percent of my clients have CB programs. Of the more than five thousand employers providing some form of child care support, about twenty-five hundred rely on a CB option that employees may elect (Friedman, 1990).

Adoptions were most common in tight labor markets where CB programs were viewed as attracting scarce skills. Our recent recessionary times have reduced this source of attraction, one speculates. This feature may again become salient, however, because of the scarcities of certain job skills already being felt and with greater supply-demand imbalances being forecast by most personnel planners. The emphasis on diversity will generate forces in the same direction.

I have never seen a public agency with a robust CB program. But many public sector menus permit some degree of choice within and between benefits.

Interaction and Structure

CB has no practical implications for these two elementals. Such programs should apply, whatever the dominant structure or pattern of interaction.

Philosophically, of course, CB is no close kin of the bureaucratic model or of degenerative interaction. Typically, in my experience, organizations adopting CB often had embarked earlier on a definite distancing from both.

5. *Job Posting*. Let us conclude this mini-set of exemplars of diversity-friendly policies and practices with an apparently innocuous case. Job posting involves getting the word around about open positions in an organization. That word can get around in various ways: in fancy advertisements in journals and newspapers; in announcements on bulletin boards throughout an organization; via grapevines of "old boy networks"; and so on. Job posting can create opportunities for individuals who are unaware of them. In sum, diversity may be served in various ways: by creating more targeted job-seeking, by getting the word to people or classes normally "out of the loop," and so on.

Job posting deals with some vital elements in organization life, and it was in many places not accepted without considerable wailing and thrashing. For example, those interested in restricting information and maintaining their favored status might well oppose even such a simple initiative.

Now, in its various forms, job posting has broad support in both law and practice. Opponents have to be subtle and knowledgeable, high-risk takers, grossly unaware, or all three in combination.

Interaction and Structure

Again, a doubleton seems likely in nature. Bureaucratic and degenerative systems are most in need of job posting. And in all probability they are more refractory to them than regenerative, flow-of-work structures.

Diversity-Friendly Representational Vehicles

Organizations have undergone a remarkable transformation over the past half-century, especially during the last decade or two. Earlier, the goal was *standardized* products in huge runs, and these were associated with the development of complex and inflexible processes and machinery. The watchwords were do it right, once, and at the top. This long-standing ideal might be labeled the *engineering of uniformity.*

More recently, market and technological conditions have required an emphasis on *customized* products of short or even individualized runs, and these require highly flexible processes and machinery. The new watchwords are continuous improvement of flexible work processes responsive to variable demands, both of which require substantial and continuing inputs from all levels and especially from operators. This requires cross-training and even job enrichment, high involvement, as well as commitment to learning and development throughout the organization. In turn, such developments are often accompanied by sharp cutbacks in middle management and overhead staff cadres (e.g., Perkins, Nieva, and Lawler, 1983).

This insistently emerging ideal can be labeled the *engineering of diversity* in people, processes, and products.

Huge costs have been involved in the general failure to appreciate this basic transition and its profound concomitants (e.g., Johnson, 1992; Johnson and Kaplan, 1987). The shortfall is particularly dramatic in manufacturing, which had fully accepted the ideology and techniques of the engineering of consent. The shortfall also is prominent in administration and in services. There, adoptions of the ideology of the bureaucratic model were no less fervent but, for varied reasons (e.g., Kouzes and Mico, 1979), could not be extended as fully as in manufacturing.

This subsection focuses on something older, and then something newer, from the tradition of efforts to bring differences in opinions, skills, roles, and hierarchical statuses to bear on organizational challenges consistent with the valuing and management of diversity, broadly viewed. In turn, the focus begins with a design for facilitating the expression of diverse opinions, then shifts to processes and products, and finally concludes with a focus on policy. In each case, the focus is on what may be called diversity-friendly representational vehicles.

Many other exemplars exist. For example, "team building" is ubiquitous nowadays (e.g., Dyer, 1977, 1987) and gets only passing notice here. Survey-feedback de-

---

Exhibit 5.5   Major Features of 3-D Image Approach to Confrontation

Involves at least two intact organization units that contribute to a common flow of work, but up to thirty-five units have been involved simultaneously, with N approximating four hundred

Involves either "upward" confrontation between a superior and his or her subordinates and/or "horizontal" confrontation between units, depending upon local objectives

Individual 3-D images are prepared on newsprint by two or more units, or by a unit and by its superior, in separate settings, with each preparing individual or group encouraged by this uncertainty to escalate truthfulness by the knowledge that others may be doing so in their deliberations

The images from units usually are consensual, but may contain minority views

Pairs of resulting images are shared publicly, with examples

The images then provide the basis for mutual problem-solving, often following an exchange process that is detailed in written form. Assume Unit A wishes a superior to stop, start, or continue certain policies, behaviors, or attitudes. The supervisor then can negotiate something in return—a stop, start, or continue from the members of Unit A.

---

signs, following appropriate practical and normative guides (e.g., Golembiewski and Hilles, 1979), also can serve as a potent representational vehicle.

1. *Confrontation Design.* Several decades ago, and especially in various high-tech, high-touch industries such as pharmaceuticals and aerospace, many saw a chronic need to induce more responsive interaction at work. The associated norms and skills were commonly seen as the building blocks of a new and more flexible social and cultural order at work. One highly successful (if sharply focused) approach uses three-dimensional images, which involve extended responses to the following questions: How do we see ourselves in relation to some relevant other? How does the relevant other see us? How do we see the relevant other?

Exhibit 5.5 details several features of 3-D confrontation designs. Basically, it seeks to engage participants in a cycle of escalating directness and authenticity, as a prelude to action planning (Golembiewski, 1979, 1:131–52).

Style of Interaction

The 3-D image design is clearly inspired by and rooted in contrasting approaches to interaction. Thus the design is an intended antidote for degenerative systems of interaction. Host organizations fit a typical profile: they "have crud in their communication pipelines"; they are "constipated"; and they ponderously and defensively generate invalid and unreliable messages. Under such conditions, the valuing and management of diversity could survive only with difficulty.

Looked at from another perspective, the 3-D design clearly intends to engage regenerative features and bring to the surface diverse opinions and reactions via supporting interaction and culture. Thus the design clearly focuses on greater openness and owning, with risk and trust being affected positively to the degree that the design works. Typically, major movement toward a regenerative profile occurs (e.g., Golembiewski and Blumberg, 1967, and many later applications). That is a very good bet, basically because people value the opportunity to be regenerative, and they also typically get a rush when once-suppressed materials are not only released but also lead to effective action planning. One can almost hear the whoosh of such energy made available for problem-solving.

Organization Structure

Typically, the consequences of bureaucratic structures provide the motivation for 3-D designs and for the upward feedback they generate. Absent structural change, periodic reinforcement experiences are required to remind organization members of regenerative values and skills (e.g., Golembiewski and Kiepper, 1988, esp. pp. 61–94). In short, bureaucratic structures tend to keep inducing degenerative tendencies, although (on occasion) some strong "normative overlays" can transcend this tendency. This is the essential promise of Total Quality Management, for example, or of customer-oriented or client-oriented programs (e.g., Albrecht and Zemke, 1985). Where the transcendence does not occur more or less permanently —which is virtually everywhere—3-D designs can serve as quick and economical reminders of the costs of backsliding into degenerative interaction.

2. *Quality Circles.* The QC intervention has been widely applied over the past decade or two, in both business and government, usually at operating levels but occasionally at middle management levels (e.g., Metz, 1981; Bowman and Steele, 1988; Park, 1990, p. 40). Basically, QCs seek to introduce greater diversity into problem-solving, typically by decreasing social distance between hierarchical levels, by empowering those at lower organization levels to apply a broader range of skills and perspectives to their work, and by creating alternative ways to influence decision making. As Se-Jeong Park explains (1990, p. 3): "QC efforts typically use intact work groups as agents of change at the shop-floor level. This involves em-

ployees in work-related decisions—allowing them to identify problems, to generate solutions, and to present them as recommendations to management. Implementation requires acceptance by management of a modified concept of authority."

QC structural variants abound, but a typical profile exists. QCs meet periodically and deal with common work problems. Structurally, QC programs usually have four components (Park, 1990, pp. 36–40): a steering committee that acts as a board of directors and may include union representatives as well as senior management; a facilitator or change agent, who helps train members of QC in problem-solving skills and less frequently in group dynamics theory and skills, helps maintain an open and supportive atmosphere, and attends individual QC meetings as a resource person (e.g., Park, 1990, pp. 167–75); a leader, often a supervisor, who presides at an individual QC's meetings; and members, typically from the same work unit or department, who with their leader typically are trained in basic problem-solving techniques and sometimes in group dynamics.

QCs have multiple attractions, consistent with a bottom, up, and participative view of work. QCs focus specifically on the continuous improvement of products or, more often, narrow processes or practices. As variously estimated, success rates are high, even substantial (Park, 1990, esp. pp. 53–56, 101–3). For example, in a batch of 154 applications selected because they all used "hard" or objective indicators of success, 74 percent of all cases were rated in the three highest of seven categories of success (Park, 1990, p. 152). Public versus business sector success favored the former, but the success rates of both were substantial. Thus 60.3 percent of all public applications fell in the three highest categories of success rates, while 80.5 percent did so in business applications (Park, 1990, p. 173). Also, success rates remain high over several significant situational differences—union versus nonunion, manufacturing versus service, size, and so on (Golembiewski and Park, 1991).

Interaction

The popularity of QCs implies the broadly perceived limits of the degenerative interaction usual at operating levels, and applications try to build a climate more supportive of problem-solving on a kind of a "cultural island" within the work setting. The intent is to release diverse resources—skills, experiences, hands-on smarts, and so on. Recent judicial decisions (e.g., *Electromation Inc. v. NLRB*, 92-4129 and 93-1169) limit some applications as unfair labor practices.

Organization Structure

QCs seemingly are schizoid. They represent a response to the constraints of bureaucratic structures, especially of "machine model" variants, and at the same time

QCs often are limited by those structures. Typically, because of functional depart-mentation and narrow specialization, QC members in Exhibit 3.1 structures are limited to narrow problems. In addition, broad ranges of real concern such as pay and benefits typically are defined as out of bounds by steering groups.

In flow-of-work structures, in contrast, QCs would have far broader vistas for problem-solving. See Exhibit 4.1 and the discussion associated with it.

3. *WAM and Related Variants.* This final diversity-friendly representational vehi-cle operates on a typically longer leash than the just discussed exemplars. Policy is the province of this class, in contrast to the largely operational orientations of the two preceding classes of exemplars.

This final class of representational vehicles has numerous variants, but certain generalizations apply. Consider WAM, or Women and Men, which was inaugurated during the 1970s because of a certain organization's growing sensitivity to a prime issue: that the numerical dominance of white and middle-aged-plus males among major corporate officers did not provide an optimal chance for gender-related con-cerns to rise to the appropriate executive levels in forceful and timely fashion—in part because all officers were males without direct experience of most of the unset-tling issues surrounding diversity, and in part because several were unsympathetic to change. Hence the CEO established a task force mandated as a "parallel system" to generate the desired visibility of such issues (e.g., Bushe and Shani, 1991). Membership included ex officio roles such as the CEO's direct report dealing with equal employment opportunities and related matters, as well as representatives se-lected from all organization levels. WAM was empowered to act on its own initia-tive, as well as to solicit suggestions for study and to respond to targets of opportunity. WAM had direct access to the CEO, both as a task force and through several of its members. Hence WAM's recommendations typically got quick and usually favorable attention from the CEO and from the board of directors.

This approach to forced-draft attention to diversity issues has a broad applica-bility at the policy level, as is illustrated by the case of one matter that troubled many in the organization. Management and executive development were very high priorities, and they led to this local lingo about the profile of the ideal executive candidate: experience in two domestic locations, as in headquarters and the field; experience in two functions; and facility with two languages, as well as service in countries using those languages. In local language, this deal was expressed as "2 by 2 by 2." So pressing was the developmental need that the rule of thumb had be-come "One strike, and you're out." That is, rejection of even one bona fide develop-mental opportunity was sufficient to remove one from the fast track.

These operating notions had "just growed," but they worked a considerable and growing hardship on many, a substantial proportion of whom carried high expec-tations relative to the efforts at racial and gender diversification under way in the organization. Many were women, but the problem set related to diversity in far

Exhibit 5.6   Foci of Interviews Regarding Career Development

How are promotions gained and awarded?

What expectations apply to gaining and awarding promotions and development?

How do employees get information about evaluations of their performance and with what specificity?

What training and development opportunities exist?

How are minorities and women progressing in management?

What are the benefits of effective diversity efforts?

broader compass. The disadvantaged included single parents with children; any parents, but especially single parents with teenaged children, for whom relocation was especially difficult; and any employees with special responsibilities, as for aged or infirm parents.

WAM got on this one like a rushing wind. In rapid sequence, a needs analysis was conducted among relevant employees, the policy was amended to "Three strikes and you're out," and a program was begun to sensitize all employees to potential issues concerning the impact of work on children and especially on adolescents. One prominent visiting speaker, for example, spoke movingly about his experience (and guilt) concerning the contribution of his tough travel schedule to the suicide of a teenage daughter, a substance abuser.

Numerous organizations have relied on, and continue to rely on, a task-force mode of spotlighting diversity. At Avon Products, for example, extensive interviews provided data for the review of policies and practices via an approach similar to that of WAM. Thomas (1991, p. 123) highlights the inputs to this policy review and also suggests the broad sweep of that review. See Exhibit 5.6.

Such ad hoc or parallel groups have been central in all movements toward managing diversity, in government as well as business. For example, the deputy administrator of the Environmental Protection Agency (EPA) established a Cultural Diversity Task Force, with a max-mix membership of forty-five including management, union, minorities, and so on. The task force encompassed four working groups (Laudicina, 1993, pp. 21–22) which focused on reviewing "good practices" in all organizational sectors, identifying EPA training and development needs, developing and administering an employee survey, and examining personnel data to identify problems and needs. The details vary in the Forest Service or Avon Products, but the basic structure and its underlying strategy are much the same.

Interaction

Clearly, WAM-like arrangements live or die on their ability to elicit multidirectional communication—up, across, and down the organization, as well as within WAM. Illustratively, WAM spent a week at start-up working on what would be generally called team building (e.g., Dyer, 1977, 1987), with an explicit focus on building values and skills associated with regenerative interaction. If members could not be open and trusting with each other, their successes with others would be sharply limited.

Organization Structure

WAM-like structures are not congenial to the bureaucratic model, which seeks uniformity rather than multiple flows of information and access. In bureaucratic structures, then, strong and continuing executive support for WAM-like structures is necessary, if not always determinative of success. Fortunately, there seems to be a growing sense of the usefulness in bureaucratic organizations of such "parallel learning structures" for decision-making (e.g., Bushe and Shani, 1991). They complement existing structures but are typically temporary and hence do not supplant existing structures for decisions and recommendations.

Flow-of-work structures can provide a more congenial home for WAM-like task forces at various levels of organization. Flow-of-work structures also can facilitate the tailoring of deliberations to specific S-units, while WAM-like structures in bureaucratic models either operate at substantial levels of abstraction or have narrow scopes and missions.

Diversity-Friendly Supports

With even modest expenditures, a management approach to diversity can provide a range of supports that help and can even make the difference. Three exemplars are discussed. They relate to parenting, mentoring, and consulting. They and related exemplars apply at all levels of organization.

1. *Aids to Parenting and Families.* These can extend to employees at all levels but have a special relevance to aiding in the valuing and management of diversity at workaday levels, as three generalizations from experience and research demonstrate. Such supports can cover a substantial range of cost and commitment. Elementally, a growing number of organizations permit limited workweeks over

extended periods for those with pressing family responsibilities (e.g., Thomas, 1990, p. 113). Costs here can be low, especially when discounted by the possibility of retaining a valued employee with potential for advancement. Big-ticket items include day care, although costs can vary widely.

Second, business organizations often have led in such regards, but legislation is beginning to play catchup. The recent federal legislation providing employee leave constitutes a case in point (Ezell, 1993), and more of the same can be expected, given that our lack of federal policy concerning families puts us in literal disgrace in the company of other developed nations (e.g., Roman and Blum, 1993).

Third, cost-benefit estimates often are attractive, even for the big-ticket items, when broad ranges of indicators are taken into account. The clear leaders in this regard are corporate wellness efforts (e.g., Falkenberg, 1987) and employee assistance programs, or EAP (e.g., Roman and Blum, 1992). Both have broad constituencies and, especially in the latter case, minorities and women are becoming frequent users. EAP offices historically emphasized substance abuse, especially alcoholism, as well as family problems. More recently, however, EAP is moving into broader consulting and counseling roles (e.g., Roman and Blum, 1992), which will involve EAP officials in their share of diversity issues.

Categoric judgments are much harder to make about such big-ticket items as on-site day care. Available studies indicate a range of likely outcomes: mixed effects on performance, especially via supervisory appraisals; strong positive impacts on recruitment and retention; and a favorable profile of attitudes about work and family responsibilities (e.g., Kossek and Nichols, 1992). At the same time, powerful intervening factors also are relevant, including such as the availability of backup caregivers and whether the primary locus is on-site or off-site.

Interaction

The special need here is for messages to be forcefully delivered to decision-making levels about the range and intensity of concerns about diversity, both already large and burgeoning. Degenerative interaction will not help, and it underlies the often monumental insensitivity of largely white and male minions who have dominated in power roles. Parenting and familial concerns had little urgency for these elites and, although arguably, perhaps were less salient for earlier generations of employees than for the diversified work forces now forming. But that was then.

Structure

Bureaucratic structures constitute major barriers here, and especially in the one-size-fits-all mentality associated with its supporting ideation and often reflected in practice. Managements often also have been leery of intruding overtly into family affairs, especially after such experiences as that with Henry Ford's Sociology Department, which reached deeply into home life in attempts to induce contented workers who consequently would be untroubled employees. Optimal diets were suggested or even prescribed, for example, after home visits.

2. *Mentoring.* The concept has received substantial attention in recent years, largely conceptual (e.g., Cahoon and Rowney, 1993) but also with a substantial mix of empirical research (e.g., Burke, McKeen, and McKenna, 1990; Dugan, 1992), and the bulk of that work generalizes to a truism. Typically, mentoring rejects the once-faddish TV commercial which, paraphrased, rested on this impatient individualism: "Please, I'd rather do it myself."

"Mentoring" varies widely in conceptual development. Some restrict it to job-related goals, while others extend the concept to encompass broader emotional well-being (e.g., Kram, 1985), and a few insist on both meanings (e.g., Thomas, 1990). This treatment accepts the broader usage, but with a tentativeness befitting the early stages of empirical research. In addition, mentoring normally "just happens," but it increasingly has been consciously planned and even institutionalized (e.g., Howard and Munch, 1991). Moreover, mentoring includes cases of someone helpful being available to an up-and-comer at the right time, and in the right place; the notion extends to those who have the knack of bringing along others to their own level, where the mentor remains while mentees go whizzing by to more senior jobs; and mentoring also encompasses long-term relationships between someone who rides the coattails of an organizational shooting star, as was the case with the premier theorist of executive action, Chester I. Barnard himself.

In its various forms, the literature on mentoring supports several generalizations, seven of which are sampled here. Mentoring appears to be ubiquitous, for reasons that relate to practical considerations but which also include deep psychological predispositions and needs. Let us resist trying to plumb the depths here. Practically, as Thomas (1991, p. 180) reminds us, moving ahead in organizations has at least three major dimensions:

Task merit, or demonstrated capacities and reasonably inferred capabilities

Cultural merit, or the fit between an individual and an organization's basic template—its dominant culture or subcultures, traditions, assumptions and expectations

Political merit, which includes a person's ability to gain the endorsement of his or her bona fides by individuals or groups with influence sufficient to reduce to acceptable levels any doubts about the person

Mentoring plays crucial roles in all three kinds of "merit assessment," especially for political merit but, if usually less so, even task merit. This provides one basic reason for the ubiquity of mentors in the careers of the organizationally success-ful. To speculate a bit, the effect is probably greatest in bureaucratic organizations and those that give uneven attention to performance appraisal, as well as in de-generative contexts.

The literature also indicates that most up-and-comers would like to develop re-lationships with a solid mentor. For example, about 94 percent of one population of managers and professionals rated mentoring as "important" or "very impor-tant" in their promotion to senior positions (Cox, 1993, p. 199). The reasons are personal and practical, with instrumental needs being dominant. Few doubt what the literature insists on—that the availability of mentors is linked directly to what mentees usually want: career advancement, greater career satisfaction, higher pay, and so on through a very attractive list (e.g., Kram, 1985). This adds an edge to mentor relationships, and influential support-reject dynamics are always at issue for both mentor and mentee.

In addition, mentoring is typically seen as involving a senior and a junior part-ner, but that is not necessarily a given. For "showing somebody the ropes," peers have on occasion proved useful (Kram and Isabella, 1985). This has useful implica-tions for the supply of mentors, although a peer cannot usually supply the organi-zation muscle of a senior mentor.

Moreover, mentoring is not only important for up-and-comers, but it may be crucial for minorities. Thus one observer (Ragins, 1989) urges that such relation-ships are vital for women, particularly because mentors may be able to run inter-ference when discrimination threatens. Similarly, *Breaking through the Glass Ceiling* devotes about 15 percent of its text to mentors and networking (Naff, 1992, pp. 29–36). Other close observers propose that many women may have a learned incapacity re "political merit." Women may be reluctant to "play politics" and to respond situationally because of cultural learning that (for example) encourages them to conform to organization norms, thereby avoiding the labels "sensitive" or "emotional" (Arroba and James, 1988).

Further, the existing literature implies some important differences between classes of mentees, but interpretations still remain chancy. For example, women in professional and managerial positions do not report less access to mentors than men, at least in some studies (Cox and Nkomo, 1991; Cox, 1993, p. 203). Even if these studies are valid, however, important issues remain open. How to interpret such a finding? Various alternatives imply very different courses of action. Among other interpretations, mentors may simply be more important to women than to men so the former consequently work harder at gaining mentors; men may tend toward greater independence than women, as contrasted with the emphasis on "connectedness" often attributed to women (Cox, 1993, p. 203); and unmentored women do not get into professional and managerial positions with any frequency and hence are not there to be counted.

Next to last on this short list of generalizations about mentoring, cross-race and cross-gender mentoring seem to induce special concerns. For example, cross-gender mentoring, plus the personal affinity and frequent interaction character-istic of mentoring, inspire in some a concern about favoritism or even "romance in the office." Both outcomes can seriously disrupt work sites (Cox, 1993, pp. 199–207) and in extreme cases can infect them with jealousy, suspicion, and backbiting.

Finally, on this short list, few mentee candidates will get all the mentoring they want or need (e.g., Ragins and Sundstrom, 1989), and this generalization applies with most force to the organizationally "different" or "diverse." Almost by defini-tion, because of the steeply narrowing character of hierarchical ladders, there will tend to be a definite supply-demand imbalance of well-placed mentors and the le-gions intent on upward mobility. Hence improvements in mentoring are much to be desired, especially in the case of those for whom "similar" mentors are in short supply because of historical patterns of staffing or because of prejudice directed against women, blacks, and others.

So mentoring shortfalls will tend to persist, even though they can be somewhat remedied. Consider the reliance on formal programs of mentoring, which do exist and seem to be growing. Some of the news seems good, on balance. Thus mentees seem to prefer informal or spontaneous mentoring relations to other alternatives, but formal mentoring is at the same time usually seen as better than none at all (e.g., Chao and Gardner, 1992). But there seems to be much bad news in too exu-berant efforts to jump-start formal programs, as when mentors are simply as-signed to mentees and self-choice does not operate (e.g., Powell, 1993, pp. 215–17).

Interaction

Where degenerative interaction exists, the case seems compelling for the greater relevance of mentoring. In short, the mine fields are more treacherous there, and a higher premium typically will be given to "going along to get along," if not to ab-ject conformity. These generalizations will apply most in cases of a "crisis of agreement," or in what Jerry Harvey (1988) has popularized as "going to Abilene." "Abilene" shares some conceptual territory with "groupthink" (Janis, 1982), but that identity is far from complete. Moreover, "Abilene" is conceptually polydimen-sional in significant ways (e.g., Golembiewski, 1990, esp. pp. 137–43). Roughly, everyone on the way to Abilene pretty much shares the same diagnosis and prefer-ences in an action setting but because of fear of exclusion, each person fails to ex-press his or her own diagnosis or prescriptions, as well as avoids inquiring about the diagnoses and prescriptions of others. Consequently, each person comes to the wrong conclusion—that he or she is the only deviant to an all-but-unanimous opinion.

No detailed studies of the criticality of regenerative interaction for mentoring exist, as far as I know. But the anecdotal evidence certainly supports this common-sense view, for the mentoring pair and perhaps especially for their organizational context. This compound generalization holds especially in connection with cross-gender mentoring—where rumors may propose romance when only workaday relationships exist, with potentially damaging effects (e.g., Cunningham, 1984). Degenerative interaction puts a chilling effect on mentoring in this specific as well as in general. As one observer notes, "Men . . . may be reluctant to mentor women, and this may impede women's developmental progress unless concerns about distance and personal intimacy are well managed" (Maniero, 1993, p. 170).

In addition, long-standing theoretical and empirical evidence seems compelling as to the salience of regenerative interaction in effective mentoring, and that evidence implies commonsense guides for setting up formal mentoring programs. For example, Cox (1993, p. 205) emphasizes that mentor-mentee matches should be made voluntarily and with mentee involvement, rather than by formal appointment only; assignments should be considered as temporary, pending a review after some period of mutual experience; and training should be provided for both mentors and mentees.

Organization Structure

Bureaucratic structures seem to raise the salience of mentoring, especially in their confounding of the subtle issue of contributions to performance, which bedevil compensation judgments for all but truly integrative roles like that of M_{ABC} in Exhibit 3.1. In bureaucratic structures, such integrative roles may exist only at the very top of towering hierarchies, or near it. For developmental purposes, this is often too late to provide progressively comprehensive challenges in integrative roles.

Put another way, bureaucratic organizations tend to place greater reliance, out of necessity, on the latter two components of assessing merit—cultural and political merit. One prime consequence is to create greater difficulties for the "different" or "diverse," who will rightly fear—in the general absence in bureaucratic structures of a record of task merit in progressively challenging integrative jobs—that progress for them requires "selling their soul to the company store." The commonly observed "type-casting" of women and minorities complicates these developmental shortfalls. Witness the often debatable placement of women and minorities in roles outside the organizational go-go because of alleged "greater sensitivity to issues of diversity," as in "staff" roles related to protected-group populations. This judgment about greater sensitivity may be correct, but whether it is or not, such assignments confound the problems of career development in bureaucratic organizations. Not only do such assignments risk identifying as "different" those in work settings in which uniformity and even conformity often get high premiums, but they keep people out of the wheelhouses of organizational life.

Even more basically, organizations apparently need to formalize mentoring relationships, for leaving this matter to an invisible hand does not seem to work (e.g., Burke, McKeen, and McKenna, 1990). Some propose that minorities "tend to be less aware of the informal networks and their . . . potential usefulness" (Cahoon and Rowney, 1993, p. 348). Perhaps. More likely, however, minorities lack access to informal relations or have been deliberately excluded from them—as many propose concerning the treatment of women by the "old boys networks" (e.g., Ragins and Sundstrom, 1989). A few organizations have begun such formalization (e.g., Thomas, 1990, pp. 113–15), but not many.

3. *Circuit Rider Consultants.* Although no reliable data on incidence are available, one clear trend relates to the reliance on what are called "circuit riders" or "shadow consultants" (e.g., Golembiewski, 1972, pp. 168–69). Their purpose is direct. Experienced persons, often beyond or near the age of retirement, serve on an as-needed basis to help those in operating roles. Typically, others in the sponsoring organization have no detailed knowledge of individual consultations or even that they exist. The relationship between consultee and consultant is as confidential as the consultee prefers. Such arrangements mostly are found at senior levels of management, but variants exist at many levels, as in programs to aid minorities over the inevitable rough spots (e.g., Thomas, 1990). More broadly, employee assistance programs also can be put in the service of diverse employee needs (e.g., Roman and Blum, 1992). See also the discussion of mentoring.

Circuit riders serve a range of purposes, which center around meeting emergent needs in timely ways before issues force themselves on the attention of senior officials. Circuit riders are not restricted to issues related to the management of diversity, but they clearly can serve such a purpose. Moreover, reliance on shadow consultants helps move toward diversity goals related to age. Although the helpers can come from all demographic groupings, because of the ways in which development has been managed in the past, today's circuit riders probably will be white males near or beyond retirement age. Our organizational tomorrows can differ greatly.

Interaction

Ideally, interaction in host organizations is regenerative because reliance on the shadow consultant inevitably raises issues of trust as well as who knows what about whom. Confidentiality in shadow consulting relationships involves trust, not only between consultee and consultant but between consultees and their formal superiors. The issues can be exotic and require goodwill as well as skill for their working resolution (e.g., Golembiewski, 1991a; Golembiewski and Gabris, 1994a, 1994b).

Structure

Traditional notions about reporting relationships—as one person, one boss—have a schizoidlike association with the reliance on circuit riders. On the one hand, tension in reporting relationships will encourage or even require helpful relationships outside the chain of command. Subordinates may be deterred by degenerative interaction and close oversight from raising some issues directly with their own superiors, perhaps especially at let's-kick-things-around stages or when the subordinate is experiencing a temporary crisis of confidence. Perhaps especially for minorities, but substantially for all, the tendency is to deliver "completed packages," which increases the probability of support-and-attack reactions after the optimal time for fine-tuning or redirection has passed.

Again, bureaucratic features complicate effective responses to their own creations. Traditional notions about one-line reporting relationships encourage suspicion about circuit riders, as well as discourage their adoption. Consider training and development efforts. There, the basic resistance to almost any innovation in bureaucratic structures often comes from first-line supervisors and middle managers, who may be more intent on creating employees like themselves than in helping in the development of those who will succeed them (e.g., Golembiewski and Kuhnert, 1994). There is no reason to expect that valuing or managing diversity are different in this fundamental regard.

Diversity-Friendly Decision Making

As a final diversity-friendly domain encompassed by a managerial approach, consider decision making at various levels. Multiple exemplars exist, and have for a long time, most prominently in business organizations (e.g., McCormick, 1938). These include junior boards of directors; the use of assessment centers as a partial bypass of, or complement to, the appraisals of potentially hostile middle managers and first-line supervisors; and the currently in vogue labor-management committees associated with Quality of Working Life and Total Quality Management efforts.

More recently, but this time in both government and business (e.g., Sussal, 1985; Bremer and Howe, 1988, esp. pp. 959–60; Thomas, 1990), diversity programs have relied on advisory or decision-making bodies to surface issues for senior levels. Thus Procter & Gamble in 1988 formed a Corporate Diversity Strategy Task Force, and Digital formed at least two novel boards of directors—one for cultural perspectives, and the other to focus on the valuing of differences.

Here, the focus will be sharply limited to two exemplars. The first relates to a participative approach to cutback, and the second deals with the use of "Work-Out" in General Electric. These exemplars relate to broad organizational ranges and suggest how differences can be taken into organizational account.

1. *Designing Your Own Cutback, within Broad Limits.* This exemplar illustrates a broad family of efforts that have extended the participative mode into alien territory. Most Organizational Development activity has dealt with the "sun," as it were: growth, tough but energizing change, and the expansion of human potential within jobs that make escalating demands. The "rain" has been harder to deal with—organizational death, reductions in force, demotions, and so on. Indeed, many change agents want none of the "rain."

The challenge is inescapable, however, on the general theory that it takes both "sun" and "rain" to make "flowers" grow. The first "rain" OD experiences of which I have direct knowledge (e.g., Golembiewski et al., 1972) were decidedly counter-cultural, inducing more than their share of raised professional eyebrows and even of verbal rumblings among colleagues (e.g., Kramer, 1972; Walton and Warwick, 1973; Golembiewski, Carrigan, and Blumberg, 1973). Nowadays, the "rain" is dealt with more frequently, if still far from routinely (e.g., Taber, Walsh, and Cooke, 1979).

The present case comes from the "oil patch," specifically, the divisional office of a multinational petroleum giant (Golembiewski, 1991b). Under energetic new leadership and in a "sun" phase, the office of four hundred employees began an OD program with a strong focus on building regenerative interaction and an associated culture. Soon, however, the "rain" came. Corporate difficulties grew, and, to make a painful story very short, the district office could do no better than levy a negotiated reduction of 20 percent in personnel costs to help pay corporate's way out of a cash-flow embarrassment.

The district officials decided to test their hard-won gains in improved interaction —higher trust, lower risk, greater openness and owning—by putting the bad news to all hands, assembled in an auditorium. Corporate conditions were fully revealed, next year's priority personnel demands were outlined, and several alternative scenarios were reviewed. Thus management could handle the cutback, as is traditional; and so on.

Soon, opinion favored seeing if the somber target could be met by a variety of self-choices by employees about the next year of work. That worked, and quickly. Employees went their various ways. Some decided to reduce their work hours to "share the work." Some decided to take long-delayed graduate courses or pursue degrees at a local university, typically with full- or part-time unpaid leaves but with tuition paid by the corporation. A few decided it was time to take advantage of a corporate plan for early retirement. Some decided on a phased reduction of work hours, leading to full-time entrepreneurial ventures. Several women decided to try to start delayed families. A few took variously long leaves, paid and unpaid. Some had responsibilities on priority projects that precluded any other choice but staying on, short of voluntary separation.

Within a full day, the goal was in sight. Human Resources computer capabilities facilitated judgments about costs, schedules, and other details. Within a week, the goal was somewhat oversubscribed, anticipated priority projects were fully staffed, and the traumata of downsizing were minimized.

This decision-making variant attended to a broad range of differences quickly and without the dismal chain of consequences often associated with cutbacks. These include rumors, building anxieties, executive overload, losing valued employees tired of waiting, or, worst of all, facing the need to mount a recruiting campaign in the midst of a reduction in force because too many of the "wrong people" leave (e.g., Slote, 1969; Sutton, 1983).

There have been other similar efforts, including some in the public sector (e.g., Drucker and Robinson, 1992).

Sad to say, there will probably be more. So no alternative exists to getting better about "rain" as well as "sun."

Interaction

The values and skills associated with regenerative interaction—especially with high trust—no doubt play important roles in such participative cutbacks. The conservative position, then, is that such designs should follow appropriate developmental work in dealing constructively with differences, as via a planned emphasis on regenerative interaction most usefully begun when things are going well in a particular organization.

Nonetheless, less dynamic and more bounded examples exist of successful applications like the present cameo (e.g., Drucker and Robinson, 1992). No prework on interaction was done in such cases, which represent both public and business sectors.

Structure

The spirit associated with bureaucratic structures is not highly compatible with such approaches, but, beyond that, there seems no inherent need to reject such approaches in bureaucracies. Indeed, the reliance on temporary parallel structures like the town meeting is growing, as more decision makers seek to overcome the clear inadequacies of bureaucratic structures, especially during periods of rapid change (Bushe and Shani, 1991). Some part of the case just sketched, in fact, relies on quite conventional management analysis, especially in the case of ultimate decisions about whether self-choices were compatible with some must-do district projects. In a small percentage of cases, perhaps 5 percent or so, self-choices were renegotiated or came to be seen as unavoidable poor fits with organizational priorities.

Organizational authorities were most overt in their desire to avoid anyone being pressured by popular opinion to announce doing more than they could handle, given their diverse circumstances—stage of life and career, family obligations, and so on. On occasion, the spirit of the moment had the quality of informal pressure to "join in" or "pay your share." Such pressures to conform were the subjects of public warnings, and resource persons sought to identify and help avoid cases of succumb now, regret later.

2. *GE's Work-Out.* The second exemplar comes from an industrial setting but seem generically applicable. Thus wide use at midmanagement levels and above at General Electric has been made of what they call a "Work-Out," a label often followed by an exclamation point to highlight its singularity. Work-Out has two meanings: to get unnecessary work *out* of the system; and to *work* out agreements for that purpose.

Indeed, if corporate prominents have their way, that technique will become a standard way of doing business in the corporation of three hundred thousand employees. Thus two observers report that CEO Jack Welch anticipates a broad cultural change that will extend to the entire work force Work-Out's "capacity for bottom-up process ownership that one might ordinarily associate with a company of 100 people" (Ashkenas and Jick, 1992, p. 165). Similar programs also exist elsewhere (e.g., Watkins and Marsick, 1993, pp. 176–78).

The Work-Out approach proposes to put into daily worklife what might be called "macro-dialoguing," which has predecessors in general concept but not in frequency of application (Golembiewski and Blumberg, 1967, 1968). GE's Work-Outs focus on a business issue or process and assemble all relevant stakeholders from all involved functions and levels of the organization. In principle, stakeholders external to the organization also might be involved (Ashkenas, 1990; Jick, 1990). Brainstorming in mixed ad hoc collectivities constitutes the basic approach to generating facts and ideas, and these are subsequently reported to a "town meeting" of all major stakeholders. Action planning then follows, often with a loop for evaluation (Ashkenas and Jick, 1992, pp. 269–70).

The Work-Out focus is determinedly on organizational learning that derives from "examining issues that have broad organizational significance, impact, or causes, and where the learnings or resolution might be transferable and leveraged across the organization" (Ashkenas and Jick, 1992, p. 172). Hence the insistence of users to differentiate Work-Out from both interpersonal dialogue, as well as from the "local" or "micro-dialogue" that occurs in most traditional Quality Circles or in teambuilding. Consistently, Work-Out has been reinforced at GE by a kind of commercial town hall—the corporate executive council—an interbusiness arena for sharing insights about problems, possibly transferable solutions, and failures (Tichy and Charan, 1989, pp. 115–16).

The originators of Work-Out understandably emphasize its uniquenesses, but the approach nonetheless shares many common features with other designs. It has generic features like those of the "decision conferences" pioneered by the Niagara Institute (e.g., Cahoon, 1992) and recently popularized by a book of cases of extensive applications (Weisbord, 1992). Earlier efforts to involve large numbers of participants in reformatting work and in cultural change also exist. One caveat: these other applications pay great attention to sensitizing participants to interaction, group dynamics, and cultural features in both the public sector (e.g., Golembiewski and Kiepper, 1988) and business (e.g., Marrow, Bowers, and Seashore, 1967). Positive consequences were observed in both sectors in several replications of the same or similar designs.

Interaction

Available reports do not dwell on the interaction characteristic of the GE decision-making approach, but various evidence suggests the need for "open" climates that are compatible with what is here called regenerative interaction. The point is not surprising, but there may be tactical reasons for proponents' failure to emphasize the role of interaction skills and values, as well as training in them. For example, as seems to have been the case with the Niagara Institute, the concern in Work-Out might well be that explicit concern with interaction would dilute the attention to the "big issues" of policy, product problems, and so on. NIH rejections—as "not invented here" and hence as inappropriate—also may motivate the strong desire to insist on Work-Out as different and distinct.

Structure

The Work-Out does not seem to be narrowly structure-bound. GE has long experience with flow-of-work structures, but bureaucratic variants no doubt also abound in its numerous units and facilities. Significantly, indeed, Work-Out seems intended as a temporary and parallel structure only for those times when traditional structures and policies do not work. This may constitute an Achilles' heel of the approach at GE, along with other features associated with the energetic style of Chief Executive Officer Welch (Watkins and Marsick, 1993, pp. 179–80).

Despite ambiguities and unclarities about Work-Out's standing with respect to the bureaucratic model, one thing seems clear. The choices of the focal issues and stakeholders always will be important, and here structural issues often will play a role. For example, representatives from a flow-of-work structure might have the internal resources to get around issues of some scope while profiting from the social and psychological integrative forces associated with common membership in a single S-unit, or a few of them. In bureaucratic structures, in sharp contrast, issues of some scope require participation from several or many functionally departmentalized units. Consequently, inter-S-unit conflicts might well surface, complicating the emergence of issues and the data appropriate for dealing with them. Possible reductions of such conflict in bureaucratic structures could derive from faith in the technique, as well as from shared commitments to overarching values, goals, or visions.

Note

1 For example, the point is overwhelmingly clear in the ongoing National Performance Review, presided over by Vice-President Albert Gore. "Bureaucracy" gets battered in the flood of official paper, but alternatives to bureaucratic structures are barely hinted at, as in Gore (1993), *Transforming Organizational Structures*, Washington, D.C.: Government Printing Office, esp. p. 17.

6 A TEMPORARY CONCLUDING,

BUT NO CONCLUSION

This is enough about structure and infrastructure for now. Perhaps even too much.

In any case, my strong sense is that this is not the end of valuing or managing diversity. Rather, it seems far more like the end of a beginning, with long and numerous ways to go. Indeed, if ever a book deserved to end indeterminately, this is such a one.

How to formalize this end of a beginning? My preconscious self, after ruminating, suggests that four points will do. Three deal with encompassing metaphors, and the fourth elaborates a caveat.

Three Central Metaphors

Although my sense is that we usually overdo it, the temptation remains strong to encapsulate complex ideation and feelings in terms of a snappy label, even a metaphor. Hence the current swirl of interest in "reinventing"—of government, business, or even a "new world order" without even a hint of self-consciousness that Hitler's Third Reich announced precisely the very same sense of itself.

At times, that temptation has shallow convenience as a motivator. A label or metaphor permits quick if often pseudo-classifications to distinguish what is au courant—this year's sheep dip, if you will—from what is really out.

But it is best not to be so harsh about what often is a self-protective device against the growing flood of books and articles spawned by our various revolutions in information technologies. Without a doubt, new labels or metaphors at times can be very useful, even evocative.

Now is one of those times, it appears. For openers, let us focus on major metaphors for, in turn, individuals and groups; organizations; and then as prototype for all levels of human development.

1. *Empowerment as Central Metaphor for Individuals and Groups.* The choice of a suggestive metaphor to encompass at the level of individuals or groups what has

been discussed here, and much more besides, is "empowerment." If nothing else, that choice puts these 1993 Ransone Lectures in good company. For example, Thomas observes (1991, p. 10) that truly managing diversity involves "developing an environment that works for all employees" and, in turn, initiatives for inducing this consequence—like the structure and infrastructure enumerated above—depend on "the ability to empower the total workforce." Morgan (1993, pp. 14–16) takes a similar position, if a bit more imperialistically, and so do many other close observers of organizational comings and goings (e.g., Handy, 1990).

So empowerment it will be, here, although the choice is made with some reservations. To be truthful, there is the clear smell of this year's enthusiasm about "empowerment," and that promises indiscriminate overuse of the concept and then discarding it before its usefulness is fully assessed, let alone exploited. So much is the concept in the air, for example, that one of today's conservative political coalitions promises to "empower America." Liberal pleas for "empowerment" are everywhere, of course.

Hence we here deal with either a conceptual chameleon or a notion that speaks to the heart of the present human condition.

However, in the final analysis—indeed, well before then—the concept of empowerment relates well to this effort toward valuing and especially managing diversity. A few comments illustrate these rich connections.

"Empowerment" relates to a yeasty collection of connotations, which cluster around a rather specific denotation. As Judith F. Vogt observes of empowerment as denotation (1992, p. 744):

> If one's true perspective is empowerment, it is seen as enhancing the well-being of individuals and of systems. Empowerment, through its synergistic properties (i.e., collaboration and mutuality), also produces energy and that energy also increases capacity.
>
> [Empowerment involves beginning to see] life as a process [of becoming], not an event. [The already beginning] fundamental changes . . . usually have meant enhancing the capacity of people and organizations by developing an ongoing infrastructure for this process of "becoming."

The associated connotations—both derivative and converging—can only be sampled here, but illustrations are both useful and suggestive. Thus "empowerment" has been seen as individually focused, as in a "process whereby an individual's belief in his or her efficacy is enhanced" (Conger and Kanungo, 1988); capacity-building, as adding to competencies and to senses of mastery rather than (e.g.) as an authority merely allowing or permitting some attempt at decision or influence (e.g., Vogt, 1989); and multileveled, in that it applies to employer as well as employed, to executives as well as hourly employees, who will all be involved in "a gradual process of transition of responsibility" (Letize and Donovan, 1990).

The last point requires a bit more attention, especially because "empowerment" is not seen as something that a higher-level "them" induces or encourages in some subordinate target, as in employees at operating levels. This is far too restrictive and often will be self-defeating. In contrast, empowerment can occur at all levels and is perhaps most important at higher hierarchical levels. To illustrate, interested readers can consult a case of "empowering at the middle" in a traditional public bureaucracy (Lewis, 1992).

Looked at in a revealing summary way, then, this analysis seeks empowerment in two basic ways. Valuing diversity, in effect, seeks to empower by acting on the more overt failures to respect differences—prejudice, racism, and so on, especially as expressed in person-to-person interaction. Managing diversity seeks to empower via dealing with more pervasive and often subtler forces against diversity. Here, the focus is on what Cox (1993, p. 207) calls "institutional bias." It is built into policies, procedures, and structures where bias springs more from the context than from persons, as it were. Embedded as it is in structure as well as infrastructure, institutional bias is more subtle and insidious than an act, a gesture, or a look—overtly prejudicial and acted out by one person toward another. This explains why Chapters 3 through 5 approach diversity as they do.

The More, More Hypothesis

There are other useful ways to view the why and how of the present approach to empowerment. In sum, "empowerment" has much in common with what I earlier called the "more, more" hypothesis, as contrasted with a "more, less" approach to life (Golembiewski, 1965, 1989a, pp. 207–12).

To explain, there are many things—but clearly not all—that can have "more, more" effects: the more one loves, the more one probably will be loved; the more one trusts, the more others reciprocally will trust and be trustworthy; the more one cooperates with others, the more cooperation is likely to be returned; and so on. Much of management, although hardly all of it, can take advantage of this basic approach to living and choice making.

Some things in life are ineluctably "more, less," in contrast; and most things in life can be made to appear or be that way, if we perversely put our minds to it. What is the approximate balance of what must be and what need not be? No doubt exists here. Some win-lose games exist in nature, but we create most of them by how we approach life and living.

Long lines of research elaborate the managerial relevance of the "more, more" approach (e.g., Edwards, 1993). Thus, following Arnold S. Tannenbaum (1966, esp. pp. 84–102), we know that work units that empower their members tend to have high satisfaction and high productivity. How does empowerment work toward such felicitous ends? It does so in various ways, one of which involves the greater power or influence attributed to all levels of an organization. In "empowered" work units, executives are seen as exercising more influence, but so are other levels of management as well as operators. Skills and attitudes underlie this "more, more" condition, but a basic contributor derives from the shared value of the legitimacy of the mutual condition.

The associated dynamics are easy enough to visualize. Briefly, the underlying mutuality often takes a direct form. Thus empowered employees can bring more of themselves to work, which often yields greater satisfaction and productivity. These effects, in turn, empower executives who are willing to trust and hence to minimize reliance on narrow control. In short, employees who are empowered will be free to be more productive and satisfied, and those outcomes can contribute to the empowerment of the managers. This is the elemental sense of the "more, more" approach.

In a "more, less" approach, the dynamics tend to differ fundamentally. An executive intent on monopolizing power is in a good position to try to do so. Such executives may consequently disempower others, but, absent great skills and good luck, they also probably will disempower themselves as well. In all probability, the disempowering executive will lower satisfaction and performance of those reporting to him. In the longer run, moreover, executives who seek to empower themselves by disempowering others often will be sowing the seeds of the limitations that later may encumber the executives themselves.

Only an obvious point needs reemphasis, to conclude this focus on empowerment as a useful guiding metaphor. In various ways, bureaucratic structures reflect the intent and dynamics of the "more, less" hypothesis. Thus the overall senses of thinking and planning at the top, as well as of doing at the bottom and close controlling by the middle, reflect the unmistakable impress of the "more, less" view of life.

In various ways, also, degenerative interaction has obvious "more, less" features and consequences. Indeed, communication is the prototypic arena of human activity in which a win-lose orientation by any actor in a system probably will result in mutual losses for all actors, at least over the long run.

The reverse arguments—for flow-of-work structures and regenerative interaction —also seem patent, in general. Thus, in effect, flow-of-work structures seek to infuse all levels with a specific responsibility for performance on measurable tasks, with the built-in emphasis on continuous improvement discussed above. This reflects and reinforces a "more, more" chain of interacting effects.

The case for regenerative interaction as a "more, more" condition is more transparent, if anything. Openness and owning can reduce the risk that important things are being repressed, goes one variant of the underlying and reinforcing dynamics. And when this vulnerability is expressed by sharing ideas and feelings, in turn, that will tend to heighten trust. And the regenerative cycle is set to build on itself.

Alternatives? Sure, but . . .

Alternatives exist to empowerment on an unprecedented scale, but none of them have much appeal to this observer. For example, we could directly adopt—or more likely, just fall into—a strategy of simultaneous upskilling and deskilling. Consider the camel as an analogy. The work force of the past can be described by a dromedarian (or one-humped) curve—a few executive jobs, many at middling levels of status and complexity, and a few brutish jobs. In contrast, the ongoing movement seems to be accelerating toward a bactrian (or two-humped) distribution of jobs, with little or no mobility between the two major clusters of jobs.

The basic problem here is that such a bactrian strategy probably would generate a massive and perhaps permanent underclass that largely will have to rely on welfare. Especially in these days of enthusiasm about "free trade," that is, we tend to overlook the fact that its better outcomes include a flight of the more menial and lower-paid jobs to Mexico, or wherever. Plenty is left to the imagination. Absent empowerment and upscaling of a growing number of American jobs at lower levels, and absent success in providing new cadres of candidates capable of (and interested in) performing such jobs, we run the risk of a job flight that will leave us with numerous unemployeds, underemployeds, and undercompensateds—with all three defined by the expectations of the recent past. This implies social dynamite, and massive welfare programs would be the major defense against turmoil.

Worse outcomes, by far, also can be envisioned. Thus the alternative to empowerment at home might have such features: domestic growth only in low-paying service jobs and the continued net export of numerous once high-paying jobs (as in auto assembly) that on relocation are robotized, with any intractable residue left to low wage earners overseas.

Middle management jobs would be sharply reduced in any such future work force model, which would provide a major push to the substantially inevitable consequence of our information technology. In practical terms, this means that any future underclass might well have a far larger leadership identified with it than has been our historic standard. This seems momentous, whatever the direction taken by that new leadership, and is definitely not a possibility that should be considered casually.

Some observers may propose that this generalization applies more to business than it does to government, given the latter's dominant service-professional character; and that may be so. But the federal government was scheduled to reduce its middle management employees by some forty thousand (Newell, 1987), which implies no shortage. Moreover, at least at the federal level, the span of control typically has been small, which generates tall structures with numerous levels of intervening supervision and middle management. Hence the generalization seems applicable in both sectors, even if more so in one of them.

2. *Flexibility as Central Metaphor for Organizations.* As the organizational complement and reinforcer of empowerment at the level of individuals and groups, Douglas T. Hall and Victoria A. Parker (1993) propose "flexibility." Their conceptual packaging resonates with the discussion above, as in challenging traditional ways to structure and to manage work; highlighting the organizational benefits of programs of valuing and managing diversity, paired with the advantages to individuals and groups; and tying various programmatic emphases, often applied at low to middle levels of organization, to a truly strategic purpose.

There is no point to recasting this proposal by Hall and Parker, but four brief points will suggest its seminal character. First, flexibility relates elementally to future organizational prospects. Directly, our future work force will be far more diverse than it has been, and is today, even if we discount as overstated the projections usually accepted as gospel. Hall and Parker (1993, p. 5) make the obvious point: "It follows, then, that the [organizations] that can attract, retain, motivate, and engage the most talented within [that diversity] will be most likely to succeed, while those that do not may not even survive." The situation does not improve when fine-tuning is attempted, as in a focus on the family in an organization that faces all-but-inevitable increases in the proportions of working women, households with single heads, and dual-career families. As Fernandez predicts (1986, p. 189): "This situation will heighten the tension caused by the conflict between work and family life, and ultimately this stress—if it is not dealt with by corporations, government, and parents themselves—will have a negative impact on this nation's capacity to be a productive and competitive society in the new world economy."

Second, every evidence suggests that business and government will be very much alike with regard to flexibility. To illustrate, Eugene B. McGregor, Jr. (1988, p. 946), calls for a new flexibility in public personnel policies, predicting that "an extraordinary amount of personnel system experimentation will be required to find the designs compatible with the knowledge-intensive systems required by modern public policy." The underlying reasons have a familiar ring. As Lane (1993, p. 11) observes: "In the federal sector and increasingly at state and local levels, not only is much of the work highly professional and technical, but task accomplishment also requires achievement of organizational objectives through the work of other public and private organizations [rather than through direct control of employees performing low-discretion work]."

Third, we need to complete an in-process bridging of a classic duality concerning work. Somewhat indelicately, I earlier referred to this as the one-buttock hypothesis (Golembiewski, 1965, 1989a, esp. pp. 161–202). Over the past decade or so, especially, real progress has been made on one part of the dualism: what Hall and Parker (1993, p. 7) refer to as "the tendency of organizations to separate employees' hands from their brains." This part of the reversal motivates job rotation and job enrichment, patently. A more challenging aspect of the dualism still demands major attention, nevertheless. To rely on Hall and Parker again (1993, pp. 7–8): "In the absence of flexibility, organizations implicitly tell employees to bring to work only the parts of themselves necessary to do the job. It is implied that the rest—those qualities that make . . . employees different . . .—can and should be left at the door."

Fourth, why try to bridge this basic dualism and via flexibility for a growing proportion of employees? No final answer is possible here, or anywhere, but several components to such an answer seem relevant. In no particular order of significance, bridging via flexibility may be the major (or even the only) way to avoid some wicked dilemmas—for example, equity may be impossible if the focus is only on protected groups, which can severely limit the options of others and often offends the rights of individuals. Moreover, flexibility probably will liberate energies that may be applied to innovation and performance, or so it seems at an everyday level; and it mirrors and requires the central role of a "learning organization," which gets so much attention nowadays; and is supported by emerging but hardly comprehensive empirical research (e.g., Hall and Parker, 1993, esp. p. 6).

In sum, in these and other regards, flexibility has much to recommend it as a guiding metaphor at the organizational level as a direct replacement for the uniformity or standardization associated with the bureaucratic model. Hall and Parker conclude that the existing evidence encourages just such a replacement. A well-known case involves the major success at Corning's program of flexibility with large reductions in turnover as well as in associated costs (Schmidt, 1988). Moreover, drawing on evidence from a recent survey (Mirvis, forthcoming), Hall and Parker broadly note that workplace flexibility has been associated with (1993, pp. 6–7) "higher morale, less absenteeism, improved productivity, and reduced turnover. . . . [And] the inclusion of views and efforts from a diverse employee population [have] the potential organizational benefit of enhancing creativity and cooperation among work groups." Sparse experimental research comes to similar conclusions, with (for example) emphasis on ethnicity as encompassing collectivist versus individualist cultural traditions (Cox, Lobel, and McLeod, 1991). Such experimental work is challenged by significant methodological issues (e.g., McLeod and Lobel, 1992), but growing research nonetheless adds momentum to the case study literature. Together, both experimental research and case studies imply multiple senses in which managing and valuing diversity can generate competitive advantages for organizations (e.g., Cox and Blake, 1991).

Flexibility and Paradoxes of Diversity

This second metaphor serves a variety of purposes, one of which preoccupies this subsection. Approaching diversity in bureaucratic work settings induces paradoxes, specifically, and these are potentially self-defeating. To illustrate, Cindy P. Lindsay urges (1993, esp. pp. 557–59) that some such closed circle often will develop in connection with the "paradox of values": "Organizations attempt to include diverse members on the basis of benefit to the existing dominant members." Even sincere efforts, especially given the bias toward uniformity in bureaucratic organizations, may be limited: early recruitment tends to include "only [or mostly those diverse] members who match the picture of existing dominant groups" and their values. Even if such organizations decide to "include greater numbers of diverse members in the valuing process," the problem shifts to having sufficient numbers of "the diverse" at decision-making levels. Again, however, the "same organizational processes which reduce variety in the selection and promotion of diverse members" remain operative in this subtle matter, thereby inhibiting the required seeding at senior levels as by the "queen bee syndrome," in which early promotees among the diverse act to restrict the promotion of others from the diverse pool (e.g., Nieva and Gutek, 1981). Various psychological processes, such as "splitting," may increase formal communication between diverse groupings but also decrease informal communication and, hence, increase social distance in contrast to the expectations inherent in the well-known "contact hypothesis" (Lindsay, 1993, pp. 557–58).

Flexibility, as reinforced by postbureaucratic structures and perhaps especially by regenerative interaction, seems to provide ways to live with such paradoxes and even to reduce their impact. For example, Lindsay (1993, p. 559) emphasizes the centrality of trust with respect to flexibility and to minimizing the paradoxes of diversity; and numerous sources (e.g., AARP, 1993, pp. 23–27, 33–48) emphasize various postbureaucratic programs in connection with giving life to flexibility and diversity.

Some sense of the future seems suggested by the efforts at Digital Equipment Corporation (e.g., Walker, 1991). Along with numerous diversity initiatives, Digital seems to have decided to cultivate regenerative interaction systems in small, voluntary, long-run "core groups" whose only agenda is to discuss diversity issues. Significant proportions of Digital's employees are participating, and their ostensible goal is to foster close interpersonal relationships that can keep diversity alive as it faces the "paradox of values" and other inhibitors in a continuous response to diversity. Otherwise, yesterday's successes can rigidify in today's policies and procedures and inhibit responses to the unfolding forms in which diversity will appear over time.

As in Chapter 1, then, the focus on flexibility assumes that there is no single balance point for the claims of diversity and uniformity. Too much of the former can set people off in different and even undercutting directions; and too much of the latter can create a convenient myopia about what is seen, and why, in an organization's responses to emerging differences.

As Chapter 1 puts it, diversity is not a terminal value. Empowerment and flexibility are two prime metaphors that will facilitate search for the several balance points that diversity-seeking organizations can expect, if they are skilled and lucky.

Flexibility and Hopscotching between Phases

Such paradoxes raise a significant issue of principle and practice. Granted the awkwardness of dealing with diversity in bureaucratic organizations (Phase II in the preface), for purposes of argument, is it possible to skip from Phase I (prebureaucratic) to Phase III (postbureaucratic)? Such hopscotching has its attractions. The question applies with greatest salience to developing countries (Grootings, Gustavsen, and Héthy, 1989), but some would propose a far broader arena that includes many troglodytic government agencies in developed settings.

The evidence is incomplete, but it leans to a largely negative answer, on three basic grounds (Grootings, Gustavsen, and Héthy, 1989, esp. pp. 27–29). Thus some impressive gains have been made in Phase I —> II transitions in developing countries. Moreover, it may be necessary to experience long term the downsides of Phase II to develop enthusiasm for postbureaucratic forms, given that early movement to Phase II is often complicated by factors that would affect employee reactions. Such factors include a frantic desire to leave impoverished rural settings, in comparison to which might pale even quite unattractive consequences of a pattern of structuring work. In addition, it seems that the movement into Phase III is "more dependent upon political, social, and cultural conditions than upon conditions controlled by the enterprise." For example, three observers note that postbureaucratic structures imply such prior underlying conditions: "Active, competent workers with a reasonable degree of self-management, [and overall social patterns] must be such that they accept and even encourage local responsibility and active political influence from the grassroots" (Grootings, Gustavsen, and Héthy, 1989, p. 19).

Alternatives? Sure, but . . .

Alternatives to flexibility certainly exist in organizations as the pair-partner of empowerment for individuals. But they seem like very bad bargains, in general.

Consider the attractiveness of uncomplicating, or decomplicating, the work force. This would not be the first place that such a suggestion has seen the light of day; indeed, it is now the alternative of choice in some quarters. To be sure, its proponents observe, diversity is in our future; and diversity implies complications and complexities. But take the bull by the horns, goes this approach. Just enlarge the cohort of "uncomplicated" or "less complicated" employees.

How could this be done? Limits can be set only at one's peril, given motivated and even desperate minds. But one need look no further than recent news stories for exemplars. To illustrate, the U.S. Marine Corps recently declared that it might just enlist only unmarrieds, apparently because enlistments and reenlistments were high enough, cutbacks were expected, or both. Whatever else can be said of this approach, and President Clinton had much negative to say about at least its procedural features, the move toward less complicated recruits seems still very much with us. Life for married marine recruits has been such that a tragic double-ton often occurs: reenlistment rates for marrieds apparently approximate only 10 percent, and marital problems are sky-high, despite a certain unreliability in estimates.

Now, the marines represent a special—even an extreme—case of the need for great control over member behavior, but two approaches to its reenlistment history are possible there, as everywhere. In combinations, perhaps: one can variously modify the employing organization; one can try to "uncomplicate" its members. The marine focus seemed definitely on the latter.

Of the various approaches to uncomplicating employees, as it were, Felice Schwartz's (1989) distinction probably has received the most attention, pro and con. She encouraged distinguishing two categories of women in management—those who are "career-primary" and those who are "career-and-family." The substantial majority of women fall in the latter category, which was popularly dubbed the "mommy track." For them, organizations were urged to provide various family supports—child care services, flexible scheduling of work, and so on. For career-primary women, upward mobility opportunities would be of central concern.

Schwartz's basic observation that women do not constitute a homogeneous category has value, but here the distinction is clearly too simple, especially in connection with women's more probable involvement in cascades of care—for children, for the elderly, for a husband, and on occasion for all three, either serially over a lifetime or even concurrently (e.g., Logue, 1993). Even if all gender discrimination were eliminated from the workplace, then, serious inequities would remain that deserve managerial and public policy attention. As Barbara J. Logue concludes (1993, p. 64): "Because women bear the brunt of negative outcomes associated with long-term care, because the nature and duration of elder care have changed substantially, and because existing policies and programs have serious limitations, policies that move toward more equitable distribution of caregiving burdens demand close attention." Otherwise, those on the "mommy track" may soon find themselves disproportionately providing basic services for parents and then husbands. As Logue observes trenchantly (1993, p. 64), "the 'mommy track' may for many women merge into the 'granny track' and then the 'hubby track'."

Worse still, a kind of General Bullmoose strategy might come to dominate. Some readers will remember him as the Al Capp cartoon-strip character of this firm opinion: "There's nothing as good for this country as a stiff recession." Thus high unemployment levels over extended periods might encourage a certain uncomplicatedness in job applicants and a consequent need for less flexibility by employing organizations. This beggar-your-neighbor policy has little to recommend it, especially in the long run. Severe social discord seems a reasonable result in such a case, an outcome to which few would deliberately contribute.

3. *The "Learning Organization" as Prototypical.* The present metaphorical trinity is completed by a third usage that is much in today's intellectual air and may even be said to dominate among many futurists.

This conceptual influence has a jagged profile, as it were, as well as great magnitude. At one level, for example, the reaction to some variants (e.g., Watkins and Marsick, 1993) of the metaphor in use is elemental—why, yes of course: the root purpose of collective life is to generate ideas with practical impact, and how appropriate to express that in terms of the "learning organization." The concept is presented as a gentle and general metaphor, with a broad array of cases in point suggesting useful ways of approaching their "learning organization." Usually, the focus is on organizational features that characterize the learning organization (e.g., Ulrich, von Glinow, and Jick, 1993), with lesser but nonetheless real concern about associated personal mentation and ideation (e.g., Watkins and Marsick, 1993).

At another level, also for example, some variants take on a Galilean quality, if not a cosmic one. Thus Fred Kofman and Peter M. Senge (1993, pp. 6–7) see their view of the "learning organization" as a direct analogy of the "heliocentric revolution." As they explain:

> In the new systems worldview, we move from the primacy of pieces to the primacy of the whole, from absolute truths to coherent interpretations, from self to community, from problem solving to creating. Thus the nature of the commitment required . . . goes beyond people's typical "commitment to their organization." It encompasses commitment to the larger world and to seeing our organizations as vehicles for bringing about such changes.

This worldview comes complete with a method—*dialogue*, "initially defined as a sustained collective inquiry into the processes, assumptions, and certainties that compose everyday experience" (Isaacs, 1993, p. 24), and elaborated in several prime sources (e.g., Bohm, 1990). This worldview also has an institutional embodiment in the MIT Center for Organizational Learning, and particularly in its Dialogue Project.

It seems all too easy to say too much about these suggestive but early forms of the "learning organization," and present purposes will be served well enough by four minimal but still useful points. First, proponents generally agree on several basics of a working definition of "learning organization." Among other features, these shared referents highlight (Watkins and Marsick, 1993, p. xii) the following:

Learning that occurs in various parts of a collectivity, and sometimes in all of it, as well as in individuals

A basic capacity for change

An acceleration of individual learning, via "mental models" that, for example, question assumptions about realities as well as via supporting organizational structures, cultures, policies, and procedures

Widespread participation and high levels of commitment

Building organizational memory in the service of systemic thinking

Second, it involves very little conceptual stretch to associate the valuing and managing of diversity with progress toward the "learning organization," in both general and specific terms. Essentially, a learning organization nowadays could hardly *not* deal successfully with diversity; and real progress toward valuing and managing diversity can reasonably be said to require ample doses of those features associated with the "learning organization."

Third, even superficial consideration supports the conclusion that bureaucratic structures provide an awkward context for "learning organizations." Thus Michael E. McGill and John W. Slocum, Jr. (1993, esp. p. 75), nicely detail this major point by putting the two at opposite ends of a continuum of "organizational approaches to experience." To the same effect, two other observers propose that bureaucratic systems are "specifically *not* designed for learning" (emphasis added), being flawed as learning systems "in at least three ways." Karen E. Watkins and Victoria J. Marsick detail these ways (1993, p. 19), revealingly: "First, choices about the values and purposes . . . are separated from the performance of those activities. Second, the learning of organizational members is focused on narrow, specific tasks with routine procedures. Third, feedback about results is so fragmented that individuals do not really learn how their performance affects the overall task." So what? Watkins and Marsick note directly: "These problems lead to a decreased potential for learning."

Fourth, organizations that favor learning tend to share central features, even as each is sui generis in responding to specific environmental, developmental, market, and technological boundary conditions. As many sources reflect (e.g., Honold, 1991; McGill and Slocum, 1993; Watkins and Marsick, 1993, esp. pp. 7–22), such organizations have similar profiles in action. They present real-time opportunities to learn from experience dealing with a flow of work; feature cultures that emphasize feedback and disclosure; encourage and reward risk-taking and experimentation that contribute to overall performance; variously seek to empower employees;

often make use of boundary-spanning structures or devices, as in cross-functional teams; and make use of decentralized modes and associated structures.

4. *Perspectives on the Metaphors.* This much having been written—about empowerment, flexibility, and the learning organization—the traditional questions remain. These may seem to increase discretion for the employees of our business and especially public organizations, but what of the traditional concerns with responsiveness and accountability? Will the present approach simply open the floodgates to a kind of agency spoils politics, heightening our insulation from popular control? Does this run the risk of "remote" or "runaway" or "renegade" administration?

Such themes require attention far beyond the present ambitions but have been dealt with fully in other sources (Golembiewski, 1995, esp. chap. 10).

Here, a bare outline deals with the traditional questions, with a focus on the public sector. Basically, the bureaucratic model poses these traditional questions in unsatisfactory and polarized forms. Thoroughgoing centralization can seek to enforce high degrees of responsiveness and accountability, but only with the serious side effects generated by long chains of command, slow-motion dynamics, the confusion of responsibilities for integrative problem-solving in pervasively fragmented and role-oriented structures, and the distancing of political and career levels. These conditions characterized much of the Reagan and Bush presidencies (e.g., Volcker, 1989, p. 20). On the other hand, decentralization in the bureaucratic model can serve to increase discretion among career bureaucrats but also at potentially severe costs. Executive review is made more tenuous and tentative in decentralized forms of the bureaucratic model. Relatedly, useful managerial discretion may easily be extended into organizational feudalities—as responses to legislative committees or subcommittees or to the importunings of narrow special interests. In effect, this condition characterized much of most presidencies (e.g., Lynn, 1981).

Put the point in a nutshell. Organizational experience oscillates between awkward polarities when the bureaucratic model dominates.

In the flow-of-work model, however, different potentials exist, although the favorable probabilities can be subverted by the mischievous or poorly informed (e.g., Pollitt, 1990). Basically, decentralization to low levels of organization is possible, and hence useful discretion can be achieved, even as responsibility is identified and performance on complete flows of work can be reliably assessed. Such probable potentials do not need to pit legislative oversight against executive direction. Both may be better targeted, assuming a movement toward the flow-of-work model. Details are available elsewhere (e.g., Golembiewski, 1987, 1994).

These perspectives may sound preachy, but the three metaphors seek to guide and motivate action, rather than to replace it with verbalisms. Specifically, many programs of change have been (and will continue to be) responsive to traumatic local situations, following the maxim "no pain, no gain." At the same time, a sub-stantial degree of conscious, planned change often is possible. Hence the attention above to guiding metaphors intended to provide direction for proactivity as well as reactivity.

A Concluding Caveat about Value-Loadedness

One caveat applies, in conclusion. A diversity-friendly managerial approach rests essentially on its normative spirit: *it is value-loaded.* So the several exemplars for valuing and managing diversity should not be seen as techniques in a tool kit—a set of convenient plug-ins when diversities threaten and rumble, but which other-wise are consigned to disuse and neglect. Rather, both structure and infrastructure should be seen as expressions of the human will in pursuit of such normative ori-entations to diversity:

> Diversity not only exists, even if menacingly to some; but it must be dealt with, as a practical matter; and it also deserves cultivation, given our history and political traditions.

> Diversity provides stimuli for an expanded sense of human consciousness in knowledge, innovation, and options for choice.

> Diversity can lead to an upwelling of the human spirit and surges in produc-tivity if tolerance and suitable institutional arrangements exist.

> Diversity often has positive instrumental effects, but its prime motivation in-heres in "doing the right things" rather than in "doing things right."

> If suppressed, diversity can lead to contradictory effects—to a diminished self-esteem, on the surface, and to a superheated mixture of emotions, often below the surface, that will at best require great resources to contain. At worst, the tragic long-run effect might only be a later and bigger explosion.

The flip side of this point has even greater implications for all of us. Diversity-friendly exemplars can always be used—and often are used—by people and insti-tutions who do not accept their value-loaded orientations. Indeed, *some adopters may have a strong animus against just such orientations.*

Many observers have reminded us about this crucial point—going back to at least Woodrow Wilson's distinction between a clever knife-sharpening technique and the range of possible intentions underlying the use of extra-sharp knives—and the same themes get vigorous contemporary reemphasis among change agents (e.g., Kramer, 1972; Walton and Warwick, 1973).

Hence the need for both wariness and concern about mindlessly institutionaliz-ing what seem to be diversity-friendly policies, procedures, interaction, and especially structures. Adoptions to "look good" or to "keep up with the Joneses" rest on shallow motivations that may result in trouble, for adopter as well as adoptee. For example, some adoptions may appear friendly to the management of diversity, that is, approach 5 distinguished in Chapter 2. For some adopters of diversity-friendly ways and means, however, today's posturings may really be temporary concessions—a veiled version of approach 1. In short, approach 1 provides for acceptance of diversity only under duress, with the former lasting only as long as the latter. Patently, then, differences in value loadings imply profound issues.

One need go no further than today's news to see the practical significance of what some may view as a subtle distinction. Consider the "remote video encoding" now being used in the U.S. Post Office, which in effect handles mail that cannot be assigned to zip codes by machine-reaching methods. That approach and its technology could be used to encourage flexibility and, if with a stretch or two, might even empower. By contrast, the approach also might be used to dilute wages and degrade working conditions in violation of collective bargaining agreements.

One's value orientations make a crucial difference, in short, in relation to diversity, as everywhere. If nothing else, employees seem to be effective at smelling out shallow-motivated adoptions (e.g., Kossek, Barber, and Winters, 1993) and perhaps especially those adoptions more or less consciously intended to deceive. Abraham Lincoln gave direct voice to this persuasion: You can't fool all of the people all of the time.

This view is opposed by a powerful tradition, one that distorts Lincoln's advice. That tradition rests on two probabilities: that you can fool all of the people much of the time and also that you can fool most of the people all of the time. To some, these suggest pretty good odds. In the present case, those playing such odds will support diversity under duress, in the terms introduced in Chapter 1, while posturing about valuing diversity.

This volume is not content with waiting to see how things will work out with respect to diversity. It attempts to contribute to the former tradition by explicit attention to valuing diversity and especially to managing diversity and to root that attention in diversity-friendly structure and infrastructure. This focus on managing diversity inhibits talking one game while walking another.

REFERENCES

Acker, Joan. (1990). "Jobs, Hierarchies, and Sexuality: Some Further Thoughts on Gender and Organizations." *Gender and Society* 4:139–58.

Alber, Antone F. (1978). "Job Enrichment Programs Seen Improving Employee Performance, but Benefits Not without Cost." *World of Work Report* 3:8–9.

Albrecht, Karl, and Ron Zemke. (1985). *Service America!* Homewood, Ill.: Dow Jones–Irwin.

American Association of Retired Persons (AARP). (1993). *Textbook Authors Conference: Presentations.* Washington, D.C.

Andersen, Kurt. (1991). "California Dreamin'." *Time*, September 23, 38–42.

Argyris, Chris. (1957). *Personality and Organization.* New York: Harper & Bros.

Argyris, Chris, and Donald Schön. (1978). *Organizational Learning.* Reading, Mass.: Addison-Wesley.

Arroba, Tanya, and Kim James. (1988). "Are Politics Palatable to Women Managers?" *Women in Management Review* 3:123–30.

Arthur, Michael B., Douglas T. Hall, and B. S. Lawrence, eds. (1989). *Handbook of Career Theory.* Cambridge, Eng. Cambridge University Press.

Ashkenas, Ronald N. (1990). "A New Paradigm for Customer and Supplier Relationships." *Human Resource Management* 29:385–96.

Ashkenas, Ronald N., and Todd A. Jick. (1992). "From Dialogue to Action in GE Work-Out." In William A. Pasmore and Richard W. Woodman, eds., *Research in Organizational Change and Development* 6:267–87. Greenwich, Conn.: JAI Press.

Atlanta Constitution (1993). "Coming to America," June 22, p. A-9.

Bailyn, Lotte. (1988). "Freeing Work from the Constraints of Location and Time." *New Technology, Work and Employment* 3(2):143–52.

Ban, Carolyn. (1991). "The Realities of the Merit System." In Carolyn Ban and Norma M. Riccucci, eds., *Public Personnel Management*, pp. 17–28. New York: Longman.

Ban, Carolyn, and Norma M. Riccucci, eds. (1991). *Public Personnel Management.* New York: Longman.

Barzelay, Michael. (1992). *Breaking through Bureaucracy.* Berkeley: University of California Press.

Bass, Bernard M. (1985). *Leadership Performance Beyond Expectations.* New York: Free Press.

Bass, Bernard M., and Bruce J. Avolio. (1993). "Transformational Leadership and Organizational Culture." *Public Administration Quarterly* 17:112–21.

———. (1990). "The Implications of Transactional and Transformational Leadership for Individual, Team, and Organizational Development." *Research in Organization Change and Development* 4:231–72.

Becker, Christine S., ed. (1988). *Performance Evaluation: An Essential Management Tool.* Washington, D.C.: International City Management Association.

Bem, S. L. (1974). "The Measurement of Psychological Androgyny." *Journal of Consulting and Clinical Psychology* 42:155–62.

Bennis, Warren G., and Burt Nanus. (1985). *Leaders.* New York: Harper & Row.

Blake, Robert R., Jane S. Mouton, Louis B. Barnes, and Larry E. Greiner. (1964). "Breakthrough in Organization Development." *Harvard Business Review* 42(6):133–35.

Blau, Peter M. (1956). *Bureaucracy in Modern Society.* New York: Random House.

Bohen, Halcyone, and Anamaria Viveros-Long. (1981). *Balancing Jobs and Family Life.* Philadelphia: Temple University Press.

Bohm, David. (1990). *On Dialogue.* Ojai, Calif.: Ojai Institute.

Boss, R. Wayne. (1978). "Trust and Managerial Problem-Solving Revisited." *Group and Organization Studies* 3(3):331–42.

Boulding, Elise. (1990). Interview. *Christian Science Monitor*, August 22, p. 12.

Bourgault, Jacques, Stephane Dion, and Marc Lemay. (1993). "Creating a Corporate Culture: Lessons from the Canadian Government." *Public Administration Review* 53(1):73–80.

Bowman, James S. (1994). "At Last, an Alternative to Performance Appraisal: Total Quality Management." Paper presented at Annual Meeting, American Society for Public Administration, San Francisco.

Bowman, James S., and Harry J. Hooper. (1991). "Dress and Grooming Regulations in the Public Service." *Public Administration Quarterly* 15:328–40.

Bowman, James S., and Jane I. Steele. (1988). "Quality Teams in a State Agency." *Public Productivity Review* 11(4):11–31.

Bremer, Kamala, and Deborah A. Howe. (1988). "Strategies Used to Advance Women's Careers in the Public Service." *Public Administration Review* 48:957–61.

Brenner, O. C., Joseph Tomkiewicz, and Virginia Ellen Schein. (1989). "The Relationship between Sex Role Stereotypes and Requisite Management Characteristics Revisited." *Academy of Management Journal* 32:662–69.

Brice, Arthur. (1994). "Bias Backlash May Be Building in U.S." *Atlanta Journal*, March 3, p. A6.

Brody, J. A. (1988). "Aging in the 20th and 21st Century." *Testimony before the Joint Economic Committee*, U.S. Congress, June 14. Washington, D.C.

Brown, Greg, and Charles C. Harris. (1993). "The Implications of Work Force Diversification in the U.S. Forest Service." *Administration and Society* 25:85–113.

Bruce, Willa, and Christine Reed. (1994). "Preparing Supervisors for the Future Work Force: The Dual-Income Couple and the Work-Family Dichotomy." *Public Administration Review* 54:36–43.

Bryne, Donn E. (1971). *The Attraction Paradigm.* New York: Academic Press.

Bullard, Angela M., and Deil S. Wright. (1993). "Circumventing the Glass Ceiling: Women Executives in American State Governments." *Public Administration Review* 53:189–202.

Burke, Ronald J., Carol A. McKeen, and C. S. McKenna. (1990). "Sex Differences and Cross-Sex Effects on Mentoring." *Psychological Reports* 61(7):1011–23.

Burns, James MacGregor. (1978). *Leadership.* New York: Harper & Row.

Bushe, Gervase R., and A. B. Shani. (1991). *Parallel Learning Structures.* Reading, Mass.: Addison-Wesley.

Bygrave, William. (1989). In *Entrepreneurship Now and Then.* Baylor University, Fall.

Bylinski, Gene. (1990). "Turning R&D into Real Products." *Fortune*, July 2, pp. 72–77.

Cahoon, Allan R. (1992). "The Search Conference Technique." In Robert T. Golembiewski, ed., *Handbook of Organizational Consultation*, pp. 109–12. New York: Marcel Dekker.

Cahoon, Allan R., and Julie Rowney. (1993). "Valuing Differences: Organization and Gender." In Robert T. Golembiewski, ed., *Handbook of Organizational Behavior*, pp. 339–54. New York: Marcel Dekker.

Calás, Marta B., and Linda Smircich. (1992). "Re-writing Gender into Organizational Theorizing." In Michael Reed and Michael Hughes, eds., *Rethinking Organization*, pp. 227–53. London: Sage.

Calista, Donald, ed. (1986). *Bureaucratic and Governmental Reform*. Greenwich, Conn.: JAI Press.

Campbell, John P., and Richard J. Campbell and Associates, eds. (1988). *Productivity in Organizations*. San Francisco: Jossey-Bass.

Campion, Michael A., Lisa Cheraskin, and Michael J. Steven. (1994). "Career-Related Antecedents and Outcomes of Job Rotation." *Academy of Management Journal* 37 (6):1518–42.

Carew, Donald K., Sylvia I. Carter, Janice M. Gamache, Rita Hardiman, Bailey Jackson III, and Eunice M. Parisi. (1977). "New York State Division of Youth." *Journal of Applied Behavioral Science* 13:327–37.

Carroll, Franklin P., W. David Patton, and Stephanie L. Witt. (1993). "The Glass Ceiling in the USDA Forest Service: Willing to Conform, Demanding Change." Paper presented at Annual Meeting, American Society for Public Administration, San Francisco.

Catton, Bruce. (1956). *This Hallowed Ground*. Garden City, N.Y.: Doubleday.

Chandler, Alfred D. (1962). *Strategy and Structure*. Cambridge, Mass.: MIT Press.

Chandler, Ralph Clark, ed. (1987). *A Centennial History of the American Administrative State*. New York: Free Press.

Chao, Georgia T., and Philip D. Gardner. (1992). "Formal and Informal Mentorships." *Personnel Psychology* 45(3):619–36.

Chapple, Eliot, and Leonard R. Sayles. (1961). *The Measure of Management*. New York: Macmillan.

Christensen, K. E. (1989). *Flexible Staffing and Scheduling*. New York: Conference Board.

———, ed. (1988a). *The New Era of Home-Based Work*. Boulder: Westview Press.

———. (1988b). *Women and Home-Based Work*. Troy, Mo.: Holt, Rinehart and Winston.

Church, Gene, and Conrad D. Carnes. (1972). *The Pit: A Group Encounter Defiled*. New York: Outerbridge and Lazard.

Cleveland, Harlan. (1993). *Birth of a New World*. San Francisco: Jossey-Bass.

Cockburn, Cynthia. (1988). *Machinery of Dominance: Women, Men, and Technical Know-How*. Boston: Northeastern University Press.

Cohen, Sharon B. (1989). "Beyond Macho: The Power of Womanly Management." *Working Woman* 14(2):77–81.

Cohen, Susan G. (1993). "New Approaches to Teams and Teamwork." In Jay R. Galbraith, Edward E. Lawler III, and Associates, *Organizing for the Future*, pp. 194–226. San Francisco: Jossey-Bass.

Cohen, Susan G., and Gerald E. Ledford, Jr. (1990). "The Effectiveness of Self-Managing Teams in Service and Support Functions." Paper presented at Annual Meeting, Academy of Management, San Francisco, August 12–15.

Conger, Jay A., and R. N. Kanungo. (1988). "The Empowerment of Practice." *Academy of Management Review* 13:471–82.

Cookson, Peter S., M. Seligson, and J. Garbarino. (1986). *When School's Out and Nobody's at Home*. Chicago: National Committee for the Prevention of Child Abuse.

Cooper, Cary, ed. (1975). *Theories of Group Processes*. New York: Wiley.

Cooper, Cary, and Ivan Robertson, eds. (1986). *International Review of Industrial and Organizational Psychology*. New York: Wiley.

Cortés, Carlos E. (1994). "Limits to *Pluribus*, Limits to *Unum*." *Natinal Forum* 74(1):6–8.

Cox, Taylor, Jr. (1993). *Cultural Diversity in Organizations*. San Francisco: Berrett-Koehler.

———. (1991). "The Multicultural Organization." *Academy of Management Executive* 5(2):34–47.

Cox, Taylor, Jr., and Stacy Blake. (1991). "Managing Cultural Diversity." *The Executive* 5:45–56.

Cox, Taylor H., Sharon A. Lobel, and Poppy Lauretta McLeod. (1991). "Effects of Ethnic Group Cultural Differences on Cooperative and Competitive Behavior on a Group Task." *Academy of Management Journal* 34:827–47.

Cox, Taylor, Jr., and Stella M. Nkomo. (1993). "Race and Ethnicity." In Robert T. Golembiewski, ed., *Handbook of Organizational Behavior*, pp. 205–29. New York: Marcel Dekker.

———. (1991). "A Race and Gender Group Analysis of Early Career Experience of MBAs." *Work and Occupations* 18:431–46.

Cregar, Michael. (1988). "Flextime Continues to Edge Upward." *Management World*, July, pp. 14–15.

Cross, Elsie Y., Judith H. Katz, Frederick A. Miller, and Edith W. Seashore, eds. (1994). *The Promise of Diversity*. Hopkins, Minn.: KJCG Enterprises.

Cummings, Thomas G. (1992). "Sociotechnical Systems Consultation." In Robert T. Golembiewski, ed., *Handbook of Organizational Consultation*, pp. 129–36. New York: Marcel Dekker.

Cummings, Thomas G., and Melvin Blumberg. (1987). "Advanced Manufacturing Technology and Work Design." In Toby D. Wall, Chris W. Clegg, and Nigel J. Kemp, eds., *The Human Side of Advanced Manufacturing Technology*, pp. 37–60. New York: Wiley.

Cunningham, Mary. (1984). *Powerplay: What Really Happened at Bendix*. New York: Linden Press.

Daley, Dennis. (1984). "Political and Occupational Barriers to the Implementation of Affirmative Action." *Review of Public Personnel Administration* 4:16–30.

Dalfiume, R. M. (1969). *Desegregation of the U.S. Armed Forces*. Columbia, Mo.: University of Missouri Press.

Dalton, Melville. (1959). *Men Who Manage*. New York: Wiley.

Davis, Stanley M., and Paul R. Lawrence. (1977). *Matrix*. Reading, Mass.: Addison-Wesley.

Deaner, C. M. Dick. (1991). "The U.S. Army Organizational Effectiveness Program." *Public Administration Quarterly* 15:12–31.

de Crèvecoeur, Michel G. (1782, 1963). *Letters from an American Farmer*. . . . New York: New American Library.

Deming, W. Edward. (1986). *Out of the Crisis*. Cambridge, Mass.: MIT Press.

———. (1982). *Quality, Productivity, and Competitive Position*. Cambridge, Mass.: MIT Press.

Desky, Joanne. (1993a). "SES Gears Up for Extensive Turnover." *PA Times* 16(2):1, 16.

———. (1993b). "Taking Work Home." *PA Times* 16(1):1, 16.

Dess, Gregory G., and Peter S. Davis. (1984). "Porter's Generic Strategies as Determinants of Strategic Group Membership and Organizational Performance." *Academy of Management Journal* 27:476–88.

Deutsch, Morton, and A. E. Collins. (1951). *Interracial Housing*. Minneapolis: University of Minnesota Press.

Deutsch, Morton, and Harold B. Gerard. (1955). "A Study of Normative and Informational Social Influences upon Individual Judgment." *Journal of Abnormal and Social Psychology* 51:629–32.

Di Tomaso, Nancy, Donna E. Thompson, and David H. Blake. (1988). "Corporate Perspectives on the Advancement of Minority Managers." In Donna E. Thompson and Nancy Di Tomaso, eds., *Ensuring Minority Success in Corporate Management*, pp. 119–36. New York: Plenum.

Doherty, Elizabeth M., and Jerry L. McAdams. (1993). In Robert T. Golembiewski, ed., *Handbook of Organizational Consultation*, pp. 173–78. New York: Marcel Dekker.

Dresang, Dennis L., and Paul J. Stuiber. (1991). "Sexual Harassment." In Carolyn Ban and Norma M. Riccucci, eds., *Public Personnel Management*, pp. 114–26. New York: Longman.

Drucker, Marvin, and Betty Robinson. (1992). "Offsetting the Downside of Downsizing." *Journal of Health and Human Resources Administration* 15:183–208.

Drucker, Peter F. (1988). "The Coming of the New Organization." *Harvard Business Review* 66(5):45–53.

———. (1954). *The Practice of Management*. New York: Harper & Brothers.

Dugan, H. Sloane. (1992). "Enlivening Developmental Relationships." In Robert T. Golembiewski, ed., *Handbook of Organizational Consultation*, pp. 179–83. New York: Marcel Dekker.

Dunnette, Marvin D., and Leaetta M. Hough, eds. (1992). *Handbook of Industrial and Organizational Psychology*, Vol. 3. Palo Alto, Calif.: Consulting Psychologists Press.

————. (1990). *Handbook of Organizational Psychology*, Vol. 2. Palo Alto, Calif.: Consulting Psychologists Press.

Dutcher, Joyce S., Carol A. Hayashida, John P. Sheposh, and David K. Dickason. (1992). *Pacer Share: Fourth Year Project Evaluation Report*. Washington, D.C.: U.S. Office of Personnel Management.

Dyer, William. (1977, 1987). *Team Building*. Reading, Mass.: Addison-Wesley.

Eccles, Robert G., and Dwight B. Crane. (1987). "Managing through Networks in Investment Banking." *California Management Review* 30 (Fall): 176–95.

Eddy, William B., ed. (1983). *Handbook on Public Organization Management*. New York: Marcel Dekker.

Edmond, Beverly C. (1993). "Federal Affirmative Action Policies and the Glass Ceiling." *Public Policy Research Newsletter* 2(3):1–4.

Edwards, David. (1993). "Institutionalized Localism." Ph.D. dissertation, University of Georgia.

Egan, Timothy. (1993). "Teaching Tolerance in Workplace." *New York Times*, p. A-18.

Elliott, Diana, and Daniel Stolle. (1993). "The Role of Employee Assessment in the Learning Organization." In Karen E. Watkins and Victoria J. Marsick, *Sculpting the Learning Organization*, pp. 171–73. San Francisco: Jossey-Bass.

Elliott, Ord, and Donald D. Penner. (1974). "The Impact of Social Structure on Organizational Change." In Howard L. Fromkin and John J. Sherwood, eds., *Integrating the Organization*, pp. 269–90. New York: Free Press.

Elliott, Robert H. (1993). "Human Resource Management and the Aging of the Workforce: Discrimination and Retirement Issues." Paper presented at Annual Meeting, American Society for Public Administration, San Francisco, July 23–26.

Evans, Karen. (1987). "Journal Peer Reveiw: A Comparison with Employee Peer Performance Appraisal." *Journal of Social Behavior and Personality* 2(4):385–96.

Ezell, Hank. (1993). "Taking Off from Job to Provide Care for Loved Ones Becomes a Basic Right." *Atlanta Constitution*, August 9, pp. E-1, E-4.

Fagenson, Ellen A., ed. (1993). *Women in Management*. Newbury Park, Calif.: Sage.

Falkenberg, Loren E. (1987). "Employee Fitness Programs." *Academy of Management Review* 12:511–22.

Faludi, Susan C. (1991). *Backlash: The Undeclared War against American Women*. New York: Crown.

————. (1990). "Sales Job." *Wall Street Journal*, February 20, p. A1.

Fannie Mae. (1993). *Diversity at Fannie Mae: Keeping the Competitive Edge*. Washington, D.C.

Federal Deposit Insurance Corporation (FDIC). (1992). *Technical Assistance Guide for the Employment of People with Disabilities*. Washington, D.C.

Fernandez, John P. (1986). *Child Care and Corporate Productivity*. Lexington, Mass.: Lexington Books.

Fernandez, John P., and Mary Barr. (1993). *The Diversity Advantage*. Lexington, Mass.: Lexington Books.

Festinger, Leon, and H. H. Kelly. (1951). *Changing Attitudes through Social Contact*. Ann Arbor: Institute of Social Research, University of Michigan.

Festinger, Leon, Henry W. Riecken, and Stanley Schachter. (1956). *When Prophecy Fails*. New York: Harper Torchbooks.

Fleishman, Edwin A. (1962). "Patterns of Leadership Behavior Related to Group Grievances and Turnover." *Personnel Psychology* 15:43–56.

Fleming, Lis. (1990). *One Minute Commuter: How to Keep Your Job and Stay at Home Telecommuting*. Davis, Calif.: Fleming Limited.

Ford Foundation. (1989). *Work and Family Responsibilities*. New York: Ford Foundation.

Ford, Robert N. (1969). *Motivation through the Work Itself*. New York: American Management Association.

Frederickson, H. George. (1992). "Painting Bull's-Eyes around Bullet Holes." *PA Times* 15(11):9.

Friedman, Dana E. (1990). *Update on Employer-Supported Child Care*. New York: Families and Work Institute.

———. (1988). "Family-Supportive Policies." In F. E. Winfield, ed., *The Work and Family Sourcebook*, pp. 101–18. Greenvale, N.Y.: Panel.

Friedman, Dana E., and Ellen Galinsky. (1992). "Work and Family Trends." In Sheldon Zedeck, ed., *Work and Family*, pp. 168–207. San Francisco: Jossey-Bass.

Fromkin, Howard L., and John J. Sherwood, eds. (1974). *Integrating the Organization*. New York: Free Press.

Fugita, Stephen S., and David J. O'Brien. (1991). *Japanese-American Ethnicity: The Persistence of Community*. Seattle: University of Washington Press.

Galbraith, Jay R. (1993a). "The Business Unit of the Future." In Jay R. Galbraith, Edward E. Lawler III, and Associates, *Organizing for the Future*, pp. 43–64. San Francisco: Jossey-Bass.

———. (1993b). "The Value-Adding Corporation." In Jay R. Galbraith, Edward E. Lawler III, and Associates, *Organizing for the Future*, pp. 15–42. San Francisco: Jossey-Bass.

Galbraith, Jay R., Edward E. Lawler III, and Associates. (1993). *Orgainzing for the Future*. San Francisco: Jossey-Bass.

Galinsky, Ellen, Dana E. Friedman, and C. A. Hernandez. (1991). *The Corporate Reference Guide to Family-Friendly Programs and Policies*. New York: Families and Work Institute.

Gallup, George, Jr. (1992). *The Gallup Poll: Public Opinion 1991*. Wilmington, Del.: Scholarly Resources.

Gard, Karen K. (1994). "MSPB Reevaluates Workforce 2000 for the 1990s." *PA Times* 17(2):1, 3, 13.

Gardenswartz, Lee, and Anita Rowe. (1993). *Managing Diversity*. Homewood, Ill.: Business One Irwin; San Diego: Pfeiffer.

Gardner, John. (1991). *Building Community*. Washington, D.C.: Independent Sector.

Garvin, David A. (1993). "Building a Learning Organization." *Harvard Business Review* 71(4):78–92.

Gerhart, Barry, and George T. Milkovich. (1992). "Employee Compensation." In Marvin D. Dunnette and Leaetta M. Hough, eds., *Handbook of Industrial and Organizational Psychology*, 3:481–569. Palo Alto, Calif.: Consulting Psychologists Press.

Gilder, George F. (1989). *Microcosm: The Quantum Revolution in Economics and Technology*. New York: Simon and Schuster.

Ginzberg, Eli. (1992). "Foreword." In Susan E. Jackson and Associates, *Diversity in the Workplace*, pp. xiii–xx. New York: Guilford Press.

Gioia, Dennis A., and Clinton O. Longenecker. (1994). "Delving into the Dark Side: The Politics of Executive Appraisal." *Organizational Dynamics* 22(3):47–58.

Glassman, Alan M., and Thomas G. Cummings, eds. (1991). *Cases in Organizational Development*. Homewood, Ill.: Irwin.

Glazer, Myron P., and Penina M. Glazer. (1989). *Whistleblowers*. New York: Basic Books.

Goldman, Eric F. (1952). *Rendezvous with Destiny*. New York: Knopf.

Goldratt, Eliyahu M., and Jeff Cox. (1992). *The Goal*. Croton-on-Hudson, N.Y.: North River Press.

Golembiewski, Robert T. (1995). *Practical Public Management*. New York: Marcel Dekker.

———. (1993a). *Approaches to Planned Change*. New Brunswick, N.J.: Transaction.

———. (1993b). "Ethical Overlays in Public Management: Toward a Comprehensive Ethical Orientation." *Korea Public Administration Journal* 2(1):67–92.

———, ed. (1993c). *Handbook of Organizational Behavior*. New York: Marcel Dekker.

———. (1992a). "Excerpts from 'Organization as a Moral Problem.'" *Public Administration Review* 52:95–98.

———, ed. (1992b). *Handbook of Organizational Consultation*. New York: Marcel Dekker.

———. (1992c). "Organization Is a Moral Problem." *Public Administration Review* 52:99–205.

———. (1991a). "American Research and Development (A–D)." In Alan M. Glassman and Thomas G. Cummings, eds., *Cases in Organizational Development*, pp. 455–79. Homewood, Ill.: Irwin.

———. (1991b). "Two Super-Optimum Solutions in a Cutback Mode." *Public Budgeting and Financial Management* 4:231–54.

———. (1990). *Ironies in Organizational Development*. New Brunswick, N.J.: Transaction.

———. (1989a). *Men, Management, and Morality*. New Brunswick, N.J.: Transaction.

———. (1989b). "Strategy and Structure." In Jack Rabin, Gerald Miller, and Bartley Hildreth, eds., *Handbook of Strategic Management*, pp. 13–58. New York: Marcel Dekker.

———. (1987). "Why Theory and Practice Should Emphasize Purpose, and How to Do So." In Ralph Clark Chandler, ed., *A Centennial History of the American Administrative State*, pp. 433–74. New York: Free Press.

———. (1986a). "OD Perspectives on High Performance." *Review of Public Personnel Administration* 7:9–26.

———. (1986b). "Organizational Analysis and Praxis: Prominences of Progress and Stuckness." In Cary Cooper and Ivan Robertson, eds., *International Review of Industrial and Organizational Psychology*, pp. 279–304. New York: Wiley.

———. (1985). *Humanizing Public Organizations*. Mt. Airy, Md.: Lomond Publications.

———. (1983). "Structuring the Public Organization." In William B. Eddy, ed., *Handbook of Organization Management*, pp. 193–225. New York: Marcel Dekker.

———. (1980). "Public-Sector Productivity and Flexible Workhours." *Southern Review of Public Administration* 4:324–39.

———. (1979). *Approaches to Planned Change*, Vols. 1 and 2. New York: Marcel Dekker.

———. (1977a). "Testing Some Stereotypes about the Sexes in Organizations: Differential Satisfaction with Work." *Human Resource Management* 16(4):21–24.

———. (1977b). "Testing Some Stereotypes about the Sexes in Organizations: Differential Centrality with Work." *Human Resource Management* 16(2):30–32.

———. (1972). *Renewing Organizations*. Itasca, Ill.: F. E. Peacock.

———. (1967). *Organizing Men and Power*. Chicago: Rand McNally.

———. (1965). *Men, Management, and Morality*. New York: McGraw-Hill.

———. (1962a). *Behavior and Organization*. Chicago: Rand McNally.

———. (1962b). "Organization as a Moral Problem." *Public Administration Review* 22:51–58.

———. (1962c). *The Small Group*. Chicago: University of Chicago Press.

———. (1962d). "Civil Service and Managing Work." *American Political Science Review* 56:961–73.

Golembiewski, Robert T., and Arthur Blumberg, eds. (1970, 1973, 1977). *Sensitivity Training and the Laboratory Approach*. Itasca, Ill.: F. E. Peacock.

———. (1968). "The Laboratory Approach to Organization Development: The Confrontation Design." *Academy of Management Journal* 11:199–211.

———. (1967). "Confrontation as a Training Design in Complex Organizations." *Journal of Applied Behavioral Science* 3:524–47.

Golembiewski, Robert, and Stokes B. Carrigan. (1973). "Planned Change through Laboratory Methods: Toward Building Organizations to Order." *Academy of Management Journal* 27:18–27.

———. (1970). "Planned Change in Organization Style Based on Laboratory Approach." *Administrative Science Quarterly* 15:79–93, 330–40.

Golembiewski, Robert T., Stokes B. Carrigan, and Arthur Blumberg. (1973). "More on 'Building New Relationships at Work.'" *Journal of Applied Behavioral Science* 9:126–28.

Golembiewski, Robert T., Stokes B. Carrigan, Walter R. Mead, Robert T. Munzenrider, and Arthur Blumberg. (1972). "Toward Building New Work Relationships." *Journal of Applied Behavioral Science* 8:135–48.

Golembiewski, Robert T., Ronald Fox, and Carl W. Proehl, Jr. (1979). "Is Flexi-Time 'Hard Time' for Supervisors?" *Journal of Management* 5:215–22.

Golembiewski, Robert T., and Gerald Gabris. (1994a). "Today's City Managers." *Public Administration Review* 54:525–53.

————. (1994b). "Tomorrow's City Management." *Public Administration Review* (in press).

Golembiewski, Robert T., and Richard Hilles. (1979). *Toward the Responsive Organization.* Salt Lake City: Brighton Publishing.

Golembiewski, Robert T., Richard Hilles, and Munro Kagno. (1974). "A Longitudinal Study of Flexi-Time Effects." *Journal of Applied Behavioral Science* 47:503–32.

Golembiewski, Robert T., and Allan Kiepper. (1988). *High Performance and Human Costs.* New York: Praeger.

Golembiewski, Robert T., and Karl W. Kuhnert. (1994). "Individual Characteristics and Performance: Pilot Study of Congruence Between Assessment Center and Bio-Data Approaches." *Public Administration Quarterly* 17:410–34.

————. (1992). "Barnard and Transformational Leadership." *Management Theory,* no. 13: 2–37.

Golembiewski, Robert T., and Mark L. McConkie. (1975). "The Centrality of Interpersonal Trust in Group Process." In Cary Cooper, ed., *Theories of Group Processes,* pp. 131–85. New York: Wiley.

Golembiewski, Robert T., Kent Nethery, Richard Hilles, and William Shepherd. (1992a). "Enhancing Worldwide Strategic Planning, Part 1." *Organization Development Journal* 10(1):31–54.

————. (1992b). "Enhancing Worldwide Strategic Planning, Part 2." *Organization Development Journal* 10(2):57–65.

Golembiewski, Robert T., and William A. Osuna. (1993). "Diversity and Organization Structure." Paper presented at Berkeley Symposium on Public Management Research, University of California at Berkeley.

Golembiewski, Robert T., and Se-Jeong Park. (1991). "Examining the Determinants of Successful QC Programs: Testing the Influence of Eleven Situational Features." *Organization Development Journal* 9(4):38–49.

Golembiewski, Robert T., and Carl W. Proehl, Jr. (1980). "Public-Sector Applications of Flexible Workhours." *Public Administration Review* 40:72–85.

————. (1978). "A Survey of the Empirical Literature on Flexible Workhours." *Academy of Management Review* 3:837–53.

Golembiewski, Robert T., Carl W. Proehl, Jr., and David Sink. (1981). "Success of OD Applications in the Public Sector." *Public Administration Review* 41:679–82.

————. (1982). "Estimating the Success of OD Applications." *Training and Development Journal* 72:86–95.

Golembiewski, Robert T., and Ben-chu Sun. (1993). "Enriching Work and Empowering Employees: Evaluating Success Rates and Methodology in Public-Sector QWL." In Robert T. Golembiewski, ed., *Handbook of Organizational Consultation,* pp. 394–405. New York: Marcel Dekker.

Goodman, Paul S., Rukmini Devadas, and Terry L. G. Hughson. (1988). "Groups and Productivity: Analyzing the Effectiveness of Self-Managing Teams." In John P. Campbell, Richard J. Campbell, and Associates, eds., *Productivity in Organizations,* pp. 295–327. San Francisco: Jossey-Bass.

Goodsell, Charles T. (1982, 1985, 1993). *The Case for Bureaucracy.* Chatham, N.J.: Chatham House Press.

Goold, Michael, and Kathleen Luchs. (1993). "Why Diversity?: Four Decades of Management Thinking." *Executive* 8:7–25.

Gouldner, Alvin W. (1954). *Patterns of Industrial Bureaucracy.* Glencoe, Ill.: Free Press.

Grootings, Peter, Björn Gustavsen, and Lathos Héthy, eds. (1989). *New Forms of Work Organization in Europe.* New Brunswick, N.J.: Transaction.

Guy, Mary Ellen. (1993a). "Three Steps Forward, Two Steps Backward: The Status of Women's Integration into Public Management." *Public Administration Review* 53:285–92.

————. (1993b). "Workplace Productivity and Gender Issues." *Public Administration Review* 53:279–82.

Guzzo, Richard A., Richard D. Jette, and Raymond A. Katzell. (1985). "The Effects of Psychologically-Based Intervention Programs on Worker Productivity: A Meta-Analysis." *Personnel Psychology* 38 (Spring):275–91.

Hall, Douglas T. (1990). "Telecommuting and the Management of Work-Home Boundaries." In Institute for Information Studies, *Paradigms Revised: Annual Review of Communications and Society*, pp. 177–208. Nashville: Northern Telecom, and Queenstown, Md.: Aspen Institute.

——, ed. (1986). *Career Development in Organizations*. San Francisco: Jossey-Bass.

Hall, Douglas T., and Victoria A. Parker, (1993). "The Role of Workplace Flexibility in Managing Diversity." *Organizational Dynamics* 22:5–18.

Hammer, Michael, and James Champy. (1993). *Reengineering the Corporation*. New York: Harper Business.

Handy, Charles. (1990). *The Age of Unreason*. Boston: Harvard Business School Press.

Hanna, David P. (1988). *Designing Organizations for High Performance*. Reading, Mass.: Addison-Wesley.

Harvey, Jerry B. (1988). "The Abilene Paradox." *Organizational Dynamics* 17:17–34.

Herberg, Will. (1960). *Protestant-Catholic-Jew*. Garden City, N.Y.: Anchor Books.

Herbst, P. G. (1962). *Autonomous Group Functioning*. London: Tavistock.

Hersey, Paul, and Kenneth H. Blanchard. (1969, 1988). *Management of Organizational Behavior*. Englewood Cliffs, N.J.: Prentice-Hall.

Herzberg, Frederick, Bernice Snyderman, and Bernard Mausner. (1959). *The Motivation to Work*. New York: Wiley.

Honold, L. (1991). "The Power of Learning at Johnsonville Foods." *Training* 28(4):55–58.

House, Robert J. (1977). "A 1976 Theory of Charismatic Leadership." In James G. Hunt and Lars L. Larson, eds., *Leadership: The Cutting Edge*, pp. 189–207. Carbondale, Ill.: Southern Illinois University Press.

Howard, Rosemary E., and Joan E. Munch. (1991). "Mentoring: A Federal Women's Program Initiative." *Bureaucrat* 20(3):13–14.

Hoy, Frank, ed. (1988). *Best Paper Proceedings*. Annual Meeting, Academy of Management, Anaheim, Calif.

Hoy, Judith. (1990). "Skills of Women Needed at the Top." *Executive Excellence* 7(6):14–15.

Hudson Institute. (1988). *Civil Service 2000*. Washington, D.C.: U.S. Office of Personnel Management.

Hummel, Ralph P. (1987). *The Bureaucratic Experience*, 3d ed. New York: St. Martin's Press.

Hunt, James G., and Lars L. Larson, eds. (1977). *Leadership: The Cutting Edge*. Carbondale, Ill.: Southern Illinois University Press.

Hyde, Albert C. (1990–91). "Rescuing Quality Measurement from TQM." *Bureaucrat* 19 (Winter): 16–20.

Hymowitz, Carol. (1990). "As Aetna Adds Flextime, Bosses Learn to Cope." *Wall Street Journal*, June 18, pp. B1–B2.

Ingraham, Patricia W., and David H. Rosenbloom, eds. (1992). *The Promise and Paradox of Civil Service Reform*. Pittsburgh: University of Pittsburgh Press.

Institute for Information Studies. (1990). *Paradigms Revised: Annual Review of Communications and Society*. Nashville: Northern Telecom, and Queenstown, Md.: Aspen Institute.

Issacs, William N. (1993). "Taking Flight: Dialogue, Collective Thinking, and Organizational Learning." *Organizational Dynamics* 22:24–39.

Jackson, Al. (1994). "Is It Diversity or Affirmative Action?" *Managing Diversity*, sample issue.

Jackson, Susan E. (1991). "Team Composition in Organizational Settings." In Stephen Worchel, Wendy Wood, and Jeffry A. Simpson, eds., *Group Process and Productivity*, pp. 138–73. Beverly Hills: Sage.

Jackson, Susan E., and Associates. (1992). *Diversity in the Workplace*. New York: Guilford Press.

Jacoby, Henry. (1973). *The Bureaucratization of the World*. Berkeley and Los Angeles: University of California Press.

Janis, Irving. (1972, 1982). *Victims of Groupthink*. Boston: Houghton Mifflin.

Jefferson, David J. (1994). "Gay Employees Win Benefits for Partners at More Corporations." *Wall Street Journal* 130 (March 18): A1, A6.

Jiang, Stephen P. (1993). "Time to Reevaluate Diversity Training." *PA Times* 16(6):8.

Jick, Todd D. (1990). "Consumer-Supplier Partnerships." *Human Resource Management* 29:435–54.

Johnson, Barry. (1992). *Polarity Management*. Amherst, Mass.: HRD Press.

Johnson, H. Thomas. (1992). *Relevance Regained*. New York: Free Press.

Johnson, H. Thomas, and Robert S. Kaplan. (1987). *Relevance Lost: The Rise and Fall of Management Accounting*. Boston: Howard Business School Press.

Joice, Wendell. (1993). *The Federal Flexible Workplace Pilot Project*. Washington, D.C.: U.S. Office of Personnel Management, Career Entry Group.

Kanfer, Ruth. (1990). "Motivation Theory and Industrial and Organizational Psychology." In Marvin D. Dunnette and Leaetta M. Hough, eds., *Handbook of Industrial and Organizational Psychology*, 2:75–170. Palo Alto, Calif.: Consulting Psychologists Press.

Kanter, Rosabeth M. (1989). "Careers and the Wealth of Nations." In Michael B. Arthur, Douglas T. Hall, and B. S. Lawrence, eds., *Handbook of Career Theory*, pp. 506–21. Cambridge, Eng.: Cambridge University Press.

———. (1977). *Men and Women of the Corporation*. New York: Basic Books.

Katzell, Raymond A. (1994). "Contemporary Meta-Trends in Industrial and Organizational Psychology." In Harry C. Triandis, Marvin D. Dunnette, and Leaetta M. Hough, eds., *Handbook of Industrial and Organizational Psychology*, 4:1–89. Palo Alto, Calif.: Consulting Psychologists Press.

Kaufman, Herbert. (1985, 1991). *Time, Chance, and Organizations*. Chatham, N.J.: Chatham House.

———. (1960). *The Forest Ranger*. Baltimore: Johns Hopkins Press.

Keenan, J. P. (1988). "Communication Climate, Whistleblowing, and the First-Level Manager." In Frank Hoy, ed. *Proceedings, Best Papers*, Academy of Management 49:247–51.

Kellough, J. Edward. (1992). "Affirmative Action in Government Employment." *Annals, AAPSS*, 523:1117–30.

———. (1991). "The Supreme Court, Affirmative Action, and Public Management: Where Do We Stand?" *American Review of Public Administration* 21:255–69.

———. (1990). "Federal Agencies and Affirmative Action for Blacks and Women." *Social Science Quarterly* 71(1):83–92.

———. (1989a). *Federal Equal Employment Opportunity and Numerical Goals and Timetables*. New York: Praeger.

———. (1989b). "The 1978 Civil Service Reform and Federal Equal Employment Opportunity." *American Review of Public Administration* 19:313–24.

Kelly, Marcia W., and Gil E. Gordon. (1986). *Telecommuting*. Englewood Cliffs, N.J.: Prentice-Hall.

Ketchum, Lyman D., and Eric Trist. (1992). *All Teams Are Not Created Equal*. Newbury Park, Calif.: Sage.

Kettl, Donald F. (1993). *Sharing Power: Public Governance and Private Markets*. Washington, D.C.: Brookings Institution.

Kilmann, Ralph H., Mary J. Saxton, Ray Serpa, and Associates. (1985). *Gaining Control of the Corporate Culture*. San Francisco: Jossey-Bass.

Kim, J. (1991). "Issues in Work Force Diversity." Paper presented at First Annual Diversity Conference, San Francisco, May 17.

Kinsman, Francis. (1987). *The Telecommuters*. New York: Wiley.

Klein, Joe. (1993). "Principle or Politics?" *Newsweek*, June 14, p. 29.

Klingner, Donald E., and John Nalbandian. (1993). *Public Personnel Management*. Englewood Cliffs, N.J.: Prentice-Hall.

Kofman, Fred, and Peter M. Senge. (1993). "Communities of Commitment: The Heart of Learning Organizations." *Organizational Dynamics* 22:5–23.

Kohlberg, Lawrence. (1981). *The Philosophy of Moral Development*. New York: Harper & Row.

Korabik, Karen. (1990). "Androgyny and Leadership Style." *Journal of Business Ethics* 9(4):283–92.

Korabik, Karen, and Roya Ayman. (1989). "Should Women Have to Act Like Men?" *Journal of Management Development* 8(6):23–32.

Kossek, Ellen Ernst. (1990). "Diversity in Child Care Assistance Needs." *Personnel Psychology* 43:769–91.

———. (1989). "The Acceptance of Human Resource Innovations by Multiple Constituencies." *Personnel Psychology* 42:264–81.

Kossek, Ellen Ernst, Alison E. Barber, and Deborah Winters. (1993). "An Assessment of Individual, Work Group and Organizational Influence on the Acceptance of Flexible Work Schedules." In Dorothy P. Moore, ed., *Best Papers Proceedings*, Academy of Management Annual Meeting, pp. 116–20.

Kossek, Ellen Ernst, and Victor Nichols. (1992). "The Effects of On-Site Child Care on Employee Attitudes and Performance." *Personnel Psychology* 45:485–509.

Kouzes, James M., and Paul M. Mico. (1979). "Domain Theory." *Journal of Applied Behavioral Science* 15:449–69.

Kram, Kathy E. (1985). *Mentoring at Work*. Glenview, Ill.: Scott Foresman.

Kram, K. E., and Lynn Isabella. (1985). "Mentoring Alternatives." *Academy of Management Journal* 28:110–32.

Kramer, Harvey. (1972). "Backfeed." *Journal of Applied Behavioral Science* 8:630.

Kraut, Allen I. (1992). "Organizational Research on Work and Family Issues." In Sheldon Zedeck, ed., *Work, Families, and Organizations*, pp. 208–35. San Francisco: Jossey-Bass.

Kuhnert, Karl W. (1993). "Leadership Theory in Postmodernist Organizations." In Robert T. Golembiewski, ed., *Handbook of Organizational Behavior*, pp. 189–204. New York: Marcel Dekker.

Lane, Larry M. (1993). "Public Sector Performance Management: Old Failures and New Opportunities." Paper presented at Annual Conference, American Society for Public Administration, San Francisco, July 18–21.

Laudicina, Eleanor V. (1993). "Managing Workforce Diversity: A Comparison of Public and Private Sector Approaches." Paper presented at Annual Meeting, American Society for Public Administration, San Francisco, July 19.

———. (1992). "Diversity and Productivity: Lessons from the Corporate Sector." Paper presented at Fifth National Public Sector Productivity Improvement Conference, Newark, N.J.

Lawler, Edward E., III. (1993). "Creating the High-Involvement Organization." In Jay R. Galbraith, Edward E. Lawler III, and Associates, *Organizing for the Future*, pp. 172–93. San Francisco: Jossey-Bass.

———. (1992). *The Ultimate Advantage*. San Francisco: Jossey-Bass.

———. (1990). *Strategic Pay*. San Francisco: Jossey-Bass.

———. (1988). "Choosing an Involvement Strategy." *Academy of Management Executive* 2:197–204.

———. (1981). *Pay and Organization Development*. Reading, Mass.: Addison-Wesley.

Lawler, Edward E., III, and Jay R. Galbraith. (1993). "New Roles for the Staff." In Jay R. Galbraith, Edward E. Lawler III, and Associates, *Organizing for the Future*, pp. 65–83. San Francisco: Jossey-Bass.

Lawler, Edward E., III, Gerald E. Ledford, Jr., and Susan A. Mohrman. (1989). *Employee Involvement in America*. Houston: American Productivity and Quality Center.

Lawler, Edward E., III, Susan A. Mohrman, and Gerald E. Ledford, Jr. (1992). *Employee Involvement and Total Quality Management: Practices and Results in Fortune 1000 Companies*. San Francisco: Jossey-Bass.

Leckie, William H. (1967). *The Buffalo Soldiers*. Norman: University of Oklahoma Press.

Ledford, Gerald E., Jr. (1993). "Employee Involvement." In Jay R. Galbraith, Edward E. Lawler III, and Associates, *Organizing for the Future*, pp. 142–71. San Francisco: Jossey-Bass.

Ledford, Gerald E., Jr., Thomas G. Cummings, and R. W. Wright. (1992). "The Design and Effectiveness of High-Involvement Organizations." Working Paper. Los Angeles: Center for Effective Organizations, University of Southern California.

Ledford, Gerald E., Jr., Edward E. Lawler III, and Susan A. Mohrman. (1988). "Groups and Productivity: Analyzing the Effectiveness of Self-Managing Teams." In John P. Campbell, Richard J. Campbell, and Associates, eds., *Productivity in Organizations*, pp. 255–94. San Francisco: Jossey-Bass.

Ledford, Gerald E., Jr., and Susan A. Mohrman. (1988). "Attitudinal Effects of Employee Participation Groups." Paper presented at Annual Meeting, Academy of Management, Anaheim, Calif., August 5–7.

Lee, Patricia. (1982). *The Complete Guide to Job Sharing*. New York: Walker.

Letize, Leta, and Michael Donovan. (1990). "The Trend toward An Empowered Work Force: The Supervisor's Changing Role." *Journal of Quality Participation* (March): 62–65.

Levinson, Harold, (1970). "Management by Whose Objectives?" *Harvard Business Review* 48(7): 125–34.

Levinson, Marc. (1993). "Playing with Fire: Empower Workers?; A Small-Town Firm Finds It Tougher Than It Sounds." *Newsweek*, June 21, pp. 46–48.

Lewis, Gregory B. (1988). "Progress toward Racial and Sexual Equality." *Public Administration Review* 48:700–707.

Lewis, Merlin. (1992). "Regional Networking." Ph.D. dissertation, Teachers College, Columbia University.

Likert, Rensis. (1967). *The Human Organization*. New York: McGraw-Hill.

Lindsay, Cindy P. (1993). "Paradoxes of Organizational Diversity." *Journal of Managerial Issues* 5:547–66.

Lindzey, Gardner, and Edward Aronson, eds. (1969). *The Handbook of Social Psychology*. Reading, Mass.: Addison-Wesley.

Little, Danity M. (1991). "Women in Government: Shattering the Glass Ceiling." *Bureaucrat* 20(3):24–28.

Littlejohn, Eric, and Hank Ezell. (1993). "Women Chip Away at 'Glass Ceiling.'" *Atlanta Constitution*, June 30, p. 1.

Locke, Edwin A., and Gary P. Latham. (1984). *Goal-Setting*. Englewood Cliffs, N.J.: Prentice-Hall.

Lockheed, M. E., and K. P. Hall. (1976). "Conceptualizing Sex as a Status Characteristic: Applications to Leadership Training Strategies." *Journal of Social Issues* 32(3):111–24.

Loden, Marilyn, and Judy B. Rosener. (1991). *Workforce America!* Homewood, Ill.: Business One Irwin.

Logue, Barbara J. (1993). "To Grandmother's House We Go?: Around the Bend on the 'Mommy Track.'" *Applied Behavioral Science Review* 1:47–67.

Loo, Robert. (1992). "Project Management for Organizational Consulting." In Robert T. Golembiewski, ed., *Handbook of Organizational Consultation*, pp. 509–19. New York: Marcel Dekker.

Lowe, Theodore A., and Gerald M. McBean. (1989). "Honesty without Fear." *Quality Progress* 22 (November): 30–34.

Lowry, Elaine. (1993). "Diversity Training Is Productivity Training." *PA Times* 16(6):8.

Lynn, Lawrence E., Jr. (1981). *Managing the Public's Business*. New York: Basic Books.

Macy, Barry A. (1978). "A Theoretical Basis for and an Assessment of the Bolivar Quality of Working Life Experiment." Paper presented at Annual Meeting, Academy of Management. San Francisco, August 9–11.

Mahfood, Phillip E. (1992). *Home Work*. Chicago: Probus.

Maniero, Lisa A. (1993). "Dangerous Liaisons?: A Review of Current Issues Concerning Male and Female Romantic Relationships in the Workplace." In Ellen A. Fagenson, ed., *Women in Management*, pp. 162–85. Newbury Park, Calif.: Sage.

Marrow, Alfred J. (1974). *Making Waves in Foggy Bottom*. Washington, D.C.: NTL Institute.

Marrow, Alfred J., David G. Bowers, and Stanley E. Seashore. (1967). *Management by Participation*. New York: Harper & Row.

Marszalek, John F. (1972). *Court Martial: A Black Man in America*. New York: Scribner's.

———. (1974). *Assault at West Point*. New York: Collier Books.

Martin, Patricia Yancey. (1992). "Gender, Interaction, and Inequality in Organizations." In Cecilia L. Ridgeway, ed., *Gender, Interaction, and Inequality*, pp. 208–31. New York: Springer-Verlag.

Matthes, Karen. (1991). "Managing Diversity: A Matter of Survival." *Personnel* 68(10):9.

Mayfield, Harold. (1960). "In Defense of Performance Appraisal." *Harvard Business Review* 38:81–87.

McConkie, Mark L. (1979). "A Clarification of the Goal-Setting and Appraisal Process in MBO." *Academy of Management Review* 4:29–40.

McCormick, Charles P. (1938). *Multiple Management*. New York: Harper & Row.

McDowell, James L., and Manindra K. Mohapatra. (1993). "Orientations of Faculty in Schools of Public Administration toward Cultural Diversity Issues." *Public Policy Research Newsletter* 11(2):1–4.

McGill, Michael E., and John W. Slocum, Jr. (1993). "Unlearning the Organization." *Organizational Dynamics* 22:67–79.

McGregor, Douglas. (1967). *The Professional Manager*. New York: McGraw-Hill.

———. (1960). *The Human Side of Enterprise*. New York: McGraw-Hill.

———. (1957). "An Uneasy Look at Performance Appraisal." *Harvard Business Review* 35:89–94.

McGregor, Eugene B., Jr. (1988). "The Public Sector Human Resource Puzzle." *Public Administration Review* 48(6):941–50.

McGuire. W. J. (1969). "The Nature of Attitudes and Attitude Change." In Gardner Lindzey and Edward Aronson, eds., *The Handbook of Social Psychology*, pp. 136–214. Reading, Mass.: Addison-Wesley.

McLeod, Poppy Lauretta, and Sharon Alisa Lobel. (1992). "The Effects of Ethnic Diversity on Idea Generation in Small Groups." In Jerry L. Wall and Lawrence R. Jauch, eds., *Best Paper Proceedings 1992*, Annual Meeting, Academy of Management, Las Vegas, Nev., pp. 227–31.

Medvedev, Z. A. (1969). *The Rise and Fall of T. D. Lysenko*. New York: Columbia University Press.

Meier, Grett S. (1979). *Job Sharing*. Kalamazoo, Mich.: W. E. Upjohn Institute for Employment Research.

Metz, Edmund J. (1981). "The Verteam Circle." *Training and Development Journal* 15(12):78–85.

Michaelson, Gerald A. (1990). "Deming in His Own Words." *Across the Board* 27 (December): 44.

Michels, Roberto. (1962). *Political Parties*. New York: Collier.

Miceli, Marcia P., J. B. Dozier, and Janet P. Near. (1991). "Blowing the Whistle on Data-Fudging." *Journal of Applied Social Psychology* 21:271–95.

Miller, Danny, and Peter H. Friesen. (1984). *Organizations*. Englewood Cliffs, N.J.: Prentice-Hall.

Miller, Katherine I., and Peter R. Monge. (1986). "Participation, Satisfaction, and Productivity." *Academy of Management Journal* 29:727–53.

Mills, Kim I. (1993). "Work at Home without Guilt." *Atlanta Constitution*, June 18, p. A-2.

Mintzberg, Henry. (1979). *The Structuring of Organizations*. Englewood Cliffs, N.J.: Prentice-Hall.

Mirvis, Philip. (Forthcoming). *Building a Competitive Work Force*. New York: Wiley.

Mobley, William H. (1982). *Employee Turnover*. Reading, Mass.: Addison-Wesley.

Moen, Ronald N. (1989). "The Performance Appraisal System: Deming's Deadly Disease." *Quality Progress* 22 (November): 62–66.

Mohapatra, Manindra K., James L. McDowell, and Enamul H. Choudhury. (1993). "State Administrators and Workforce 2000." Paper prepared for delivery at Annual Meeting, Midwest Political Science Association, Chicago: April 15–17.

Mohrman, Susan. (1993). "Integrating Roles and Structure in the Lateral Organization." In Jay R. Galbraith, Edward E. Lawler III, and Associates, *Organizing for the Future*, pp. 109–41. San Francisco: Jossey-Bass.

Mohrman, Susan A., and Allan M. Mohrman. (1993). "Organizational Change and Learning." In Jay R. Galbraith, Edward E. Lawler III, and Associates, *Organizing for the Future*, pp. 87–108. San Francisco: Jossey-Bass.

Mohrman, Susan A., and Luke Novelli, Jr. (1985). "Beyond Testimonials: Learning from a Quality Circles Programme." *Journal of Occupational Behaviour* 6:93–110.

Moore, Dorothy P., ed. (1993). *Best Papers Proceedings*, Academy of Management, Annual Meeting, Atlanta, Ga.

Morgan, Gareth. (1993). *Imaginization*. Newbury Park, Calif.: Sage.

Morrison, Ann M. (1992). *The New Leaders*. San Francisco: Jossey-Bass.

Morrison, Ann M., and Mary A. von Glinow. (1990). "Women and Minorities in Management." *American Psychologist* 45:200–208.

Muczyk, Jan P. (1979). "A Common Surrogate for OD: Dynamics and Hazards of MBO Applications." In Robert T. Golembiewski, *Approaches to Planned Change*, 2:166–78. New York: Marcel Dekker.

Mueller, Kenneth J. (1992). *Health Care Policy in the United States*. Lincoln: University of Nebraska Press.

Murphy, Kevin R., and Jeanette N. Cleveland. (1991). *Performance Appraisal*. Boston: Allyn and Bacon.

Naff, Katherine C., Project Director. (1992). *Breaking through the Glass Ceiling*. Washington, D.C.: National Capital Area Chapter, American Society for Public Administration.

Nalbandian, John. (1989). "The U.S. Supreme Court's 'Consensus' on Affirmative Action." *Public Administration Review* 49:38–45.

National Industrial Conference Board. (1965). *The Product Manager System*. New York: National Industrial Conference Board.

National Performance Review. (1993). *From Red Tape to Results: Creating a Government That Works Better and Costs Less—Executive Summary*. Washington, D.C.: U.S. Government Printing Office.

Near, Janet P., Melissa S. Baucus, and Marcia P. Miceli. "The Relationship between Values and Practice: Organizational Climates for Wrong-Doing." (1993). *Administration and Society* 25:204–26.

Neave, Henry R. (1990). *The Deming Dimension*. Knoxville: SPC Press.

Newell, Terry (1987). "Myth of the Disappearing Manager." *Bureaucrat* (Summer): 37–41.

Newland, Chester A. (1992). "The Politics of Civil Service Reform." In Patricia W. Ingraham and David H. Rosenbloom, eds., *The Promise and Paradox of Civil Service Reform*, pp. 63–89. Pittsburgh: University of Pittsburgh Press.

New York Times. (1994). "Seeking 'Fair Deal' for a Black Cadet." January 31, p. A10.

———. (1993). "Army's Monument to the Unsung." July 26, p. A-8.

Newsweek, (1993a). "Teaching Minds to Fly with Discs and Mice." May 31, p. 47.

———. (1993b). "White Male Paranoia: Are They the Newest Victims, or Just Bad Sports?" March 29, pp. 48–53.

Nicholas, John M. (1982). "The Comparative Impact of Organization Development Interventions on Hard Criteria Measures." *Academy of Management Review* 7:531–42.

Nieva, Veronica F., and Barbara Gutek. (1981). *Women and Work*. New York: Praeger.

Nollen, Stanley D. (1982). *New Work Schedules in Practice*. New York: Van Nostrand Reinhold.

Ogburn, Charlton. (1959). *The Marauders*. New York: Harper & Row.

Olson, M. H. (1988). "Corporate Culture and the Home Worker." In K. E. Christensen, ed., *The New Era of Home-Based Work*, pp. 126–34. Boulder: Westview Press.

———. (1987). *An Investigation of the Impact of Remote Work Environments and Supporting Technology*. New York: New York University, Graduate School of Business Administration, Center for Research on Information Systems.

Osborne, David, and Ted Gaebler. (1992). *Reinventing Government*. Reading, Mass.: Addison-Wesley.

Osuna, William A. (1993). "Notes on the Background, Enactment, Implementation and Impact of Executive Order 9981." Working Paper, Athens, Ga.

O'Toole, James, and Warren G. Bennis. (1992). "Our Federalist Future." *California Management Review* 35(2):73–90.

Ott, E. M. (1989). "Effects of the Male-Female Ratio at Work: Policewomen and Male Nurses." *Psychology of Women Quarterly* 13:41–57.

Ouchi, William G. (1984). *The M-Form Society*. Reading, Mass.: Addison-Wesley.

Park, Se-Jeong. (1990). "A Critical Assessment of Evaluative Studies on Quality Circles Change Programs." Ph.D. dissertation, University of Georgia.

Pasmore, William. (1988). *Designing Effective Organizations*. New York: Wiley.

Pasmore, William A., and Richard W. Woodman, eds. (1992). *Research in Organizational Change and Development*, Vol. 6. Greenwich, Conn.: JAI Press.

Patkai, P., K. Petterson, and T. Akerstedt. (1973). "Effects of Flexible Working Hours and Individual Diurnal Rhythms." *Reports from the Psychological Laboratories, 406*. Stockholm, Sweden: University of Stockholm.

Paul, Robert J. (1993). "Managing the Older Worker." *Executive* 7(3):67–74.

Perin, Constance. (1990). "The Moral Fabric of the Office." In Pamela S. Tolbert and Stephen R. Barley, eds., *Research in the Sociology of Organizations*, Vol. 8: *Organizations and Professions*, pp. 241–68. Greenwich, Conn.: JAI Press.

Perkins, Donald N. T., Vera F. Nieva, and Edward E. Lawler III. (1983). *Managing Creation*. New York: Wiley Intersciences.

Perry, James L. (1991). "Linking Pay to Performance: The Controversy Continues." In Carolyn Ban and Norma M. Riccucci, eds., *Public Personnel Management*, pp. 73–86. New York: Longman.

Peters, Thomas J., and Robert H. Waterman, Jr. (1982). *In Search of Excellence*. New York: Harper & Row.

Pierce, Jon L., John W. Newstrom, Randall B. Dunham, and Alison E. Barber. (1989). *Alternative Work Schedules*. Needham Heights, Mass.: Allyn and Bacon.

Pollitt, Christopher. (1990). *Managerialism and the Public Services*. Oxford: Basil Blackwell.

Polmar, Norman, and Thomas B. Allen. (1982). *Rickover*. New York: Simon and Schuster.

Pomerleau, Raymond. (1993). "A Desideratum for Managing the Diverse Workplace." Paper presented at the Berkeley Symposium on Public Management Research, University of California at Berkeley, July 19.

Porter, Lyman W. (1974). "Communication: Structure and Process." In Howard L. Fromkin and John J. Sherwood, eds., *Integrating the Organization*, pp. 216–46. New York: Free Press.

Powell, Gary N. (1993). *Women and Men in Management*. Newbury Park, Calif.: Sage.

Pressman, Jeffrey L., and Aaron B. Wildavsky. (1973). *Implementation*. Berkeley and Los Angeles: University of California Press.

Prokesh, S. (1991). "Kinder, Gentler Plant a Failure." *Chicago Tribune*, July.

Rabin, Jack, Gerald Miller, and Bartley Hildreth, eds. (1989). *Handbook of Strategic Management*. New York: Marcel Dekker.

Ragins, Belle Rose. (1989). "Barriers to Mentoring." *Human Relations* 42:1–22.

Ragins, Belle Rose, and Eric Sundstrom. (1989). "Gender and Power in Organizations." *Psychological Bulletin* 105(1):51–58.

Rainey, Glenn W., Jr., and Hal G. Rainey. (1986a). "Breaching the Hierarchical Imperative: The Modularization of the Social Security Claims Process." In Donald Calista, ed., *Bureaucratic and Governmental Reform*, pp. 171–96. Greenwich, Conn.: JAI Press.

———. (1986b). "Structural Overhaul in a Government Agency: Implications of Social Security Claims Modularization for Central OD Principles and Techniques." *Public Administration Quarterly* 10:206–28.

Rainey, Hal G. (1991). *Understanding and Managing Public Organizations*. San Francisco: Jossey-Bass.

Raleigh (N.C.) *News and Observer.* (1993). "New Freedoms at Work." September 5, pp. 1A, 12A, 13A.

Ramsower, Regan Mays. (1985). *Telecommuting.* Ann Arbor: UMI Research Press.

Raven, Bertram. (1974). "The Nixon Group." *Journal of Social Issues* 30:297–320.

Reed, Michael, and Michael Hughes, eds. (1992). *Rethinking Organization.* London: Sage.

Riccucci, Norma M. (1991). "Affirmative Action in the Twenty-first Century." In Carolyn Ban and Norma M. Riccucci, eds., *Public Personnel Management*, pp. 89–99. New York: Longman.

Ridgeway, Cecila L., ed. (1992). *Gender, Interaction, and Inequality.* New York: Springer-Verlag.

Rieff, David. (1991). *Los Angeles: Capital of the Third World.* New York: Simon and Schuster.

Ritter, James W. (1978). "Army Organizational Effectiveness and Navy Organizational Development: A Comparison." U.S. Army OETC, *OE Communique*, January, pp. 54–58.

Rogers, Everett M. (1962). *Diffusion of Innovations.* Glencoe, Ill.: Free Press.

Roman, Paul M., and Terry C. Blum. (1993). "Work-Family Role Conflict and Employer Responsibility." In Robert T. Golembiewski, ed., *Handbook of Organizational Behavior*, pp. 299–326. New York: Marcel Dekker.

———. (1992). "Employee Assistance Programs as Sources of Consultation." In Robert T. Golembiewski, ed., *Handbook of Organizational Consultation*, pp. 627–40. New York: Marcel Dekker.

Romzek, Barbara S. (1991). "Balancing Work and Nonwork Obligations." In Carolyn Ban and Norma M. Riccucci, eds., *Public Personnel Management*, pp. 227–39. New York: Longman.

Ronen, Simcha. (1981). *Alternative Work Schedules.* New York: McGraw-Hill.

Rosenbloom, David H. (1984). "The Declining Salience of Affirmative Action in Federal Personnel Management." *Review of Public Personnel Administration* 4:31–40.

———. (1981). "Federal Equal Employment Opportunity." *Southern Review of Public Administration* 5:63–72.

———. (1987). *Federal Equal Employment Opportunity.* New York: Praeger.

Rynes, Sara L., Caroline Weber, and George T. Milkovich. (1989). "Effects of Market Survey Rates, Job Evaluation and Job Gender on Job Pay." *Journal of Applied Psychology* 74:114–23.

Sandroff, Ronni. (1988). "Sexual Harassment in the Fortune 500." *Working Woman* (December): 69–73.

Sargent, Alice G. (1981). *The Androgynous Manager.* New York: AMACOM.

Savage, Charles M. (1990). *Fifth Generation Management: Integrating Enterprises through Human Networking.* Bedford, Mass.: Digital Press.

Sayles, Leonard R., and Margaret Chandler. (1992). *Managing Large Systems.* New Brunswick, N.J.: Transaction.

———. (1971). *Managing Large Systems.* New York: Harper & Row.

Schachter, Hindy L. (1993). "A Case for Moving from Tolerance to Valuing Diversity." *Review of Public Personnel Administration* 13:29–44.

Schein, Virginia E., Elizabeth H. Maurer, and Jan F. Novak. (1977). "Impact of Flexible Working Hours on Productivity." *Journal of Applied Psychology* 62:463–65.

Schmidt, Peggy. (1988). "Women and Minorities." *New York Times*, October 16, pp. 25–27.

Schneider, E. L. (1989). "Options to Control the Rising Health Care Costs of Older Americans." *Journal of the American Medical Association* 26:907–8.

Schneier, Craig E., Richard W. Beatty, and Lloyd S. Baird. (1988). "How to Conduct a Successful Performance Appraisal System." In Christine S. Becker, ed., *Performance Evaluation: An Essential Management Tool*, pp. 74–81. Washington, D.C.: International City Management Association.

Schwartz, Felice. (1989). "Management Women and the New Facts of Life." *Harvard Business Review* 89:65–76.

Scott, Jewel D. (1992). "Past Success, Future Challenges." *Public Administration Review* 52:105–7.

Scott, William G., and D. K. Hart. (1979). *Organizational America.* Boston: Houghton Mifflin.

Selznick, Phillip. (1949). *TVA and the Grass Roots.* Berkeley: University of California Press.

Shamir, Boas. (1992). "Home: The Perfect Workplace?" In Sheldon Zedeck, ed., *Work, Families, and Organizations*, pp. 272–311. San Francisco: Jossey-Bass.

Sherif, Muzafer. (1935). "A Study of Some Social Factors in Perception." *Archives of Psychology* 28, no. 187.

Sherwood v. *Brown*, 1980. 619 F.2d, 47.

Simon, Herbert. (1947, 1957, 1976). *Administrative Behavior*. New York: Macmillan.

Slavin, Seymour. (1993). "Multiculturalism—The Next Stage: Implications for the Public Services and Public Administration." Paper presented at Annual Meeting, American Society for Public Administration, July 24–26, San Francisco.

Slote, Alfred. (1969). *Termination*. Indianapolis: Bobbs-Merrill.

Smith, Kenwyn K., and David K. Berg. (1987). *Paradoxes of Group Life*. San Francisco: Jossey-Bass.

Stalk, George, Jr., and Thomas M. Hout. (1990). *Competing against Time: How Timebased Competition Is Reshaping Global Markets*. New York: Free Press.

Stanley, J. D. (1981). "Dissent in Organizations." *Academy of Management Review* 6:13–19.

Stewart, Debra. (1976). "Women in Top Jobs: An Opportunity for Federal Leaders." *Public Administration Review* 36(4):357–64.

Stewart, John M. (1965). "Making Project Management Work." *Business Horizons* 8 (Fall): 54–70.

Sussal, Carol M. (1985). "Group Work with Federal Employees." *Social Work with Groups* 8(3):71–79.

Sutton, Robert I. (1983). "Managing Organizational Death." *Human Resource Management* 22:391–412.

Taber, Thomas D., Jeffrey T. Walsh, and R. A. Cooke. (1979). "Developing a Community-Based Program for Reducing the Social Impact of a Plant Closing." *Journal of Applied Behavioral Science* 15:133–55.

Tannenbaum, Arnold S. (1966). *Social Psychology of the Work Organization*. Belmont, Calif.: Wadsworth.

Taras, Daphne. (1991). "Breaking the Silence." *Public Administration Quarterly* 14:401–18.

Tavernier, Gerard. (1980). "How America Can Manage Its Flexible Benefits Program." *Management Review* 64(8):8–13.

Taylor, Dalmas A. (1974). "Should We Integrate Organizations?" In Howard L. Fromkin and John J. Sherwood, eds., *Integrating the Organization*, pp. 340–62. New York: Free Press.

Taylor, Frederick W. (1911). *The Principles of Scientific Management*. New York: Harper.

Thomas, D. A. (1990). "The Impact of Race on Managers' Experiences of Developmental Relationships." *Journal of Organizational Behavior* 11:479–92.

Thomas, R. Roosevelt, Jr. (1991). *Beyond Race and Gender*. New York: AMACON.

———. (1990). "From Affirmative Action to Affirming Diversity." *Harvard Business Review* 68 (March–April): 107–17.

Thompson, Donna E., and Nancy Di Tomaso, eds. (1988). *Ensuring Minority Success in Corporate Management*. New York: Plenum.

Tichy, Noel, and R. Charan. (1989). "Speed, Simplicity, and Self-Confidence: An Interview with Jack Welch." *Harvard Business Review* 67(5):112–20.

Tipple, Terence J., and J. Douglas Wellman. (1991). "Herbert Kaufman's Forest Ranger Thirty Years Later." *Public Administration Review* 51:421–28.

Tolbert, Pamela S., and Stephen R. Barley, eds. (1991). *Research in the Sociology of Organizations*, Vol. 8: *Organizations and Professions*. Greenwich, Conn.: JAI Press.

Torres, Cresencio, and Mary Bruxelles. (1992). "Capitalizing on Global Diversity." *HR Magazine*, December, pp. 30–33.

Towers Perrin & Hudson Institute. (1990). *Workforce 2000*. Valhalla, N.Y.: Towers Perrin.

Triandis, Harry C. (1974). "Person Perception." In Howard L. Fromkin and John J. Sherwood, eds., *Integrating the Organization*, pp. 177–215. New York: Free Press.

Triandis, Harry C., Marvin D. Dunnette, and Leaetta M. Hough, eds. (1994). *Handbook of Industrial and Organizational Psychology*, Vols. 1–4. Palo Alto, Calif.: Consulting Psychologists Press.

Triandis, Harry C., Lois L. Kurowski, and Michele J. Gelfand. (1994). "Workplace Diversity." In Harry C. Triandis, Marvin D. Dunnette, and Leaetta M. Hough, eds., *Handbook of Industrial and Organizational Psychology* 4:769–827. Palo Alto, Calif.: Consulting Psychologists Press.

Tsiu, Anne S., Terri D. Egan, and Charles A. O'Reilly III. (1992). "Being Different." *Administrative Science Quarterly* 37:549–79.

Ulrich, Dave, Mary Ann von Glinow, and Todd Jick. (1993). "High-Impact Learning." *Organizational Dynamics* 22:52–66.

U.S. Congress, House Committee on Armed Services. (1974). *Report*, Special Subcommittee on Disciplinary Problems in the U.S. Navy, esp. pp. 17674–79.

U.S. Department of Defense, Defense Equal Opportunity Management Institute. (1993). *Program of Instruction*. Washington, D.C.

U.S. Department of Labor. (1991). "*A Report on the Glass Ceiling Initiative*. Washington, D.C.

U.S. Environmental Protection Agency (1992). *EPA Headquarters Cultural Diversity Survey*. Washington, D.C., December 4.

U.S. General Accounting Office (GAO). (1993a). "Federal Performance Management: Agencies Need Greater Flexibility in Designing Their Systems." Washington, D.C.

———. (1993b). *Federal Performance Management*, Report to the Subcommittee on Federal Services, Post Office, and Civil Service, Committee on Governmental Affairs, U.S. Senate. Washington, D.C.

U.S. Office of Personnel Management, Personal Systems and Oversight Group. (1992). *Broad-Banding in the Federal Government*. Washington, D.C., December.

Vancil, Richard F. (1987). *Passing the Baton: Managing the Process of CEO Succession*. Boston: Harvard Business School Press.

Verba, Sidney. (1961). *Small Groups and Political Behavior*. Princeton: Princeton University Press.

Vicere, A. A. (1990). "The Changing Paradigm of Executive Development." *Journal of Management Development* 10(3):44–47.

Vogt, Judith F. (1992). "Consulting as Empowerment." In Robert T. Golembiewski, ed., *Handbook of Organizational Consultation*, pp. 743–52. New York: Marcel Dekker.

———. (1989). "Participatory Research in the Empowerment of People." *Convergence* 14(13):20–29.

Vogt, Judith F., and Kenneth L. Murrell. (1990). *Empowerment in Organizations*. San Diego: University Associates.

Volcker, Paul A., chair. (1989). National Commission on the Public Service. *Leadership for America*. Washington, D.C.

Waldman, David A., and Ron S. Kenett. (1990). "Improve Performance by Appraisal." *HR Magazine* 35(3):66–69.

Waldo, Dwight. (1979). "Public Management Research." Paper presented at the Public Management Research Conference. Washington, D.C., Brookings Institution.

Walker, Barbara A. (1991). "Addressing Diversity through Core Groups." Paper presented at Annual Conference, Organizational Behavior Teaching Conference, Bellingham, Wash.

Walker, Barbara A., and W. C. Hanson. (1992). "Valuing Differences at Digital Equipment Corporation." In Susan E. Jackson and Associates, eds., *Diversity in the Workplace*, pp. 119–37. New York: Guilford Press.

Walker, Tom. (1993). "Glass Ceiling Is Cracking in Wake of Cutbacks." *Atlanta Constitution*, June 27, p. R-1.

Wall, Jerry, and Lawrence R. Jauch, eds. (1992). *Best Paper Proceedings*. Annual Meeting, Academy of Management, Las Vegas, Nev.

Wall, Toby D., Chris W. Clegg, and Nigel J. Kemp, eds. (1987). *The Human Side of Advanced Manufacturing Technology*. New York: Wiley.

Walton, Richard E. (1979). "Work Innovations at Topeka." *Journal of Applied Behavioral Science* 13:422–33.

―――. (1972). "How to Counter Alienation in the Plant." *Harvard Business Review* 50:70–81.

Walton, Richard E., and Donald P. Warwick. (1973). "The Ethics of Organization Development." *Journal of Applied Behavioral Science* 9:681–98.

Wamsley, Gary, R. N. Backer, Charles T. Goodsell, P. S. Kronenberg, John A. Rohr, Camilla M. Stivers, Orion F. White, and J. F. Wolf. (1990). *Refounding Public Administration*. Newbury Park, Calif.: Sage.

Wamsley, Gary L., Charles T. Goodsell, John A. Rohr, Camilla M. Stivers, Orion F. White, and J. F. Wolf. (1983). "The Public Administration and the Governance Process: Shifting the American Political Dialogue." Mimeo.

Watkins, Karen E., and Victoria J. Marsick. (1993). *Sculpting the Learning Organization*. San Francisco: Jossey-Bass.

Watson, Warren E., Kamalesh Kuman, and Larry K. Michaelsen. (1993). "Cultural Diversity's Impact on Interaction Process and Performance." *Academy of Management Journal* 36:590–602.

Webster, S. W. (1961). "The Influence of Interracial Contact on Social Acceptance in a Newly-Integrated School." *Journal of Educational Psychology* 52:292–96.

Weick, Karl. (1979). *The Social Psychology of Organizing*. Reading, Mass.: Addison-Wesley.

Weinstein, Deena. (1979). *Bureaucratic Opposition*. New York: Pergamon.

Weisbord, Marvin R. (1992). *Discovering Common Ground*. San Francisco: Barrett-Koehler.

Wheatley, Margaret J. (1992). *Leadership and the New Science*. San Francisco: Barrett-Koehler.

White, Glen. (1989). "Groupthink Reconsidered." *Academy of Management Review* 14:40–57.

Whyte, William H., Jr. (1956). *The Organization Man*. Garden City, N.Y.: Doubleday Anchor Books.

Wilcox, Herbert. (1968). "The Culture Trait of Hierarchy in Middle Class Children." *Public Administration Review* 48:222–35.

Wilkins, Alan L., and William G. Ouchi. (1983). "Efficient Cultures." *Administrative Science Quarterly* 28:468–81.

Williams, G. W. (1888). *A History of the Negro Troops in the War of the Rebellion, 1861–1865*. New York: Harper & Bros.

Williams, Lena. (1992). "Companies Capitalizing on Worker Diversity." *New York Times*, December 15, pp. A1, D20.

Winfield, Fairlee, ed. (1988). *The Work and Family Sourcebook*. Greenvale, N.Y.: Panel.

Woll, Jerry L., and Lawrence R. Jauch, eds. (1992). *Best Paper Proceedings*, Academy of Management.

Womack, James P., Daniel T. Jones, and Daniel Roos. (1990). *The Machine That Changed the World*. New York: Rawson Associates.

Worchel, Stephen, Wendy Wood, and Jeffry A. Simpson, eds. (1991). *Group Process and Productivity*. Beverly Hills: Sage.

Yukl, Gary, and David D. Van Fleet. (1992). "Theory and Research on Leadership in Organizations." In Marvin D. Dunnette and Leaetta M. Hough, eds., *Handbook of Industrial and Organizational Psychology*, 3:147–97. Palo Alto, Calif.: Consulting Psychologists Press.

Zand, Dale. (1972). "Trust and Managerial Effectiveness." *Administrative Science Quarterly* 17:229–39.

Zander, Alvin. (1982). *Making Groups Effective*. San Francisco: Jossey-Bass.

Zedeck, Sheldon, ed. (1992). *Work, Families, and Organizations*. San Francisco: Jossey-Bass.

Zilbert, Edward R. (1991). "Management in the 1990s." *Journal of Management Development* 10(2):7–14.

INDEX

Acker, J., 79

Aetna Insurance, 148

Affirmative Action: and "equal outcomes," 35–36; and "group rights," 31–32; historical highlights of, 31–33; mixed consequences of, 33–35

Afro-Americans: and Buffalo Soldiers, 26–29; and civil service employment, 30–31, 33–35; in Civil War, 27

Akerstedt, T., 139, 145

Alber, A. F., 70, 107

Albrecht, K., 158

Allen, T. B., 45

Andersen, K., 12, 117

Argyris, C., 13, 68–69, 84, 90, 95–96

Army, U.S.: and Organizational Effectiveness, 45–46

Arroba, T., 165

Ashkenas, R. N., 172

Avolio, B. J., 86–87, 127

Avon Products, Inc., 3, 161

Ayman, R., 102

Backer, R. N., 51

Bailyn, L., 145

Baird, L. S., 78

Ban, C., 2

Barber, A. E., 140–41, 189

Barnes, L. B., 67

Barr, M., 4–5

Barzelay, M., 59, 92

Bass, B. M., 86–87, 127–29

Baucus, M. S., 83, 125

Beatty, R. W., 78

Bem, S. L., 64

Ben and Jerry's Ice Cream, 13

Bennis, W. G., 86, 91, 120, 127

Blake, D. H., 12, 117

Blake, R. R., 67

Blake, S., 11, 46, 181

Blanchard, K. H., 84, 86

Blau, P. M., 83

Blum, T. C., 163, 168

Blumberg, A., xii, 38, 60, 158, 170, 172

Bohen, H., 140

Bohm, D., 185

Boss, R. W., 59, 103

Boulding, E., 5

Bourgault, J., 19

Bowers, D. G., 173

Bowman, J. S., 52, 75, 113–14, 158

Bremer, K., 169

Brenner, O. C., 102

Brice, A., 33

Brody, J. A., 7

Brown, G., 5, 47

Bruce, W., 135

Bruxelles, M., 36

Bryne, D. E., 124

Bullard, A. M., 35

Bureaucratic structure as diversity-unfriendly: and "culture," 60–61, 87; and degenerative interaction, 54, 56–64; as distinct from bureaucrats, 51–52; and dress codes, 52–53; features of, 56–57; and homogeneous grouping,

ABOUT THE AUTHOR

Robert T. Golembiewski is Research Professor
of Political Science at the University of Georgia.
He received his bachelor's degree from Princeton
and his master's and doctorate from Yale. He has
written or edited more than 50 books, the latest
of which is *Practical Public Management*. He
also has published more than 500 scholarly
articles and contributions in various journals.
His work appears in about a dozen languages.
Golembiewski is the only dual winner of the
major awards given in business and in public
administration for contributions to management
and research.